COACHING STUDENTS II SECONDARY SCHOOLS

This practical, evidence-based guide provides a comprehensive introduction to the coaching of secondary school students. Using a clear, step-by-step structure, the book explores how coaching can help students improve performance, enhance well-being, develop skills and achieve goals. The ultimate aim is to help the student become his or her own coach.

Divided into six parts, *Coaching Students in Secondary Schools* explores all of the key aspects of coaching, from basic coaching skills to effective methods of evaluation. Having explained why coaching benefits students, the book shows readers how to adopt a 'coaching approach', structure a formal session, launch a coaching programme and measure its success.

Topics covered include:

- the uses and benefits of coaching
- the evidence for coaching
- core coaching skills
- conducting coaching sessions
- the practicalities of coaching
- evaluating the impact of coaching.

With real-life scenarios and examples embedded throughout, *Coaching Students in Secondary Schools* will be essential reading for practising secondary school teachers, classroom assistants and student support staff.

Adam Abdulla is a highly experienced coach and coach trainer and a member of the Association for Coaching. He also has several years of experience as a secondary school teacher. Trained by the pioneers of cognitive behavioural coaching, he has worked with students, teachers, leaders and heads as well as hundreds of clients outside education.

COACHING STUDENTS IN SECONDARY SCHOOLS

Closing the Gap between Performance and Potential

Adam Abdulla

LONDON AND NEW YORK

First published 2018
by Routledge
2 Park Square, Milton Park, Abingdon, Oxon OX14 4RN

and by Routledge
711 Third Avenue, New York, NY 10017

Routledge is an imprint of the Taylor & Francis Group, an informa business

British Library Cataloguing in Publication Data
A catalogue record for this book is available from the British Library

Library of Congress Cataloging in Publication Data
Names: Abdulla, Adam, author.
Title: Coaching students in secondary schools : closing the gap between performance and potential / Adam Abdulla.
Description: Abingdon, Oxon ; New York, NY : Routledge, 2018. | Includes bibliographical references and index.
Identifiers: LCCN 2017020821| ISBN 9781138080485 (hardback) | ISBN 9781138080492 (pbk.) | ISBN 9781315113494 (ebook)
Subjects: LCSH: Mentoring in education. | Education, Secondary. | Achievement motivation. | Motivation in education. | Educational psychology.
Classification: LCC LB1731.4 .A29 2018 | DDC 371.102–dc23
LC record available at https://lccn.loc.gov/2017020821

ISBN: 978-1-138-08048-5 (hbk)
ISBN: 978-1-138-08049-2 (pbk)
ISBN: 978-1-315-11349-4 (ebk)

Typeset in Interstate
by Swales & Willis Ltd, Exeter, Devon, UK
Printed and bound by CPI Group (UK) Ltd, Croydon, CR0 4YY

CONTENTS

PREFACE

This book is aimed at education professionals who are interested in *coaching* students. As will become clear in later chapters, a 'coaching approach' can benefit students of all ages, including primary school children and undergraduates at university. However, this book focuses on students in secondary schools, particularly those in the later stages.

In writing this book, I have drawn heavily on the academic literature. You will therefore find numerous references not only to other books on coaching but also to scientific papers, journals and theses. I make no apologies for this. Like any other educational intervention, coaching should be supported by evidence. If you would like to know more about the relevant research then the references may be of interest. That said, throughout most of this book I assume that your interest in coaching is practical rather than academic. There is therefore a constant emphasis on the nuts and bolts. Techniques and strategies are carefully explained and almost every chapter includes extended examples of coach-student dialogue.

I have tried to make the book as readable as possible. The chapters vary in length and detail but in each one the topics to be covered are listed at the beginning and the main points are summarised at the end. In addition, the Appendices include a number of practical coaching resources. Finally, a brief summary of each chapter can be found towards the end of the Introduction.

ACKNOWLEDGEMENTS

Many different people have made it easier to write this book. In terms of my own training, I count myself extremely fortunate to have learnt from several of the pioneers of cognitive behavioural coaching, including Stephen Palmer, Gladeana McMahon and Nick Edgerton. Windy Dryden also needs to be mentioned. Indeed, Part IV of this book owes more to his work than to anybody else's. I therefore want to thank Professor Dryden for engaging in stimulating correspondence over a number of years.

Coaching is a goal-focused activity. It has been my great pleasure, therefore, to discuss the topic of goals with the world's leading experts on goal-setting: Dr Edwin Locke and Dr Gary Latham. I would like to thank both for taking the time to clarify several important issues. I must also acknowledge the help of Dr Gerard Seijts, who read a draft of the Appendix on learning goals. If there is any value in that appendix then Dr Seijts deserves much of the credit. Dr Dominique Morisano – an expert on the use of goal-setting in academic settings – also offered an invaluable perspective.

Professor Dale Schunk took the time to address several queries about grades, learning and motivation. Gabriele Oettingen and Peter Gollwitzer – professors of psychology at New York University – confirmed points about 'mental contrasting' and 'if-then plans' respectively. Professor Gollwitzer also read and tweaked my account of his work in Chapter 10. Input from Dr Anthony Grant helped me to improve Chapter 3 on the evidence for coaching. Dr Christian van Nieuwerburgh generously supplied additional sources. Professor Aylet Fishbach helped me to develop a way of highlighting progress without undermining commitment. David Peterson – Director of Executive Coaching at Google – kindly shared his thoughts on part of Chapter 20. Professor Jonathan Passmore helped me to interpret the results of the longitudinal study described in Chapter 3. Professors Ronald Landis and Scott Morris vetted some of the material on statistical significance and effect sizes. Professors Ray Engel, Matthew Burns, Rangasamy Ramasamy, and Robert Haccoun commented helpfully on my exposition of single-case designs. Dr Gordon Spence read through the material on goal attainment measurement whilst Pat Dugard answered several questions about data analysis.

Professor Keith Morrison deserves a special mention. I sent Professor Morrison several drafts of Chapter 19 on randomised controlled trials. The thoroughness of his responses was staggering. What I have ultimately written in that chapter hardly does justice to the depth and quality of his feedback. In fact, I am not sure that I would have written much at all without Professor Morrison's unflagging support and encouragement. He has been an inspiration to me as I have worked on this book.

Many others have made important contributions. To my great surprise and joy, I even received input from a Nobel Prize winner – Daniel Kahneman. I wrote to Professor Kahneman about his theory of 'loss aversion' and its relevance to student motivation. He not only replied but also shed considerable light on the matter that I was considering.

I would also like to thank all of the teachers, leaders and students that I have coached or worked with. This includes my colleague Amanda Triccas – a senior leader and great champion of coaching. Ever enthusiastic about professional development, Amanda has helped me to make coaching and training an integral part of professional development at Godolphin and Latymer School.

My Editor Clare Ashworth and Editorial Assistants Sarah Richardson and Matt Bickerton have been extremely patient and insightful in responding to my many queries. I am also grateful to Annamarie Kino for initially welcoming my proposal.

Finally, I would like to thank my parents. I am always inspired by my father's optimism and zest for life and by my mother's kindness and generosity of spirit. I therefore dedicate this book to them both.

INTRODUCTION

In this chapter

- Who this book is for
- The plan of the book
- Important notes and caveats.

Who this book is for

This book is designed for education professionals who are interested in coaching students. Originating in the field of sport and then migrating to the world of business, coaching now features in many schools, universities and educational institutions. There is coaching for teachers (Costa and Garmston, 2002), coaching for leaders (Reiss, 2007) and even coaching for parents (Bamford, Mackew and Golawski, 2012). This book, however, focuses entirely on the coaching of students. It will therefore be most useful for teachers, tutors, supervisors, assistants and indeed anybody else who works closely with students.

The approach in this book is primarily designed to work with students in the later stages of secondary school. You should therefore assume that most of the 'coachees' in the examples are aged between 15 and 18. This certainly does not mean that coaching should be confined to students in this age bracket. Almost all of the material in the book could be used equally well with undergraduates. In fact, Dawson and Guare (2012) note that a coaching approach can be effective with students of *any* age, so long as they have the required maturity. Suggett (2012), for example, describes the positive effects of coaching in a primary school. And much of the best research on coaching has involved students at university (e.g. Grant, 2001). One should therefore not be surprised to find that a coaching approach is just as effective with an 11-year-old in Year 6 as it is with a 17-year-old in a secondary school or a 20-year-old at university. It all depends on the student.

And of course the coach. In order for coaching to be effective practitioners need to understand the key *principles*. They must also be proficient in the *techniques*. One of the main aims of this book is to help readers acquire that understanding and develop that proficiency.

This book is also designed for schools that want to take an *evidence-based* approach to interventions. If you are a senior leader or head teacher, you will probably want to know that what you are providing for your students is supported by the research. You may also want to know how you can conduct your *own* research. If so, you will be pleased to discover that this book not only covers the evidence for coaching but also explains how you can evaluate the effectiveness of your own programme.

The plan of the book

Different readers will have different intentions. Perhaps you are a teacher and would like to adopt more of a 'coaching style'. Or perhaps you want to go further and conduct formal coaching sessions. If you are a school leader, you may be more interested in the practicalities of launching a coaching programme or the process of evaluating impact. Before anything else, you may want to know whether coaching really 'works'. Whatever your interests, the following overview should help you to find the most relevant material.

The book is divided into six parts:

Part I: **Background and prerequisites** (Chapters 1–4)

Part II: **Core coaching skills** (Chapters 5–7)

Part III: **Coaching sessions and coaching programmes** (Chapters 8–13)

Part IV: **Emotional obstacles** (Chapters 14–16)

Part V: **The practicalities of coaching** (Chapters 17–18)

Part VI: **Evaluating impact** (Chapters 19–20).

As you can see, each part of the book consists of 2 chapters or more. What follows is a brief summary of each chapter.

Part I: Background and prerequisites

Chapter 1 covers the potential *uses* of coaching as well as its benefits. It might seem odd to present the uses and benefits of coaching before explaining what 'coaching' is. However, many readers will want to know what sorts of *rewards* they can expect before they invest in the process. Chapter 1 therefore describes some of the most significant ways in which coaching helps students. As will be seen, the benefits are both practical and psychological. Moreover, they extend far beyond the achievement of grades.

In **Chapter 2** we answer the question: '*What is coaching?*' Many of the defining features of coaching are illustrated in an example and then explained throughout the rest of the chapter. We also cover the differences between coaching, mentoring and counselling. Finally, the chapter distinguishes between (purely) *behavioural coaching* and cognitive behavioural coaching (CBC).

In **Chapter 3** we consider the *evidence* for coaching. In the first half of the chapter, we see how research has established the value of key features of coaching (e.g. goal-setting, action-planning, feedback). In the second half, we look at studies of coaching as a whole. The chapter also explains important concepts in quantitative research, e.g. 'randomised controlled trial', 'statistical significance', 'effect size'.

Chapter 4 outlines the *mindset* that is required for effective coaching. In order to be of genuine assistance to students, would-be coaches must have a certain philosophy. The chapter elucidates this philosophy in terms of a few key beliefs. We explain how each of these beliefs can be developed and maintained throughout coaching.

Part II: Core coaching skills

Chapter 5 is the first of three chapters on core coaching *skills*. We explore *rapport-building, listening* and *reflecting* - essential tools for any coach. The importance of these skills is explained and we consider how each can be improved and developed through reflection and practice.

Chapter 6 is devoted to *questioning*. This is arguably the most distinctive feature of coaching and is therefore treated at length. We cover the criteria for good coaching questions and explain how coaches can elicit the most useful answers from students. The chapter also introduces the *solution-focused* approach to questioning and coaching.

In **Chapter 7** we move on to *affirming*. One of the coach's most important roles is to provide the coachee with verbal encouragement. But how should this be done? What sorts of praise or recognition are appropriate in coaching? Chapter 7 answers these questions and shows how effective 'affirming' can boost a student's perceived self-efficacy.

Part III: Coaching sessions and coaching programmes

Chapter 8 introduces the GROW model and summarises each of its four phases. A concrete example is used to illustrate the whole process. We begin to see how a coaching model such as GROW can be used to structure a coaching session.

Chapter 9 covers the first phase of GROW - *Goal-setting (G)*. Goal-setting is the foundation of all coaching and this chapter is accordingly thorough. First, we cover the criteria for effective goals. Then we explain the various *types* of goals that students can and should set. Two crucial distinctions are drawn. The first is between *ultimate* goals and *proximal* goals. The second is between *performance* (or outcome) goals and *learning* goals. These goals - and their relationships - are carefully explained.

Chapter 10 moves on to the second phase of GROW - *Reality (R)*. In this chapter, we see how the coach helps the student to take stock of her current situation. How much of her goal has she already achieved? What is helping her to achieve it? What obstacles stand in her way? And what resources does she have at her disposal? The answers to these questions will serve as a launch pad.

In **Chapter 11** we explore the third phase of GROW - *Options (O)*. The coach helps the student to think of several ways of achieving her goal, i.e. to come up with 'options'. We then see how the coach helps her to *evaluate* these options in terms of effectiveness and feasibility - how practical is each option? Which ones will be most effective in helping her achieve her goal?

Chapter 12 covers the final phase of GROW - *Will (W)*. In this chapter, we see how the student turns her options into action-steps. Through focused questioning and attention to detail the coach helps her to decide exactly what she *will* do to achieve her goal.

In **Chapter 13** we take a tour through a coaching programme. We begin by considering what should happen before the first session. Then we examine the structure of the first session, subsequent sessions and finally the student's last coaching session.

Part IV: Emotional obstacles

Chapter 14 introduces the topic of *emotional obstacles*. When students become angry, anxious, dejected (and so on), they often struggle to achieve their goals. This chapter explains when it is appropriate for a coach to address emotions. We also introduce the ABC model used in cognitive behavioural coaching (CBC). As this model makes clear, when students hold *rigid* and *extreme* beliefs ('I've *got* to get an A!' 'It would be *awful* if I fail!') they make it harder to achieve their goals.

In **Chapter 15** we see how a coach can use the ABC model to help a student identify the rigid and extreme beliefs that largely hold her back. The student comes to see that in order to overcome problematic emotions she will need to modify those beliefs.

In **Chapter 16** we consider how a coach can help a student to replace rigid and extreme beliefs with *flexible* and *non-extreme* alternatives. By developing and rehearsing helpful beliefs, the student makes it easier to achieve her goal.

Part V: The practicalities of coaching

Chapter 17 covers the *logistics* of coaching. Where and when should coaching sessions take place? How should students enrol? What sort of paperwork should be kept? Chapter 17 addresses these matters and is a useful starting point for schools that intend to launch their own coaching programmes.

Chapter 18 covers the issue of *contracting*. Before a coaching programme begins, coach and student need to be clear about key terms and conditions. This chapter points out the sorts of things that need to be agreed in advance and explains how many common problems can be avoided.

Part VI: Evaluating impact

In **Chapter 19** we cover the most rigorous and respected approach to coaching evaluation - the *Randomised Controlled Trial (RCT).* The chapter explains how a school can conduct its own RCT, collecting quantitative data. We also consider how the results of the experiment may be analysed. As will become clear, RCTs can provide extremely strong evidence that coaching is effective.

In **Chapter 20** we explain how a school can take a quantitative approach to evaluation *without* using a randomised controlled trial. The chapter focuses on *single case design,* which allows us to assess the impact of coaching on individual students or small groups of students. This is often more practical than conducting a large RCT. At the end of the chapter we briefly discuss *qualitative* data, which can be extremely revealing.

Finally, the **Appendices.** These will be most useful for readers who conduct formal coaching sessions. **Appendix A** provides a list of ways to help a student generate 'options.' **Appendix B** distinguishes the performance goal from the learning goal and explains when each is appropriate. **Appendix C** is the student's coaching form. **Appendix D** is an example of a coaching contract. **Appendix E** helps students to identify performance-interfering thoughts (PITs) and to replace them with performance-*enhancing* thoughts (PETs).

Important notes and caveats

Finally, a few points need to be made about the content, style and limitations of this book.

1. **Confidentiality**
   Coach-student dialogues feature in almost every chapter. In some cases, these dialogues are based on sessions that actually took place. However, for the sake of confidentiality certain details have been changed or omitted. In addition, names have been invented and do not refer to real people.
2. **The limits of this book**
   This book covers a lot of ground. However, no book can ever hope to replace real training. Readers who wish to become truly effective coaches will need to go on a course. Many schools are now having their staff trained in coaching skills and subsequently developing an internal cadre of coaches. By the end of this book I hope that you (or your school) will want to do likewise.
3. **The limits of coaching**
   Anybody engaged in coaching should be aware not only of its potential but also of its limits. It is important, for instance, to distinguish coaching from counselling and psychotherapy (see Chapter 3). Students suffering from anxiety disorders, clinical depression or other mental health issues will need to work with counsellors or therapists rather than coaches. Similarly, students with learning difficulties may need support from a 'Special Educational Needs Coordinator' (SENCO) or in some cases an educational

psychologist. As powerful as coaching is, it is not always the right intervention. Responsible coaches should know when to refer students to more appropriate sources of support.

4 **A note on language**

In this book, I refer to the person being coached as the 'student' or 'coachee'. These terms are used interchangeably, as are 'teacher[1] ' and 'coach', which of course refer to the person offering the coaching. In addition, for the sake of clarity, I always make the student female ('she/her') and the coach male ('he/him'). Two possible objections should be addressed. The first concerns the use of the term 'coachee' which, according to some commentators, suggests that something is being *done to* the person and that she is largely passive in the process (e.g. Peterson 2006). I do not think this is a necessary connotation. 'Coachee' need only mean 'the person being coached'. After all, somebody *is* being coached. We do not need to assume that this person is passive. Indeed, as we shall see throughout this book, coachees are very much active participants.

The second objection concerns gender. Some may consider it sexist to reserve 'he' for the coach and 'she' for the coachee. However, constantly writing 'he or she' or alternating between the two pronouns would make the text confusing (Whitmore, 2009). In any case, it should be obvious that coaches can be female as well as male and coachees boys as well as girls.

Note

1 Throughout this book, I use the term 'teacher' as a catch-all term for various educational roles, e.g. teacher, advisor, supervisor, tutor etc.

References

Bamford, A., Mackew, N. and Golawski, A. (2012). Coaching for parents: empowering parents to create positive relationships with their children. In C. van Nieuwerburgh (ed.), *Coaching in Education: Getting Better Results for Students, Educators and Parents*. London: Karnac.

Costa, A.L. and Garmston, R.J. (2002). *Cognitive Coaching: A foundation for Renaissance schools.* Norwood, MA: Christopher-Gordon.

Dawson, P. and Guare, R. (2012). *Coaching students with executive skill deficits*. New York: Guilford Press.

Grant, A. (2001). Towards a Psychology of coaching. Unpublished PhD thesis, University of Sydney.

Peterson D.B. (2006). People are complex and the world is messy: A behaviour-based approach to executive coaching. In D. Stober and A.M. Grant (eds), *Evidence-based coaching handbook*. Hoboken, NJ: John Wiley & Sons.

Reiss, K. (2007). *Leadership coaching for educators: Bringing out the best in school administrators.* Thousand Oaks, CA: Corwin Press.

Suggett, N. (2012). Coaching in primary schools: A case study. In C. van Nieuwerburgh (ed.), *Coaching in Education: Getting Better Results for Students, Educators, and Parents*. London: Karnac.

Whitmore, J. (2009). *Coaching for Performance.* (4th edn). London: Nicholas Brealey.

Part I

Background and prerequisites

1 The benefits of coaching

In this chapter

- The many uses of coaching
- The benefits for students
- What makes coaching so effective?

The uses and outcomes of coaching

All educators (one hopes) want to *get the most out of their students*. Sadly, however, that aim is often not achieved. Students regularly run into obstacles that prevent them from fulfilling their potential. They may, for example, have difficulty in:

- settling in
- managing workload
- meeting deadlines
- revising for tests
- preparing for exams.

How can we help students with these challenges? One answer is *coaching*. In the next chapter, we explore what coaching actually is. Here we consider some of its major benefits for students. Coaching can and often does lead to significant improvements in all of the following:

- commitment
- perseverance
- resilience
- perceived self-efficacy[1]
- well-being
- performance.

Given these benefits, it is not difficult to see how coaching can complement and supplement teaching. Teaching focuses on the knowledge and skills required for academic success. Coaching contributes to that success by enabling students to *manage themselves more effectively*. It helps them to sharpen their focus, marshal their resources and make the most of their abilities. It allows them to overcome many common barriers to learning, e.g. inadequate self-discipline, poor time management and lack of self-awareness. Ultimately, it enables students to close the gap between their performance and their potential.

It is important, however, not to see coaching as merely a remedial intervention. True, coaching may be used to help students who are 'underperforming' in some respect. But it can also help students who are already doing well to do even better - what we might call 'Coaching for Excellence'. In fact, coaching is an extremely versatile intervention. Consider the following scenarios in which coaching might be useful:

1. A student in Year 10 wishes to set up a society but does not know where to start.
2. A student in Year 11 is on course for straight As but believes she is capable of A*s.
3. A new Year 12 student is keen to settle in and become part of the school community.
4. A student in Year 13 wants to maximise her chances of getting into a good university.

In each of these cases coaching could be of considerable benefit to the student. Notice too that only one of the above cases is explicitly about academic performance. Coaching is much more than a tool for improving grades (though of course it can and does serve that end). In fact, there are countless scenarios that lend themselves to coaching. Generally speaking, coaching can be helpful whenever a student is keen to:

- deal with a practical *challenge*;
- accomplish a specific *task*;
- develop a particular *skill*.

There are of course a great many challenges, tasks or skills that a student might be concerned with. Coaching therefore has wide application when it comes to students.

What makes coaching so effective?

This is not the place to examine the coaching process in detail. We do that in the rest of the book. However, it may be useful to point out some of the ways in which coaching brings about the results mentioned earlier (e.g. improved performance). What is it that makes coaching so effective? There are many important factors. Below we consider four of them:

1. Self-determination

As we shall see throughout this book, coaching encourages students to *take ownership* of their lives. This results in a 'proactive acceptance of responsibility for their own futures' (Ives and Cox, 2012, p. 41). Coachees set their own goals, determine their own action-steps and make whatever adjustments *they* deem appropriate. This self-determination has several positive effects. For one thing, research has shown that students who are encouraged to be autonomous show greater motivation than students whom teachers 'control' (Ryan and Deci, 2000). In addition, when students take the initiative - as they are encouraged to do in coaching - then they are on their way to becoming *self-regulated learners*. As Zimmerman (1990) notes, self-regulated learners select, structure and create their own learning environments, proactively seek out information, take responsibility for their own achievement outcomes and report high perceived self-efficacy. In addition, 'students who assume personal responsibility for self-regulating their academic activities not only outperform students who fail to self-regulate (Krouse and Krouse, 1981; Zimmerman and Martinez-Pons, 1990), but have higher self-esteem and self-concepts, and are less anxious and more self-accepting (Borkowski and Thorpe, 1994)' (Grant, 2001, p. 4). Most schools would regard these as ideal outcomes. They are thoroughly promoted by coaching.

2. Expanded awareness

One of the primary functions of coaching is to raise the coachee's *awareness* (Whitmore, 2009). This is extremely important within education. Many students are barely conscious of the way they approach their studies, manage their time or tackle assignments. This can be a serious problem. Fortunately, coaching is a powerful remedy. Coaching helps students to *see* what they are doing. It encourages them to reflect on their approach in light of their goals. Two typical coaching questions are: 'What are you doing to achieve your goal?' and 'How *effective* is that?' In addition, coaching helps students to become aware of their strengths. Consider another typical coaching question: 'What *skills* do you have that you could bring into play here?' (Rogers, 2012). By expanding their awareness, coaching empowers students to overcome their challenges and achieve their goals.

3. Optimised decision-making

Another significant benefit of coaching is that it leads to optimised decision-making (Bresser and Wilson, 2016). This will be especially clear in Chapters 11 and 12, where we see how the coach helps the student first to explore her options and then to determine her action-steps. This is a very thorough process at the end of which the student decides what she is going to do to achieve her goal. With the help of the coach, she carefully weighs up the pros and cons of different options and chooses the ones that are the most feasible and effective. Going through this process not only helps the student to make progress in school. It also prepares her for the future. As many commentators have argued, students need to be equipped with the decision-making skills that are required in later life (e.g. Conklin, 2011). Coaching is an excellent way to accomplish this goal.

4. Improved time management

Coaching helps students improve their time management (Bettinger and Baker, 2011; Dawson and Guare, 2012). Typically, coaches help students to decide what tasks are most important, when to carry them out and how much time to allocate to each one. This can make a huge difference. There is good reason to think that many students underperform not because they lack ability but because they struggle to manage their time (Krouse and Krouse, 1981). Conversely, students who feel they have *control* over their time report less stress, greater satisfaction with life and improved academic performance (Macan *et al.*, 1990). In helping students to improve their time management, coaching therefore promotes a wide range of positive outcomes.

There are many other features of coaching that make it especially effective with students, including goal-setting, action-planning and performance and progress feedback. These are discussed in Chapter 3 so nothing will be said about them here. By this point, however, you should have a reasonably good idea of the benefits of coaching.

It is now time to define 'coaching' more precisely. In the next chapter, we therefore address the fundamental question: 'What *is* coaching?'

Chapter summary

- Coaching complements and supplements traditional teaching.
- Coaching helps students to manage themselves more effectively.
- Coaching can be used to help students who are struggling. But it can also be used to help 'high-flyers' make further progress ('Coaching for Excellence').
- Coaching is more than a tool for improving grades. In fact, it can be used to help students (i) deal with challenges, (ii) accomplish tasks or (iii) develop skills in a wide range of scenarios.
- Many different factors make coaching effective. These include: self-determination, expanded awareness, optimised decision-making and improved time management.

Note

1 The concept of (perceived) 'self-efficacy' was introduced by Bandura (1977). It is akin to self-belief. A student with a strong sense of self-efficacy is confident that she can do what it takes to succeed in a given domain (e.g. her school work).

References

Bandura, A. (1977). Self-efficacy: Toward a unifying theory of behavioural change. *Psychological Review*, 84, 191–215.

Bettinger, E. and Baker, R. (2011). The effects of student coaching in college: An evaluation of a randomized experiment in student mentoring (NBER Working Paper No. 16881). Cambridge, MA: National Bureau of Economic Research.

Borkowski, J.G. and Thorpe, P.K. (1994). Self-regulation and motivation: A life-span perspective on underachievement. In D.H. Schunk and B.J. Zimmerman (eds), *Self-regulation of learning and performance: Issues and educational applications*. Hillsdale, N.J.: Erlbaum.

Bresser, F. and Wilson, C. (2016). What is coaching? In J. Passmore (ed.), *Excellence in Coaching: The Industry Guide* (3rd edn). London: Kogan Page.
Conklin, W. (2011). *Higher-Order Thinking Skills to Develop 21st Century Learners*. Huntington Beach, CA: Shell Education.
Dawson, P. and Guare, R. (2012). *Coaching students with executive skill deficits*. New York: Guilford Press.
Grant, A. (2001). Towards a Psychology of coaching. Unpublished PhD thesis, University of Sydney.
Ives, Y. and Cox, E. (2012). *Goal-focused coaching: Theory and practice*. New York: Routledge.
Krouse, J.H. and Krouse, H.J. (1981). Toward a multimodal theory of academic achievement. *Educational Psychologist*, 16, 151–164.
Macan, T.H., Shahani, C., Dipboye, R.L. and Phillips, A.P. (1990). College students' time management: Correlations with academic performance and stress. *Journal of Educational Psychology*, 82, 760–768.
Rogers, J. (2012). *Coaching Skills: A Handbook*. Maidenhead: Open University Press.
Ryan, R.M. and Deci, E.L. (2000). Self-determination theory and the facilitation of intrinsic motivation, social development, and well-being. *American Psychologist*, 55, 68–78.
Whitmore, J. (2009). *Coaching for Performance*. (4th edn). London: Nicholas Brealey.
Zimmerman, B. (1990). Self-regulated learning and academic achievement: An overview. *Educational Psychologist*, 25, 3–17.
Zimmerman, B.J. and Martinez-Pons, M. (1990). Student differences in self-regulated learning: Relating grade, sex, and giftedness to self-efficacy and strategy use.
Journal of Educational Psychology, 82, 51–9.

2 What is coaching?

In this chapter

- Key features of coaching
- Taking a 'coaching approach'
- Coaching sessions and coaching programmes
- The differences between coaching, mentoring and counselling
- Behavioural Coaching vs. Cognitive Behavioural Coaching (CBC).

Coaching in action

Many books on coaching begin with a definition. Verbal definitions, however, are of limited use. In order to understand what 'coaching' is people need to *see* and *hear* it in action. The next best thing is to read transcripts of coaching conversations.

Below we consider two conversations. In both cases a teacher is attempting to help a student - Lara - with her time management. In the first conversation, the teacher takes a didactic *approach*. In the second, the teacher takes a *coaching* approach. By comparing these two approaches we shall be able to tease out many of the key features of coaching.

Approach A - The didactic approach

Teacher: 'You've got an issue with time management, Lara. '

Lara: 'Yeah, I know. . .'

Teacher: *(frowning)* 'The problem is you're spending all your time on extracurricular stuff when you should be focusing on your work.'

Lara: 'Yes, but it's hard. . .'

Teacher: 'You did the same last year and it affected your results.'

Lara: 'I know.'

Teacher: 'You remember what happened - you spent all your time on hockey and left revision to the last minute.'

Lara: 'That was a mistake.'

Teacher: 'If you're not careful, your A-levels will suffer. You need to allocate more time to work.'

Lara: 'I know, but I don't have the time.'

Teacher: 'Why don't you set aside a couple of hours per evening for study?'

Lara: 'Evenings are really difficult for me. I've got to deal with my brother, help my mum. . .'

Teacher: 'It's about priorities. You'll need to do it if you want to do well in the exams.'

Lara: 'Er. . .ok.'

Approach B - The coaching approach

Teacher: 'How are things going Lara?'

Lara: *(looking distressed)* 'Not great. I've got too much going on.'

Teacher: 'I'm sorry to hear that. How would you *like* things to be?'

Lara: 'I just need more time. I've got 4 A-levels to work for.'

Teacher: 'Ok, so you'd like more time to work for your A-levels?'

Lara: 'Yes.'

Teacher: 'When *are* you finding time for work at the moment?'

Lara: 'Sometimes in the evenings, but I don't get much done. I have to deal with my brother, help my mum and other stuff too.'

Teacher: 'So you find some time in the evenings but don't get as much done as you'd like? *(Lara nods.)* What could you do to get more time?'

Lara: *(thinks for a moment)* 'I guess I could cut back on extra-curricular stuff.'

Teacher: 'What do you mean exactly?'

Lara: 'Well I could play less hockey. Maybe just once a week.'

Teacher: 'To what extent would that give you time for work?'

Lara: 'Well I'd have about 4 or 5 extra hours per week.'

Teacher: 'Ok, so if you cut back on hockey and play just once a week, you'll gain about 4 or 5 hours. And that would give you time to work?'

Lara: *(looking slightly unsure)* 'Yeah, it would.'

Teacher: 'You look a bit unsure.'

Lara: 'It's just that I love hockey. I don't really wanna cut back.'

Teacher: 'Ok, so on the one hand you love hockey and don't like the idea of cutting back.'

Lara: 'Not really, no.'

Teacher: 'On the other hand, you want more time to work for your A-levels.'

Lara: 'Definitely.'

Teacher: 'When you weigh those two things up, what do you think you should do?'

Lara *(thinks for a moment and then speaks decisively)* 'Right now work is more important. I need to work for my A-levels.'

Teacher: 'And what about hockey?'

Lara: 'I can start playing more later. . .after the exams.'

Teacher: 'Great. It sounds like you may have found a solution.'

Lara: *(looking more optimistic)* 'Yeah, I think so.'

Key features of coaching

1. Coaching is largely non-directive or 'coachee-led'

A good coach does not attempt to push the coachee down any particular path (Stober, 2006). Instead he allows her to find her own way. We call this approach *non-directive or coachee-led*. In Approach A, the teacher *told* Lara what the 'problem' was and then advocated a particular solution. In Approach B, the teacher helped Lara to find her own solution. Notice too how the teacher in Approach A tried to shape Lara's motivation ('If you're not careful, your A-levels will suffer. You need to allocate more time to work.') In Approach B, the coach drew on Lara's *own* motivation ('so you'd like more time to work for your A-levels?') In this respect too, Approach B is coachee-led. As Peterson (2006, p. 53) puts it, 'the coach's purpose is not to change a person's motivations. . .but to see how the person being coached can most effectively use these [existing] motivations to guide, shape and reinforce desired behaviour.'

Note, however, that coaching is *largely* but not *absolutely* non-directive. It is doubtful whether any intervention can be entirely non-directive. In coaching the coach clearly asks some questions rather than others and in doing so he will be directing a student's *attention* to some things rather than others. In this book, this is perhaps especially true of the approach taken in Part IV. However, even then you will notice that the coach never foists his views on the student. Rather he helps her to make up her own mind. This is the essence of the *non-directive* approach.

2. Coaching is non-judgemental

A coach is there to *help the coachee achieve her goals*. Outright criticism is rarely conducive to this end. A good coach therefore never expresses disapproval and never passes judgement (Stober, 2006).

In Approach A, the teacher criticises Lara's approach. In Approach B, on the other hand, the teacher refrains from passing judgement. It is Lara who judges the situation to be bad and the teacher simply helps her to make it better. If students feel they are being criticised or attacked, they are likely to clam up ('er. . .ok') or become defensive ('Yes, but. . .'). On the other hand, if a student feels that she is being listened to *non-judgementally*, she will normally experience a sense of freedom. This makes it much more likely that she will engage in the conversation, contribute ideas and eventually find her own solutions, as Lara did in Approach B.

3. Coaching is action-oriented

All forms of coaching put a premium on *action* (e.g. Ives and Cox, 2012). Of course, a coach who completely neglects a coachee's thoughts and feelings will be overlooking a crucial element (Auerbach, 2006). As we shall see in Part IV, a coachee's *beliefs* might be her biggest obstacle. What we mean, therefore, is not that thoughts and feelings are ignored but rather that they are addressed *only in so far as they are related to action*

(Stober, 2006). This focus on action is crucial. A key question throughout coaching is: 'What can you *do* to achieve this goal?' (e.g. Starr, 2016). And for one well-known coach the core of coaching boils down to one simple question: 'What are you going to do differently?' (Peterson, 2006).

Notice how in Approach B the coach asks *action-oriented* questions, e.g. 'What could you do to get more time?' The aim is to help Lara think in terms of immediate behaviour - what steps could she take to achieve the outcome she desires?

4. Coaching focuses on the present and future

Good coaches acknowledge that a person's past is an important part of that person's identity (O'Connell *et al.*, 2012). However, effective coaching focuses primarily on the *present* and *future*. Lengthy discussions about what happened last month or last year are generally out of place in coaching. Much more important is what is happening *right now*. Most important of all, what does the coachee *want* to happen in the (near) future? This does not mean that there is nothing to be gained from discussing the past; only that any discussion of the past should be in the interests of the present and future. For example, a good coach may encourage the coachee to 'mine the past' for solutions that might be useful to her in the present (Jackson and McKergow, 2007). And of course, the point of applying them to the present is to help her attain her preferred future (O'Connell *et al.*, 2012).

Consider the two approaches again. When Lara says that her work is suffering, the teacher could ask her when the 'problem' started, or point out that she has had similar problems in the past. This is what the teacher does in Approach A. On the other hand, the teacher's first question in Approach B is: 'How would you *like* things to be?' In other words, he encourages a *forward focus* (Ives and Cox, 2012). Whatever the origins of the 'problem', whatever Lara's issues in the past, the most important thing in coaching is to help her improve the present and attain her desired future.

5. Coaching is solution-focused[1]

This point is closely related to the last two. Just as coaching focuses on the present and the future, so it favours 'solution construction' over 'problem analysis' (Grant, 2016). Initially, the coach may listen to the coachee describe her 'problem.' However, he will then try to focus attention on possible *solutions*. Notice how the teacher in Approach B moves from acknowledging Lara's concern ('I'm sorry to hear that') to enquiring about solutions ('when *are* you finding time for work at the moment?' 'What could you do to get more time?').

6. Coaching is based primarily on questioning and 'reflecting'

We have already said that coaching is non-directive. This means that the coach does not *tell* the coachee to do this or that. Instead he spends most of his time *asking questions* and *reflecting* back what the coachee has told *him*. Again, the two conversations should make this clear.

In Approach A the teacher does a lot of 'telling.' The only question he asks is: 'Why don't you set aside a couple of hours per evening for academic work?' Even this is more of a suggestion than a question. In Approach B, on the other hand, the teacher asks several questions: 'How are things going Lara?' 'How would you *like* things to be?' 'What do you mean exactly?' Unlike the teacher's 'question' in Approach A, these are all *real* questions in the sense that the teacher genuinely wants to know what Lara thinks.

In addition, the teacher in Approach B tries to capture the essence of what Lara has said ('So you sometimes find time for work in the evenings but you don't get as much done as you'd like. . .'). This is what we mean by 'reflecting'. Reflecting not only makes Lara feel heard but also enables her to consider and build on what she has said. When combined, the processes of questioning and reflecting have the effect of making Lara's thoughts - not the coach's - the focal point of the conversation.

The fact that coaches ask and 'reflect' but rarely 'tell' comes as a surprise to many people. This may have something to do with the word 'coaching', which (in a sports context at least) suggests guidance or instruction. A 'coach' in *our* sense of the word does not give instruction. In fact, he is confident that if he asks the right questions and reflects back the answers he can more or less help a student to instruct herself.

A definition at last?

It may be helpful to summarise what we have learnt so far. Coaching is:

- *non-directive ('coachee-led')*
- *non-judgemental*
- *solution-focused*
- *action-oriented*
- *present-focused* and *future-focused*
- based *on questioning* and *reflecting.*

We also said that the coach's role is to *help the coachee achieve her goal*, which in Lara's case was to find more time for work. A definition of coaching, incorporating all of the above, might therefore run something like this:

> *Coaching is a largely non-directive ('coachee-led'), non-judgemental, solution-focused approach designed to help people achieve their goals. It is action-oriented, present-and-future-focused and operates through a process of questioning and reflecting rather than 'telling'.*

This is arguably a rather cumbersome definition. However, the discussion above should have illuminated its components.

Taking a 'coaching approach' vs. conducting a coaching session

Having clarified the nature of coaching, we now need to draw a contrast between taking a 'coaching approach' and conducting a coaching session.

Taking a 'coaching approach'

Teachers can take a 'coaching approach' in any interaction with a student. By now you probably know what this entails (if not you may wish to re-read the dialogue in Approach B). Teachers who take a coaching approach will listen non-judgementally to what students have to say, encourage them to specify a preferred outcome, find out how much of that outcome they have already achieved, ask them how they might make further progress, whilst all the while focusing on action, reflecting back the students' thoughts and allowing students to come to their own conclusions.

Taking a 'coaching approach' may be very much an impromptu affair. For example, a student might find her teacher after a lesson and explain that she is having trouble with her homework. He might quickly put on his 'coaching hat' and act like the teacher in Approach B (i.e. listen, question and reflect). The conversation might last only a few minutes and the teacher and student may never revisit the topic again. This is sometimes known as 'corridor coaching' (e.g. Greene and Grant, 2003).

Coaching sessions and coaching programmes

What then does it mean to conduct a coaching *session*? And how does it differ from what we've just described? In terms of conversational technique there is actually no difference. A teacher conducting a coaching session will listen non-judgementally to what students have to say, encourage them to specify a preferred outcome, and so on and so forth. The difference between taking a 'coaching approach' and conducting a coaching *session* lies at a higher level. Coaching sessions are normally scheduled in advance. Most importantly, they are much more *structured* than 'corridor coaching' conversations. In Part III of this book we cover the structure of coaching sessions in detail. Here we should explain how they fit into coaching *programmes*.

Although stand-alone coaching sessions are possible, sessions in this book are always part of a coaching *programme*. The point of a coaching programme is to help a student attain her *ultimate* goal, which is simply what she wants to achieve *by the end of coaching*. This could be to have completed a piece of coursework, to have learnt a particular skill, or to have mastered a specific topic. In order to achieve her ultimate goal, the student sets successive *proximal goals*. A proximal goal is simply what the student wants to have achieved *by her next coaching session*. Each proximal goal can be seen as a stepping stone to her ultimate goal. Figure 2.1 provides a bird's eye view of what we have just described.

In Figure 2.1 the student's ultimate goal for her coaching programme is to have completed her coursework by 21 September. Her first *proximal* goal is to have produced a plan for her coursework (see the box at the bottom). If all goes well, she will have achieved this by the next session, in which case she will set a *new* proximal goal. If you follow the arrow up to the second box from the bottom you will see that the student's second proximal goal is to have written a first draft of her coursework. Once again, she will strive to achieve this before her next coaching session. By the final session, the student will (ideally) have achieved her ultimate goal, which, as we said, was to have completed her coursework by 21 September.

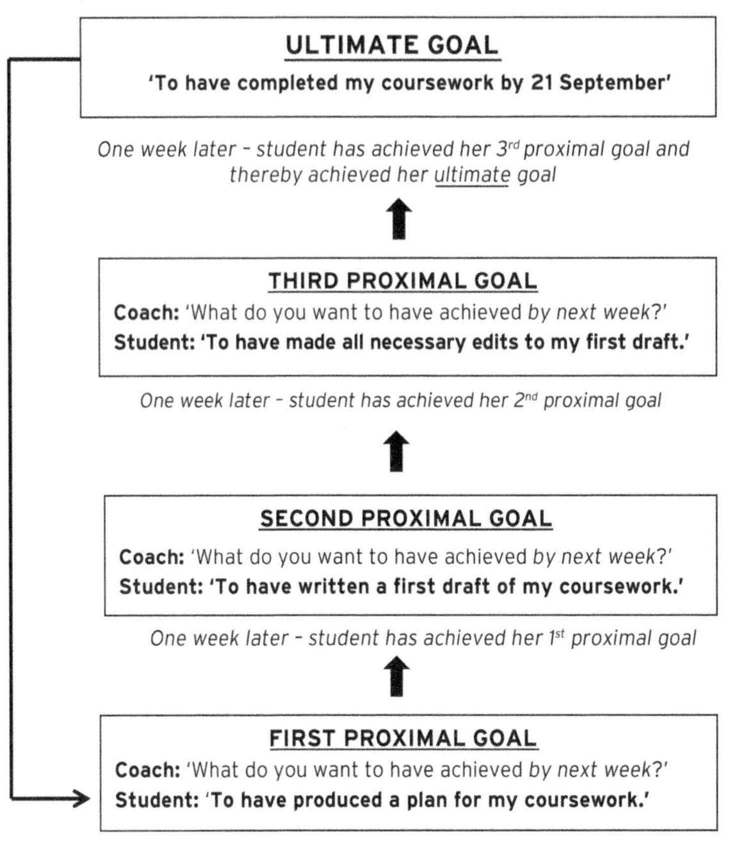

Figure 2.1 Proximal Goals and the Ultimate Goal in a student's coaching programme.

As should now be clear, a coaching programme is made up of a number of coaching sessions. It is designed to help a student achieve her *ultimate goal* by means of successive *proximal goals*. Each proximal goal brings her a little closer to her ultimate goal, which, if all goes well, she will have achieved by the end of the programme.

What is coaching? A second answer

We can now see that there are *two* ways of answering the 'What is coaching?' question. On the one hand, we can talk about coaching as a helpful style of communication (e.g. Kimsey-House *et al.*, 2011). In this case, we would emphasise all of the elements discussed at the beginning of this chapter (e.g. its use of questioning and reflecting). We could also refer to the definition we gave on (p. 12).

On the other hand, we can now also talk about coaching as a *structured intervention*. In this case, an answer to 'What is coaching?' might go something like this:

Coaching is a structured one-to-one intervention based on a series of sessions that make up a programme. Sessions are undertaken with the aim of helping the coachee achieve a distal or 'ultimate' goal by means of successive proximal goals.

We say much more about coaching sessions and programmes in Part 3. For now, the definition above is sufficient. In the rest of this chapter we shall be using this definition as opposed to the one on (p. 12). When we speak of 'coaching,' that is, we mean the *structured intervention*, not merely the style of communication.

The differences between coaching, mentoring and counselling

At this point you may want to know how coaching differs from other interventions such as *mentoring* and *counselling*. Unfortunately, in spite of (and in some cases *because of*) several publications, a great deal of confusion prevails.

Coaching vs. mentoring

First, how does coaching differ from mentoring? There has been an unfortunate tendency in the literature to conflate the two practices. In fact, the terms are sometimes used interchangeably (Wisker *et al.*, 2008). This gives people the impression that coaching and mentoring are two sides of the same coin. They are not. Coaching and mentoring differ from each other in terms of approach, techniques and underlying philosophy. Table 2.1 summarises some of the key points. For similar treatments, see O'Connell *et al.* (2012) and Passmore (2016).

It should be clear from Table 2.1 that coaching is in many ways fundamentally different from mentoring. In mentoring, there is generally a *transfer of knowledge or expertise from the mentor to the mentee*. In coaching, on the other hand, the coach's main role is to draw out the coachee's *own* knowledge. The aim of coaching is therefore to *elicit* rather than *instil*.

Many schools already make use of mentoring, not only for NQTs and newly appointed heads but also for students. In fact, the prevalence of mentoring in education may explain

Table 2.1 Differences between coaching and mentoring.

Coaching	*Mentoring*
encourages the coachee to come up with her own solutions *('How could you accomplish that?')*	**supplies the 'mentee' with advice** *('I'd recommend that you. . .')*
treats the coachee as the expert *('What strategy do you think is best?')*	**treats the mentor as the expert** *('The best strategy is. . .')*
is based on the coachee's experience *('What's worked well for you in the past?')*	**is based on the mentor's experience** *('When I was in your position, I. . .')*
is often conducted within a set time-frame (e.g. six scheduled sessions beginning on 1 January and ending on 6 February)	**takes place within a looser time-frame** (i.e. no precise start or end date)
is based on structured and comparatively formal sessions (e.g. weekly 1 hour sessions using the 'GROW' model)	**is based on relatively informal meetings** (e.g. less structured conversations - scheduled as and when the mentee requires)
is designed to help people achieve precise goals or enhance performance in a specific area (e.g. to have completed a piece of coursework by a certain date; to have improved work-life balance)	**is designed to help people settle in, 'learn the ropes' or develop in broader terms.** (e.g. an established teacher might 'mentor' an NQT).

why coaching is so often confused or conflated with it (van Nieuwerburgh, 2012). Admittedly, there are some similarities. For example, coaching and mentoring are (normally) both one-to-one interventions. And both can be said to have the aim of helping people make progress.

There is no doubt that mentoring can be highly effective. Good mentors can provide invaluable advice and pass on great wisdom. Coaching, however, assumes that people already *have* their own wisdom. Rather than turning to a mentor to pick *his* brain, a student working with a coach learns to make better use of her own. Of course, there is nothing to stop her from having the best of both worlds, i.e. a coach *and* a mentor.

Coaching vs. counselling

Coaching is also sometimes confused with *counselling* or psychotherapy.[2] In many ways, this particular confusion is more dangerous than the last (viz. the confusion with mentoring). For ethical, legal and professional reasons, distinguishing between coaching and counselling is of the utmost importance (Peterson, 2011). Unfortunately, it is not unusual to meet people who think or say that coaching is 'like counselling'. Of course, some similarities should be acknowledged. Like coaching (and mentoring), counselling is often a one-to-one intervention. And like coaches, counsellors tend to listen non-judgementally and 'reflect' back what they hear whilst respecting the client's autonomy and agenda.

However, there is a crucial distinction between coaching and counselling that all students and teachers should understand. Students who see counsellors may be dealing with bullying, bereavement, or even sexual and emotional abuse (e.g. Bor *et al.*, 2002). Let us be clear: these issues are *not* addressed in coaching. Coaches may help students who are *dissatisfied* with school life but they should not work with students who are deeply distressed or disturbed. Similarly, students in coaching may wish to overcome emotional *obstacles* (e.g. dejection after poor marks) but they are not there to address emotional *disorders* (e.g. clinical depression). It should always be remembered that the aim of coaching is to help students improve performance and achieve goals, not to tackle mental health issues.

More could be said about the differences between coaching and counselling but we have established the main point: students whose primary concern is to reduce emotional distress are best served by a counsellor not a coach. Students who are psychologically healthy[3] but keen to improve performance are best served by a coach not a counsellor.

Behavioural coaching vs. cognitive behavioural coaching (CBC)

There is one last issue for us to address in this chapter and that is the distinction between (purely) *behavioural* coaching and *cognitive* behavioural coaching *(CBC)*. Behavioural coaching, as you might expect, focuses on students' behaviour, i.e. on what they *do*. It involves setting measurable goals, creating action plans and helping coachees observe the impact of their behaviour on their progress (Passmore, 2008). In the UK, behavioural coaching is commonly associated with the GROW model (Alexander, 2016). We explore this model in detail in Chapters 8 to 13. The key point to note is that in behavioural coaching there is an outward focus on actions - what is the student *doing* to achieve her goal? And what else could she do to make progress?

Cognitive behavioural coaching (CBC) also stresses action. However, it addresses, in addition, the coachee's *thinking*, particularly if this thinking is making it difficult to achieve the goal. CBC is based on the same fundamental principles as CBT – cognitive behavioural therapy. The key premise of any cognitive behavioural approach is that the way we *feel* is largely determined by the way we *think* (e.g. Neenan and Dryden, 2014). As we shall see in Part IV, the beliefs a student holds are sometimes her biggest obstacle. For example, imagine a student who believes that she '*can't bear*' writing long essays and that she '*shouldn't* have to' do so. This student is likely to feel angry whenever she is set an essay. She may also put off the task until the last minute. Needless to say, this way of thinking, feeling and behaving is not conducive to goal attainment.

CBC therefore helps coachees not only to engage in effective action but also to overcome any unhelpful beliefs or 'performance-interfering thoughts' that may be impeding their progress (e.g. Palmer and Szymanska, 2008). Wisker *et al.* (2008, p. 29) say that '[a] coachee's practical problems will inevitably have emotional aspects *but exploring these is not the coach's responsibility*' (italics added). This statement would be true of purely behavioural coaching. But it is not true of CBC. CBC *does* involve addressing the 'emotional aspects' – *if this is necessary for the coachee to achieve her goal.*

Is cognitive behavioural coaching a form of counselling or therapy?

In a word, no. The additional focus on a person's beliefs and emotions does not make CBC a form of counselling or therapy. CBC is not CBT. A key difference between the two is 'that people seeking coaching usually focus on achieving personal and/or professional fulfilment, not on psychological difficulties that significantly impair their well-being or functioning' (Neenan and Palmer, 2012, p. 2).

What type of coaching is described in this book?

This book takes a *cognitive-behavioural* approach to coaching. However, since the book is aimed at educators with little coaching experience, much of it addresses the behavioural basics. In fact, there are several reasons why people should focus initially on the *behavioural* aspects. Behavioural coaching

- *is comparatively easy to learn* (Devine *et al.*, 2013)
- *does not require any psychological training* (Alexander, 2016)
- *is already widely used in education* (Creasy and Paterson, 2005)
- *has had demonstrable success with students* (e.g. Passmore and Brown, 2009)
- *can be taught to and used by students themselves* (Devine *et al.*, 2013).

Some commentators, however, argue that the most powerful form of coaching combines the cognitive and behavioural elements (e.g. Neenan, 2012). And empirical evidence does indicate that a combined cognitive-behavioural approach is in many ways more effective than a behavioural (or a cognitive) approach alone (Grant, 2001a; Grant, 2001b; see also Chapter 3).

We therefore also cover the cognitive dimension, particularly in Part IV. It should be noted, however, that coaching can be highly effective even without the cognitive dimension. Indeed,

'CBC will not be necessary where action-oriented models will suffice to generate the desired change in behaviour' (Williams, Edgerton and Palmer, 2014, p. 47). Finally, it should be remembered that cognitive behavioural coaching (CBC) requires additional training. The material in Part IV should therefore be considered advanced. If you are new to coaching you would do well to focus initially on the other parts of the book before attempting to get your head around CBC.

Concluding remarks

This has been a long chapter and we have covered a lot of ground. By now you should have a good idea of what coaching is and how it differs from counselling and mentoring. You also know the difference between a (purely) behavioural and a *cognitive*-behavioural approach to coaching. One very important question has yet to be addressed - what is the *evidence* for coaching? How do we know that it actually works? Most importantly, how do we know that it works *with students?* We address these questions in the next chapter.

Chapter summary

- Coaching is non-directive, non-judgemental, action-oriented and solution-focused.
- Coaching focuses on the present and future, rather than the past.
- Coaching is based primarily on questioning and 'reflecting' rather than 'telling'.
- A teacher can take a 'coaching approach' in any interaction with a student. Teachers can also conduct formal coaching sessions as part of a coaching programme.
- In a coaching programme, students first decide on their ultimate goal, i.e. what they want to have achieved by the end of the programme. They then set successive proximal goals, i.e. what they want to have achieved by the next session.
- Whereas mentoring involves a transfer of knowledge or expertise from the mentor to the mentee, coaching is about helping a person draw on her *own* expertise.
- Coaching should be distinguished from counselling or therapy. Counselling helps students alleviate emotional distress. Coaching helps students improve performance or achieve personal development goals.
- Behavioural coaching involves setting goals, creating action-plans and monitoring progress. Behavioural coaching is most often associated with the GROW model.
- Cognitive-behavioural coaching (CBC) addresses an additional dimension - the coachee's *thinking*. A student's beliefs ('I *can't bear* long essays') might be a major obstacle to goal attainment. CBC addresses such beliefs and enables students to overcome emotional obstacles.
- The 'emotional obstacles' that CBC addresses are not mental health issues (e.g. depression).
- This book takes a cognitive-behavioural approach to coaching. Whilst most of the chapters are devoted to the behavioural basics, Part IV focuses specifically on the cognitive dimension.

Notes

1 Readers should be aware of a potential ambiguity here. In one sense, *all* forms of coaching can be described as 'solution-focused' (Ratner and Yusuf, 2015) However, 'solution-focused coaching' is also a distinct *type* of coaching (e.g. O'Connell *et al.*, 2012).
2 In the rest of this section 'counselling' should be taken to mean 'counselling *or psychotherapy*'. There are those who argue that counselling and psychotherapy are two different things. However, for the purposes of this chapter they are sufficiently similar to be taken together and contrasted with coaching. I would like to thank my colleague Dr Mary Hill for drawing attention to this point.
3 This sentence may appear to suggest a simple dichotomy: people are either psychologically healthy or psychologically unhealthy. Some prefer to see mental health in terms of a *continuum* (see Scheid and Brown, 2010). However, even on this model coaching and counselling can and should be distinguished. For instance, we could say that they address different *parts* or *ends* of the continuum (e.g. Kinder and Buon, 2015).

References

Alexander, G. (2016). Behavioural coaching: the GROW model. In J. Passmore, (ed.), *Excellence in coaching: The Industry Guide* (3rd edn). London: Kogan Page.
Auerbach, J. (2006). *Cognitive coaching.* In D.R. Stober and A.M. Grant (eds), *Evidence based coaching handbook: Putting best practices to work for your clients.* Hoboken, NJ: John Wiley & Sons.
Bor, R., Ebner-Landy J., Gill., S. and Brace, C. (2002). *Counselling in schools.* London: Sage.
Creasy, J. and Paterson, F. (2005). *Leading coaching in schools.* London: National College for School Leadership.
Devine, M., Meyers, R. and Houssemand, C. (2013). How can Coaching Make a Positive Impact within Educational Settings? *Procedia - Social and Behavioral Sciences*, 93, 1382-1389.
Grant, A. (2001a). Towards a Psychology of coaching. Unpublished PhD thesis, University of Sydney.
Grant, A. (2001b). Coaching for enhanced performance: comparing cognitive and behavioural approaches to coaching. Paper presented at the 3rd International Spearman Seminar: Extending intelligence: enhancement and new constructs, Sydney, Australia.
Grant, A.M. (2016). Solution-focused coaching. In J. Passmore (ed.), *Excellence in Coaching: The Industry Guide* (3rd edn). London: Kogan Page.
Greene, J. and Grant, A.M. (2003). *Solution-focused Coaching: Managing people in a complex world.* Harlow: Pearson Education Limited.
Ives, Y. and Cox, E. (2012). *Goal-focused coaching: Theory and practice.* New York: Routledge.
Jackson, P.Z. and McKergow, M. (2007). *The solutions focus: Making coaching & change SIMPLE* (2nd edn). London: Nicholas Brealey.
Kimsey-House, H., Kimsey-House, K., Sandahl, P. and Whitworth, L. (2011). *Co-active coaching: Changing business, transforming lives* (3rd edn). Boston, MA: Nicholas Brealey.
Kinder, A and Buon, T. (2015). The role of coaching in supporting organizations to address mental health issues. In L. Hall (ed.), *Coaching in Times of Crisis and Transformation: How to Help Individuals and Organizations Flourish.* London: Kogan Page.
Neenan, M. (2012). Understanding and tackling procrastination. In M. Neenan and S. Palmer (eds), *Cognitive Behavioural Coaching in Practice: An Evidence Based approach.* Hove: Routledge.
Neenan, M. and Dryden, W. (2014). *Life coaching: A cognitive behavioural approach* (2nd edn). Hove: Routledge.
Neenan, M. and Palmer, S. (2012). Introduction. In M. Neenan and S. Palmer (eds), *Cognitive Behavioural Coaching in Practice: An Evidence Based approach.* Hove: Routledge.
O'Connell, B., Palmer, S. and Williams, H. (2012). *Solution Focused Coaching in Practice.* Hove: Routledge.
Palmer, S. and Szymanska, K. (2008). Cognitive behavioural coaching: An integrative approach. In S. Palmer and A. Whybrow (eds), *Handbook of coaching psychology: A guide for practitioners.* London: Routledge.
Passmore, J. (2008). Behavioural coaching. In S. Palmer and A. Whybrow (eds), *Handbook of coaching psychology: A guide for practitioners.* London: Routledge.

Passmore, J. (2016). Introduction. In J. Passmore (ed.), *Excellence in Coaching: The Industry Guide* (3rd edn). London: Kogan Page.

Passmore, J. and Brown, A. (2009). Coaching non-adult students for enhanced examination performance: a longitudinal study. *Coaching: An International Journal of Theory, practice and research.* 2, 1, 54–64.

Peterson, D.B. (2006). People are complex and the world is messy: A behaviour-based approach to executive coaching. In D.R. Stober and A.M. Grant (eds), *Evidence based coaching handbook: Putting best practices to work for your clients.* Hoboken, NJ: John Wiley & Sons.

Peterson, D.B. (2011). Executive coaching: A critical review and recommendations for advancing the practice. In S. Zedeck (ed.), *APA Handbook of Industrial and Organizational Psychology.* Washington, DC: American Psychological Association.

Ratner, H. and Yusuf, D. (2015). *Brief Coaching with Children and Young People: A Solution focused approach.* London: Routledge.

Scheid, T.L. and Brown, T.N. (2010). Approaches to mental health and illness: Conflicting definitions and emphasis. In T.L. Scheid and T.N. Brown (eds), *A handbook for the study of mental health: Social contexts, theories and systems.* New York: Cambridge University Press.

Starr, J. (2016). *The coaching manual* (4th edn). Harlow, England: Pearson.

Stober, D. (2006). Coaching from the humanistic perspective. In D.R. Stober and A.M. Grant (eds), *Evidence Based Coaching Handbook: Putting Best Practices to Work for Your Clients.* Hoboken, NJ: John Wiley & Sons.

van Nieuwerburgh, C. (2012). Coaching in education: An overview. In C. van Nieuwerburgh (ed.), *Coaching in Education: Getting Better Results for Students, Educators, and Parents.* London: Karnac.

Williams, H., Edgerton, N. and Palmer, S. (2014). Cognitive behavioural coaching. In E. Cox, T. Bachkirova and D. Clutterbuck (eds), *The Complete handbook of Coaching* (2nd edn). London: Sage.

Wisker, G., Exley, K., Antoniou, M. and Ridley, P. (2008). *Working one-to-one with students.* Abingdon: Routledge.

3 The evidence for coaching

In this chapter

- The research on key elements of coaching
- The evidence for coaching as a whole
- Making sense of quantitative research.

Introduction

In Chapter 1 several claims were made about coaching. We said, for example, that coaching improves performance and enhances students' well-being. It is now time to corroborate these assertions. Many education professionals will want to be sure that coaching 'works' before they invest valuable time in it. In addition, with more and more authorities calling for education to be 'evidence-based' (e.g. Bridges, Smeyers and Smith, 2009; Goldacre, 2013), coaching too will have to prove its effectiveness. In this chapter, we therefore consider the evidence for coaching. First, we look at the research that has been carried out on key elements of coaching. Then we consider studies that have been conducted on coaching *as a whole*, particularly as it relates to students.

Remember, however, that coaching comes in different shapes and forms. Even coaches who subscribe to the same general approach will differ somewhat in their practice. When we speak of the key elements of 'coaching', therefore, this should be taken to mean the key elements of a widely-practised form of coaching or, better still, the key elements of coaching *as it is described in this book*.

The research on key elements of coaching

This book takes a (largely) solution-focused, goal-oriented, cognitive behavioural approach to coaching. The basic model we adopt is an adapted version of 'GROW' (see Part III). Passmore (2008, p. 76) describes GROW as 'perhaps the most well-known coaching model'.

Whilst there are clearly different ways to apply the model, coaching with GROW invariably includes certain elements, such as:

- *Goal-setting*
- *Action-planning*
- *Feedback* (i.e. *Performance Feedback* and *Progress Feedback*).

In the first part of this chapter we shall see that the value of these things has been firmly established. After we have considered these three features we shall then consider a fourth:

- *Reality-checking.*

As will become clear, the reality-checking of coaching is very similar to a process known as 'mental contrasting'. Mental contrasting has been thoroughly researched and its effectiveness is now beyond question. It may therefore be speculated that coaching that includes reality-checking benefits from the principles of mental contrasting.

We begin, however, with the three staples of coaching: goal-setting, action-planning and feedback.

1. Goal-setting

i. How does it feature in coaching?

As Ives and Cox note, 'goals are the core of the coaching enterprise' (Ives and Cox, 2012, p. x). Consider an example. A student - Tilly - is keen to do well in French. In her first coaching session, she sets her *ultimate goal*:

Box 3.1 Tilly's ultimate goal.

Ultimate goal

To have mastered both of my A2 cultural topics by the end of term.

At the beginning of each coaching session, Tilly sets herself a *proximal goal*, which is what she wants to have achieved by the next session. Tilly's first proximal goal is:

Box 3.2 Tilly's first proximal goal.

Proximal goal

To have made notes on Albert Camus' L'étranger covering all of my teacher's bullet-points.

If Tilly's ultimate goal is the 'final destination', then her proximal goals can be seen as milestones on the way. Many coaching texts advocate setting both ultimate (or 'distal') and proximal goals (e.g. Stober and Grant, 2006; Ives and Cox, 2012; Dawson and Guare, 2012). In addition, goals in coaching are often made "SMART',[1]" i.e. specific, measurable, achievable, rewarding and time-bound.

ii. What does the research tell us?

More than a 1000 studies have been conducted on goal-setting (Morisano, 2013). Locke *et al.* (1981) reported that 96 per cent of studies demonstrated the benefit of setting a specific, challenging goal, which is precisely what students do in coaching (see Chapter 8). Morisano and colleagues studied the effect of goal-setting on students (Morisano et al., 2010). They found that goal-setting resulted in a significant improvement not only in academic performance but also in students' ability to manage workload. In addition, students who set goals experienced less stress and anxiety than those who did not set goals and they attributed this result specifically to goal-setting. The significance of this should be clear: setting and working towards proximal goals is exactly what happens in coaching (Ives and Cox, 2012; Grant, 2012; Dawson and Guare, 2012). For more on goal-setting see Chapters 8 and 9 and Appendix B.

2. Action-planning

i. How does it feature in coaching?

Another crucial element of coaching is *action-planning*. At the end of each session, our student Tilly will decide what steps she is going to take before the next session. Recall that her first proximal goal was to have made notes on Camus' *L'étranger* covering all of her teacher's bullet-points. Her first action-step might therefore be as follows:

> *When it is 4pm on Monday 6th February, then I will go to the library, find three books on Camus and write a 250-word biographical profile.*

Notice how specific this step is. In coaching, one of the major characteristics of action-planning is precision (e.g. Whitmore, 2009; Alexander and Renshaw, 2005). Coachees are typically asked: '*What* are you going to do?' '*When* are you going to do it?' '*Where* are you going to do it?' Some students and teachers may wonder whether this level of detail is necessary.

ii. What does the research tell us?

Once again, the coaching approach is supported by research. It turns out that in making plans we *do* need to be specific. That is, we need to spell out not only *what* we are going to do but also *when* and *where* we are going to do it. This has been powerfully demonstrated by Peter Gollwitzer and his colleagues (e.g. Gollwitzer and Brandstatter, 1997; Gollwitzer, 1999; Gollwitzer and Sheeran, 2006). In one study, students were required to write and submit a report during the Christmas holidays. Half of the students were asked to specify *when* and *where* they would write their report (e.g. right after breakfast on Christmas day in a quiet corner of the living room). The other half were not asked to be specific. Of the students who were *not* asked to be specific only 32 per cent sent back the report by the deadline. However, of the students who *were* asked to be specific, 71 per cent sent back the report on time (Gollwitzer and Brandstatter, 1997, p. 191).

We can see, then, that students need to be precise when making plans, as they inevitably are in coaching. In fact, in the model presented in this book students are asked to go a little further. At the end of each session, they are encouraged to express their plans in an *'if. . .then'* or *'when. . .then'* format, e.g. *'**When** it is 4pm on Monday 6 February, **then** I will go to the library. . .'* These 'if/when. . .then' plans are known as 'implementation intentions'. Research shows that when students form such plans they are much more likely to take action (e.g. Oettingen, Hönig and Gollwitzer, 2000).

3. Performance and progress feedback

i. How does it feature in coaching?

Another key feature of coaching is *feedback* (Grant, 2012; Dawson and Guare, 2012). We have already seen how the coach helps Tilly to set a proximal goal and create a plan of action. However, coaching does not stop there. In the very next session, Tilly's coach will ask the following questions:

1) *'Did you carry out your action-plan?'*
2) *'On a scale from 0 to 10, to what extent did you achieve your proximal goal?'*
3) *'On a scale from 0 to 10, how close are you now to your **ultimate** goal?'*

Answers to (1) and (2) constitute *performance feedback*. Tilly's first proximal goal was: *'To have made notes on Albert Camus' L'étranger covering all of my teacher's bullet-points.'* Tilly and her coach will find out whether she executed her plan to achieve this goal and how successful she was in achieving it. Did she make the notes? Did she cover all of her teacher's bullet-points? If not, what did she manage to do?

Answering question (3) yields *progress feedback*. Tilly's ultimate goal was: *'To have mastered both of my A2 cultural topics by the end of term.'* After one week of coaching (and one proximal goal), how close is she now to mastering those topics? Ideally, she will see that she has made at least a little progress. By 'feedback', therefore, we mean objective 'information that tells a performer how well he or she is performing a task or progressing with respect to a goal' (Ashford and De Stobbeleir, 2013, p. 51).

ii. What does the research tell us?

It turns out that feedback is crucial. People need to see the *results* of their actions. This helps them to determine whether to keep doing what they are doing or to try something different (Locke and Latham, 2002; Locke and Latham, 2013). But feedback not only provides information. It also *motivates* students to act. Experiments show that students who discover how well they are doing with respect to their goals outperform students who do not obtain such feedback (e.g. Bandura and Cervone, 1983). In addition, progress feedback enhances perceived self-efficacy and enables students to take greater strides in their learning (Schunk, 1991; Schunk and Rice, 1991).

You may wonder, however, whether coaching is really necessary for feedback. Surely students can acquire knowledge of their performance without the help of a coach. In theory, this is true. Our student Tilly could set herself a goal (*'To have mastered both of my A2 cultural topics by the end of term'*) and then periodically discover and reflect on how she is doing with respect to it. There are, however, two problems. The first is that when students are left to their own devices they often find it difficult to measure their progress (e.g. Schunk, 1983). Coaches solve this problem by measuring it *with* them (see Chapters 9 and 13). The second problem is that without support from a coach students may not make the best *use* of feedback. Feedback on its own does not improve performance (Locke and Latham, 2013). People must use that feedback to modify their approach and set new goals. This is exactly what happens in coaching. When Tilly and her coach find out how successful she was in making her notes on *L'étranger*, the coach will ask her: 'What did you learn that could help you in future?' and 'What would be a sensible goal for *this* week?' These questions are a powerful way to accelerate her progress. As McDowall and Millward (2010, p. 61) note, 'behaviour changes are more likely to take place if feedback is supported by. . .coaching. . .compared with feedback that is *not* paired with coaching, because the latter facilitates effective goal setting' (italics added).

We have now considered the evidence for *goal-setting*, *action-planning* and *performance* and *progress feedback* - all key features of coaching. Another aspect of coaching, which we may call 'reality-checking', should also be considered.

4. Reality-checking

i. How does it feature in coaching?

A key feature of coaching is its focus on *reality*. Indeed, the second phase of the GROW model - the most widely used model in coaching - is actually entitled 'Reality' (see Chapter 10). When a coachee has identified a rewarding goal, her coach will typically bring her down to earth by asking questions such as: 'What could *stop* you from achieving that?' or 'What might *get in your way*?' Tilly's first proximal goal was to have made detailed notes on Camus' L'étranger. As part of the 'Reality' phase, her coach will ask her: 'What could *stop* you from making those notes?' This question may help Tilly to see that there are aspects of her behaviour or routine that could prevent her from achieving her goal (see Ives and Cox, 2012). For example, perhaps she has a tendency to procrastinate. Or perhaps she gets distracted by friends. By drawing attention to 'Reality' coaching helps students realise that if they want to achieve their goals then they will have to overcome certain obstacles.

ii. What does the research tell us?

The sequential focus on 'Goal' and 'Reality' *in that order* is very much supported by the evidence. The key figure here is Gabriele Oettingen - a professor of psychology at New York University. Oettingen has spent over 20 years studying the effects of elaborating on a desired future (i.e. a 'Goal') and then reflecting on current obstacles (i.e. 'Reality') - a process she calls 'mental contrasting' (see Oettingen, 2014). Research has shown that mental contrasting is extremely effective in enhancing students' commitment and improving academic performance (e.g. Oettingen *et al.*, 2001).

To appreciate the relevance of this to coaching, look at Table 3.1, focusing on the **rows**. The first row presents typical questions used in mental contrasting studies. The rows beneath present typical questions used in coaching. Notice the similarities.

You can no doubt see the parallels between Oettingen's 'mental contrasting' (first row) and the approach taken in coaching (the other rows). In all cases attention is focused first on the goal or desired future and then on reality or present obstacles. Moreover, the coaching questions are remarkably similar - indeed almost identical - to the ones used in mental contrasting studies (e.g. Oettingen *et al.*, 2001; Oettingen, 2014; Gollwitzer *et al.*, 2011).

Of course, this does not mean that coaches are consciously employing mental contrasting. They may never have heard of the process. However, many coaches *do* ask their coachees to consider first what they want to achieve and then what may prevent them from achieving it. It therefore seems fair to suggest that coaches and coachees adopting this approach (e.g. by using GROW) may be unconsciously benefitting from the principles of 'mental contrasting' (Oettingen, personal communication[2]).

This may be a good point to summarise what we have learnt so far. Research shows that optimum performance results from *goal-setting*, *action-planning*, and performance and progress *feedback*. All three of these things are major components of coaching. In addition, evidence

Table 3.1 Similarities between coaching and 'mental contrasting.'

Source	*Focusing on the Goal*	*Drawing attention to Reality (i.e. obstacles)*
'Mental contrasting facilitates academic performance in school children' (Gollwitzer et al., 2011)	*'Imagine [statement of goal]. What would be the best thing about this?'*	*'Which behaviour of yours could stand in the way of [statement of goal]?'*
'The Coaching Manual' (Starr, 2016)	*'Imagine [statement of goal]. . . What would that feel like?'*	*'As you think about the journey towards this, what might stand in your way?'*
'The Key to Coaching' (Ali and Chan, 2016)	*'What are the benefits of achieving the goal?'*	*'What are you doing that is getting in the way of your goal?*
'Essential Coaching Skills' (Dunbar, 2009)	*'What will that give you?'*	*'What's stopping you from getting what you want?'*
'Coaching Successfully' (Eaton and Johnson, 2001)	*'What will you feel when the goal is reached?'*	*'What might hinder you as you progress towards the goal?'*

makes it clear that students benefit from contrasting a desired outcome (i.e. their goal) with present obstacles (i.e. reality). This too is a common feature of coaching. A compelling argument can therefore be made that coaching 'incorporates multiple techniques already shown to be effective in facilitating learning' (Peterson, 2011, p. 552).

The evidence for coaching as a whole

We now know that many of the elements of coaching are very much supported by the research. But how do we know that students benefit from coaching *as a whole*? To answer this question, we shall consider a number of studies that focus squarely on coaching. First, however, we need to introduce a few key concepts:

i. Randomised controlled trials (RCTs)

In a randomised controlled trial (RCT) or 'true experiment' participants are randomly selected from the population of interest (e.g. a school's sixth form) and then randomly assigned to either the 'experimental group', which receives coaching, or the 'control group', which does not. At the end of the experiment the results of the two groups are compared to see whether there are any statistically significant differences (see below for 'statistical significance').

Randomly assigning students to each group should give us roughly equivalent groups that differ systematically in just one respect - *whether or not they receive coaching*. This allows us to attribute any difference in outcomes to coaching and nothing else. RCTs are regarded by many researchers as the 'gold standard' for testing the effectiveness of an intervention (e.g. Brown and Baker, 2007; Stufflebeam and Coryn, 2014).

ii. Statistical significance

Suppose we conduct an RCT to see whether coaching improves students' examination performance. We randomly select 100 students and randomly assign them to either the coaching group or control group. Lo and behold - the coaching group achieves a higher average score than the control group. Can we conclude that coaching had an effect? Not necessarily. The difference could have arisen through chance alone. However, if a difference is *statistically significant* then *it is very unlikely to arise through chance alone*. By convention, a difference is considered 'statistically significant' if the probability of obtaining it by chance alone is less than 5 per cent. In such a case, we reject the 'chance' hypothesis and assume that the intervention (i.e. coaching) had an effect.

Statistical significance is a prominent feature of educational research. However, it has its critics (see Cohen, Manion and Morrison, 2017). Many researchers now believe that it should be replaced or at least supplemented by the calculation of an *effect size*.

iii. Effect size

Imagine that we have conducted our RCT with proper random selection and assignment. The students in the coaching group did - on average - outperform those in the control group. In addition, the difference is 'statistically significant', i.e. unlikely to come about through

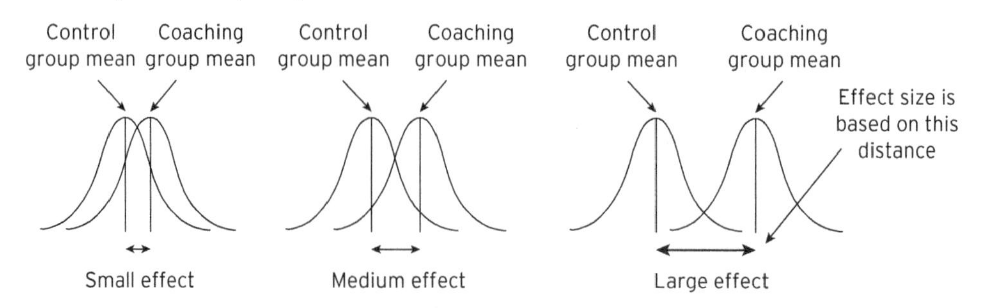

Figure 3.1 A small, medium and large effect size - adapted from Coolican (2014)

chance alone. Is it time to celebrate? Again, not necessarily. The difference between the two groups may be *statistically* significant, but is it large enough to be *practically* significant? We can answer this question by considering the *effect size*. Calculating an effect size is a way of *quantifying* the difference between the coaching and control group and thereby measuring the effectiveness of the intervention (see Coe, 2000). Figure 3.1 illustrates the difference between a small, medium and large effect.

Notice that the *effect size* depends (partly) on the distance between the two means, i.e. the mean for coached students and the mean for non-coached ('control') students. All other things being equal, the greater this distance, the greater the effect size. Cohen (1988) suggested thresholds of 0.2, 0.5 and 0.8 for small, medium and large effect sizes respectively. These thresholds are widely used by researchers. Cohen's own examples may provide further illumination: a *small* effect is equivalent to the (mean) difference in height between 15- and 16-year-old girls; a *medium* effect is equivalent to the difference in height between 14- and 18-year-old girls; and a *large* effect size is equivalent to the difference in height between 13- and 18-year-old girls. It may be helpful to bear these comparisons in mind whenever an 'effect size' is mentioned.

With the above in mind, we can now consider three different studies of coaching, each of which focused on students. These studies involved either secondary school students or undergraduates. Students were between 15 and 22 years old, which is close to our target age range. There is also evidence that coaching benefits students in primary schools (e.g. Madden, Green and Grant, 2011) and older students at university (e.g. Bettinger and Baker, 2011). Dawson and Guare (2012) therefore appear to be right in saying that coaching can be effective with students of *any* age.

Study 1: Coaching for cognitive hardiness and hope - (Green, Grant and Rynsaardt, 2007)

Background

This study involved 56 female students aged between 16 and 17 at a private school in Australia. Half of the students were randomly assigned to a coach while the other half were assigned to a control group. Students who were coached completed a 10 session programme conducted by teachers who had been trained in coaching. The aim was to see whether coaching would have a positive impact on well-being, in particular students' 'cognitive hardiness' and 'hope'. The coaching involved 'setting goals, developing action plans [and] monitoring and evaluating progress' (Green *et al.*, 2007, p. 27). In other words, precisely the elements discussed earlier in this chapter.

Results

Results of the experiment revealed statistically significant increases in both hope and cognitive hardiness for the students who were coached but no such changes for the students in the control group. The authors do not give effect sizes. However, these can easily be calculated from their data and come out as 1.15 for 'cognitive hardiness' and 0.82 for 'hope'.[3] Using Cohen's (1988) guidelines, we can describe both of these as large effects.

The authors note that 'cognitive hardiness' is a key dimension of *resilience*. Students who are high in hardiness find it easier to face stressful situations and are better protected from possibly damaging experiences (Green *et al.*, 2007; Maddi, 2002). The experiment showed, therefore, that coaching can enhance resilience and have a positive effect on students' psychological well-being. In addition, individuals with high levels of hope enjoy several other benefits, including better physical health, enhanced psychosocial adjustment and higher academic achievement (Kauffman, 2006; Snyder, 2000). The authors therefore conclude that this study 'provides encouraging empirical support for the usefulness of evidence-based life coaching interventions in an educational setting'.

A couple of additional points should be noted about this study. The first is that it is a good example of a randomised controlled experiment. Recall that randomised controlled trials or 'true' experiments are often regarded as the gold standard in research. The second point concerns the type of coaching that was provided. We said above that it included exactly the features discussed earlier in this chapter (e.g. goal-setting and action-planning). However, it also included a *cognitive* dimension. Coaches helped students not only to identify effective action-steps but also to develop helpful *thoughts* and *self-talk* that would enable them to achieve their goals. This too is consistent with the approach taken in this book.

Study 2: Coaching for results at GCSE (Passmore and Brown, 2009)

Background

This longitudinal study was known as the 'Sandwell Coaching Project' or 'ACES' - 'Academic Coaches Ensuring Success'. Sandwell - an educational area in England - had been suffering from low grades at GCSE. Eighteen schools took part in the project and almost 2000 students were coached over a period of 3 years. The average age of the students was 15. The prospective coaches undertook a 4-day training course based on a behavioural, goal-focused model of coaching (involving GROW). Each coach then went on to work with between 20–25 students, covering study skills, work topics, individual challenges and personal goals. Note that this study used a 'comparison group' rather than a true control group. The results of the schools in the study were compared with national figures and neighbouring authorities.

Results

The project was rigorously evaluated for three years. With regard to A*-C performance at GCSE, the results showed an upward trend from 53 per cent in Year 1 to 73.6 per cent in Year 3. Although Passmore and Brown (2009) do not calculate effect sizes we can use the data they provide to estimate the impact of coaching.[4] Neighbouring schools that did *not* use coaching - the 'comparison group' - saw an improvement in GCSE grades from 48 per cent to 55 per cent[5] from Year 1 to Year 3. That is, there was a 7 per cent improvement for non-coached schools but a 20.6 per cent improvement for the coached schools. The difference in improvement was therefore 13.6 per cent. In addition, Sandwell's rate of improvement was significantly above the UK national average (14.5 per cent greater to be precise). As Passmore and Brown conclude, this study shows 'that coaching can be an effective intervention. . .in helping students enhance examination results' (Passmore and Brown, 2009, p. 62).

Study 3: Coaching for academic performance, study-skills and well-being (Grant, 2001a; Grant, 2001b)

Background

This was a series of three studies involving second-year undergraduate students - aged between 19 and 22. In each case, students were randomly assigned to either a coaching group or a control group. One of the key aims of the study was to compare three different approaches to coaching: (i) *cognitive-only*, (ii) *behavioural-only*, and (iii) *combined cognitive-behavioural* coaching (see Chapter 2 for discussion of behavioural and cognitive-behavioural coaching). The researcher - Anthony Grant - wanted to see what effects these approaches would have on students' academic achievement, approaches to learning and study, self-regulation, study-related anxiety, non-study-related anxiety, private self-consciousness and self-concept. All three coaching programmes (cognitive-only, behavioural-only and combined cognitive-behavioural) were made up of six separate sessions. To assess the longevity of the effects, academic performance was tracked for an additional semester and a follow-up study was conducted.

Results

In terms of effect sizes, the *cognitive-only* coaching programme had its greatest impact on 'achieving' approaches to study, study-related self-regulation and intellectual ability self-concept. In all of these cases a large effect was observed. There was a smaller but still medium-to-large effect on 'deep' approaches to study, scholastic competence self-concept, test anxiety and non-study-related anxiety (i.e. these types of anxiety were significantly reduced). Crucially, however, academic performance did *not* improve. In fact, the academic performance of the control group improved whilst that of the cognitive-only coaching group actually declined.

In terms of effect sizes, the *behavioural-only* coaching programme had its greatest impact on test anxiety (which was significantly reduced) and academic performance (which significantly improved). In both cases a large effect was observed. However, there was virtually no effect on self-regulation, surface or achieving approaches to learning or self-concept.

Finally, consider the results of the combined cognitive-behavioural coaching programme. In terms of effect size, this programme had its greatest impact on academic performance, deep approaches for learning and test anxiety (which, once again, was significantly reduced). In all of these cases a large effect was observed. There was also a statistically significant impact on scholastic competence self-concept, achieving approaches to learning, non-study-related self-regulation, global self-worth, study-related self-regulation and intellectual ability self-concept. Crucially, the improvement in academic performance was still evident in the follow-up study one semester later. In contrast, the academic performance of the students in the behavioural-only programme had declined by this point.

In summary, the *combined cognitive-behavioural* coaching programme emerged as superior to the cognitive-only and behavioural-only coaching programmes in several key respects. The results suggest that a *cognitive-only* approach to coaching can enhance well-being and self-concept but does not actually improve students' performance. On the other hand, the *behavioural-only* approach improved academic performance (in the short term at least) but did not enhance students' sense of self. In terms of long-term performance enhancement, it certainly appears that a *combined* cognitive-behavioural approach is the most effective. Moreover, the combined approach also improved students' approaches to learning and – like the other two approaches – led to a reduction in test anxiety. Grant (2001a, p. 157) concludes that '[c]oaches who seek to enhance *both* performance *and* well-being should incorporate similar cognitive-behavioural techniques into their coaching programmes,' (italics added). That is exactly what we do in this book.

Conclusion

We have now considered a sample of the evidence for coaching. Some (but not all) of this evidence is based on the results of randomised controlled trials or experiments – often seen as the gold standard in research. It should be clear that coaching can lead to a wide range of positive outcomes for students, including improvements in resilience, well-being and performance. The evidence also suggests that coaching can be effective with students of all ages. Of course, this does not mean that the research is perfect. For one thing, as we saw in the examples, not all studies of coaching have included a control group. In 2005, Anthony Grant argued that more randomised controlled trials of coaching were needed (Grant, 2005). This is still the case today.

Two things, however, should be clear. First, the core elements of coaching (i.e. goal-setting, action-planning and feedback) are thoroughly supported by research. Second, the studies that have focused on coaching as a whole have shown that it can be a highly effective intervention. We may therefore conclude that '[t]here is an emerging evidence-base that coaching is a powerful tool to support learning and development for students' (Devine, Meyers and Houssemand, 2013, p. 1382).

Chapter summary

- A huge amount of research supports the core elements of coaching: goal-setting, action-planning and feedback.
- Many forms of coaching involve a reality-checking stage after goal-setting. This closely resembles the process of 'mental contrasting', the value of which has been established. Many coaches and coachees using 'GROW' (or something similar) may therefore be benefitting from the principles of mental contrasting.
- Randomised controlled experiments have shown that coaching can be a powerful way to enhance students' resilience, well-being and academic performance.
- Evidence suggests that a purely behavioural approach to coaching can be effective. However, a combined cognitive-behavioural approach is likely to serve students better in the long-run.
- There is evidence that coaching can be effective with students of all ages.

Notes

1 In the coaching literature, the letters of 'SMART' do not always represent the same things. For example, some take 'R' to stand for 'realistic' rather than 'rewarding.'
2 Professor Oettingen reminds me that "mental contrasting" invariably involves *imagery* (i.e. visualisation), which is not always used in coaching (Oettingen, personal communication). In this book, imagery is included.
3 These effect sizes were calculated by subtracting the mean of the control group (at the end of the experiment) from the mean of the coaching group (at the end of the experiment) and dividing the result by the pooled standard deviation. Morris (2008) suggests a slightly different formula. However, this produces almost exactly the same results.
4 I would like to thank Professor Passmore for confirming the accuracy of these calculations.
5 These percentages refer to the proportion of students achieving at least 5 A–C grades at GCSE.

References

Alexander, G. and Renshaw, B. (2005). *Supercoaching*. London: Random House.
Ali, A. and Chan, E. (2016). *The Key to Coaching: Learning, Application and Practice*. North Carolina: Lulu Press.
Ashford S. and De Stobbeleir K. (2013). Feedback, goal-setting and task performance revisited. In E. Locke and G. Latham (eds.), *New developments in goal setting and task performance*. New York: Routledge.
Bandura, A. and Cervone, D. (1983). Self-evaluative and self-efficacy mechanisms governing the motivational effects of goal systems. *Journal of Personality and Social Psychology*, 45, 1017–1028.
Bettinger, E. and Baker, R. (2011). *The effects of student coaching in college: An evaluation of a randomized experiment in student mentoring* (NBER Working Paper No. 16881). Cambridge, MA: National Bureau of Economic Research.
Bridges, D., Smeyers, P. and Smith, R. (2009). *Evidence-Based Education Policy*. Oxford: Wiley-Blackwell.
Brown, B.J. and Baker, S. (2007). *Philosophies of research into higher education*. London: Continuum International Publishing Group.
Coe, R. (2000). What is an 'effect size'? A brief introduction. Unpublished manuscript, Durham University, UK.
Cohen, J. (1988). *Statistical power analysis for the behavioral sciences*. Hillsdale, NJ: Lawrence Erlbaum Associates.

Cohen, L., Manion, L. and Morrison, K. (2017). *Research Methods in Education* (8th edn). New York: Routledge.

Coolican, H. (2014). *Research Methods and Statistics in Psychology* (6th edn). Hove: Psychology Press.

Dawson, P. and Guare, R. (2012). *Coaching students with executive skill deficits*. New York: Guilford Press.

Devine, M., Meyers, R. and Houssemand, C. (2013). How can Coaching Make a Positive Impact within Educational Settings? *Procedia - Social and Behavioral Sciences*, 93, 1382–1389.

Dunbar, A. (2009). *Essential life coaching skills*. Abingdon: Routledge.

Eaton, J. and Johnson, R. (2001). *Coaching Successfully*. London: Dorling Kindersley.

Goldacre, B. (2013). Building Evidence into Education, available at: www.gov.uk/goverment/news/building-evidence-into-education (accessed 13 February 2016)

Gollwitzer, P.M. (1999). Implementation intentions: Strong effects of simple plans. *American Psychologist*, 54, 493-503.

Gollwitzer, P. and V. Brandstatter (1997). Implementation intentions and effective goal pursuit. *Journal of Personality and Social Psychology*, 73, 1, 186–199.

Gollwitzer, P.M. and Sheeran, P. (2006). Implementations and goal-achievement: A meta-analysis of effects and processes. *Advances in Experimental Social Psychology* 38, 69–119.

Gollwitzer, A., Oettingen, G., Kirby, T., Duckworth, A. and Mayer, D. (2011). Mental contrasting facilitates academic performance in school children. *Motivation and Emotion*, 35, 403–412.

Grant, A. (2001a). Towards a Psychology of coaching. Unpublished PhD thesis, University of Sydney.

Grant, A. (2001b). Coaching for enhanced performance: comparing cognitive and behavioural approaches to coaching. Paper presented at the 3rd International Spearman Seminar: Extending intelligence: enhancement and new constructs, Sydney, Australia.

Grant, A.M. (2005). Workplace, Executive and Life Coaching: An Annotated Bibliography from the Behavioural Science Literature. Unpublished paper, Coaching Psychology Unit, University of Sydney, Australia.

Grant, A. (2012). An integrated model of goal-focused coaching: An evidence-based framework for teaching and practice. *International Coaching Psychology Review*, 7, 2, 146–165.

Green, S., Grant, A. and Rynsaardt, J. (2007). Evidence-based life coaching for senior high school students: Building hardiness and hope. *International Coaching Psychology Review*, 2, 24-32.

Ives, Y. and Cox, E. (2012). *Goal-focused coaching: Theory and practice*. New York: Routledge.

Kauffman, C. (2006). Positive psychology: The science at the heart of coaching. In D.R. Stober and A.M. Grant eds), *Evidence based coaching handbook: Putting best practices to work for your clients*. Hoboken, NJ: John Wiley & Sons.

Locke, E. and Latham, G.P. (2002). Building a practically useful theory of goal setting and task motivation: A 35-year odyssey. *American Psychologist*, 57, 705–717.

Locke, E. and Latham G. (2013). *New Developments in Goal Setting and Task Performance*. New York: Routledge.

Locke, E.A., Shaw, K.N., Saari, L.M. and Latham, G.P. (1981). Goal setting and task performance: 1969–1980. *Psychological Bulletin*, 90, 1, 125–152.

Madden, W., Green, S. and Grant, A. (2011). A pilot study evaluating strengths-based coaching for primary school students: Enhancing engagement and hope. *International Coaching Psychology Review*, 6, 1, 71–83.

Maddi, S.R. (2002). The story of hardiness: Twenty years of theorising, research, and practice. *Consulting Psychology Journal*, 54, 173–185.

McDowall, A. and Millward, L. (2010). Feeding back, feeding forward and setting goal. In S. Palmer and A. McDowall (eds), *The coaching relationship: Putting people first*. Hove: Routledge.

Morisano, D. (2013). Goal setting in the academic arena. In E.A. Locke and G.P. Latham (eds), *New developments in goal and task performance*. New York: Routledge.

Morisano, D., Hirsh, J.B, Peterson, J.B., Pihl, R.O. and Shore, B.M. (2010). Setting, elaborating, and reflecting on personal goals improves academic performance. *Journal of Applied Psychology*, 95, 255-264.

Morris, S.B. (2008). Estimating effect sizes from pretest-posttest-control group designs. *Organizational Research Methods*, 11, 364–386.

Oettingen, G., Hönig, G. and Gollwitzer, P.M. (2000). Effective self-regulation of goal attainment. *International Journal of Educational Research*, 33, 705–732.

Oettingen, G., Pak, H. and Schnetter, K. (2001). Self-regulation of goal setting: Turning free fantasies about the future into binding goals. *Journal of Personality and Social Psychology*, 80, 736-753.

Oettingen, G. (2014). *Rethinking positive thinking*. New York: Penguin Random House.

Passmore, J. (2008). Behavioural coaching. In S. Palmer and A. Whybrow (eds), *Handbook of coaching psychology: A guide for practitioners*. London: Routledge.

Passmore, J. and Brown, A. (2009). Coaching non-adult students for enhanced examination performance: A longitudinal study. *Coaching: An International Journal of Theory, Practice and Research*. 2, 1, 54-64.

Peterson, D.B. (2011). Executive coaching: A critical review and recommendations for advancing the practice. In S. Zedeck (ed.), *APA Handbook of Industrial and Organizational Psychology*. Washington, DC: American Psychological Association.

Schunk, D.H. (1983). Progress self-monitoring: Effects on children's self-efficacy and achievement. *Journal of Experimental Education*, 51, 89-93.

Schunk, D.H. (1991). Self-efficacy and academic motivation. *Educational Psychologist*, 26, 207-231.

Schunk, D.H. and Rice, J.M. (1991). Learning goals and progress feedback during reading comprehension instruction. *Journal of Reading Behavior*, 23, 351-364.

Snyder, C. (2000). *Handbook of hope: Theory, measures, and applications*. San Diego, CA: Academic Press.

Starr, J. (2016). *The coaching manual* (4th edn). Harlow, England: Pearson.

Stober, D. and Grant A.M. (2006). Toward a contextual approach to coaching. In D.R. Stober and A.M. Grant (eds), *Evidence Based Coaching Handbook: Putting Best Practices to Work for Your Clients*. Hoboken, NJ: John Wiley & Sons.

Stufflebeam, D.L. and Coryn, C.L.S. (2014). *Evaluation theory, models, & applications* (2nd edn). San Francisco, CA: Jossey-Bass.

Whitmore, J. (2009). *Coaching for Performance*. (4th edn). London: Nicholas Brealey.

4 The coaching mindset

In this chapter

- What every coach needs to believe about coaching
- What every coach needs to believe about the coachee.

In coaching the mindset one has makes all the difference. In fact, it could be argued that mindset is even more important than skillset. Of course, anybody offering coaching will have to know how to formulate questions, elicit ideas, structure sessions and so on. But these things will do no good whatsoever unless they are underpinned by the right philosophy. This philosophy consists of certain fundamental *beliefs* about the coach, the coachee and the process of coaching. In this chapter we discuss some of these beliefs. For those who are familiar with person-centred counselling much of the following will sound familiar. Indeed, as Joseph (2014, p. 71) points out, '[t]he ideas first associated with the person-centred movement underpin the practice of many coaches.'

Belief 1: The coachee has the potential to make progress

Coaches must genuinely believe in the potential of their coachees. Students themselves will have varying degrees of confidence. Some may have a strong sense of self-efficacy. But others will be experiencing self-doubt. Coaches therefore need to be confident that students can improve their performance. This confidence is likely to benefit the student in several ways. First, people find it much easier to believe in themselves when significant others express faith in their abilities (Bandura, 1997). Second, evidence suggests that students are more likely to develop intellectually when teachers have positive expectations of their progress (Rosenthal and Jacobson, 1968; Crano and Mellon, 1978). Third, when coaches believe that students can succeed, they allow those students to stand on their own two feet. They work *with* the coachee, rather than *on* the coachee (Stober, 2006). This is particularly important for students. As students are allowed to solve their own problems and succeed at real tasks they experience a growing sense of self-efficacy (Schunk, 1989).

Whitmore summarises the point nicely: 'For people to build their self-belief, in addition to accumulating successes they need to know that other people believe in them, which means being trusted, allowed, encouraged and supported to make their own choices and decisions.' (Whitmore, 2009, p. 19). We can see, then, how important it is for the coach to believe in the coachee.

How to develop, maintain and act on this belief

Coaches need to find *reasons* to believe in their coachees (Boniwell, Kauffman and Silberman, 2014). There is more than one way to do this. Before coaching starts, the coach may wish to read up on the coachee. Her profile or reports may offer a glimpse of her potential. For instance, it might be useful to know that she participates in several societies or that many of her teachers are impressed by her commitment. On the other hand, the coach should remember that past performance and present potential are two different things (Whitmore, 2009). Coaching focuses primarily on the present and future. The coach should therefore always be on the look-out for *current* strengths and successes. Perhaps most importantly of all, he should remember that *all* human beings have the potential to develop, provided they are given the right encouragement.

Belief 2: The coachee has more at her disposal than she currently realises

One of the key functions of coaching is to raise the coachee's *awareness* (Whitmore, 2009). If she cannot see a way forward, then she is probably not seeing the whole picture. She may not be aware of the *skills* she possesses. Or she may be forgetting past successes. Or perhaps she does not realise how many people are there to help her. Whatever the case, if she is not performing at the level she desires, then she is probably using only a fraction of her resources. By raising her awareness of these resources the coach not only boosts her morale but helps her to identify the means by which she can achieve her goals. In short, the coach must always remember that the coachee has *more at her disposal than she currently realises.*

How to develop, maintain and act on this belief

At the beginning of the programme the coach may invite the coachee to draw up a list of 'resources'. She could make a note of everything she has that could help her achieve her goal. This could include (i) relevant skills, (ii) past experiences, (iii) personal qualities, (iv) useful tools (e.g. books, websites), (v) helpful people, and so on. Later on in coaching, if ever she feels stuck, the coach could remind her of her list.

Belief 3: The solutions tend to lie with the coachee not the coach

As educators, we may assume that we know more than our students. After all, we are older and more experienced than they are. However, it is a fundamental tenet of coaching that the coachee tends to know best. Some commentators rightly point out that there are times when coachees do *not* have the solutions (e.g. Cavanagh, 2006). Input from the coach may therefore occasionally be helpful. But generally speaking, the coach should assume that the student can find her *own* answers. His job is to ask the right questions.

How to develop, maintain and act on this belief

This belief is not always easy to hold onto. Students sometimes struggle to think of answers. And teachers may assume that they need to 'impart their wisdom'. However, there are at least three points that every coach should bear in mind:

(i) **Remember that the student knows more about *the situation* than the coach.** It is the *student* - not the coach - who is experiencing the challenge or working towards the goal. She is the one taking action. She is the one who sees the results. It is therefore safe to assume that since she is *in* the situation she will know more about it than the coach, who is necessarily at some remove from it. Coachees are the experts on their own experience (Stober, 2006).

(ii) **Remember that the student knows more about *herself* than the coach does.** The coach should also remind himself that he knows much less about the coachee than she knows about herself. Unlike him, she will have intimate, first-hand knowledge of her thoughts, values, and personality. She knows what she likes and dislikes, what she finds easy and what she finds difficult, what leaves her cold and what inspires her to act. She is therefore probably more likely than the coach to know what sort of solution will work for her and what sort of solution will not (Berg and Szabo, 2005).

(iii) **Remember that the student has probably already *found* at least part of the solution.** Imagine a student who is late for almost every lesson. Doesn't she need input or guidance from her coach? Not necessarily. The key lies in the word 'almost'. The student is late for *almost* every lesson. This implies that she is at least sometimes on time. The coach could therefore help her to recall the occasions on which she has been punctual and then ask her: 'How did you do that?'

Belief 4: Coaching is about building on success

In solution-focused coaching we assume that coachees do not start from zero. As we saw above, no matter what the challenge or goal, it can be shown that students are *already succeeding* - at least in part. Consider a student who achieves a low mark in an exam, say 50 per cent. A concerned teacher might ask: 'What happened with the questions you got wrong?' However, a solution-focused coach would ask: 'What happened with the questions you got *right*?' Once the student has answered this ('I revised those topics well,' 'I planned my answers in rough,') he can then ask: 'How could you *build* on that to get an even higher mark?' Or 'How could you do that for the *other* questions now?' In short, coaching takes a student's success (not her failure) as its starting point. No matter how small that success may seem, it is always there and should be used as a platform.

How to develop, maintain and act on this belief

This is a belief that is best developed through action. In later chapters we shall see how a coach's questions can reflect and enhance the 'glass half full' mentality. Every coach should get into the habit of asking: 'What's going *well*?' 'How much have you *already achieved*?' 'What did you get *right*?' 'What's *working* for you at the moment?' After such questions the coach can ask: 'How could you do *more* of that?' or 'What's the *next step*?'

Belief 5: The coachee is responsible for her own performance

It is not up to the coach to improve the student's performance. Only the student can do that. A coach is there to facilitate and (sometimes) collaborate. He can help a student to set goals. He can help her to construct action plans. But '[u]ltimately a coach is not responsible for what his coachee does and doesn't do' (Alexander and Renshaw, 2005, p. 265).

How to develop, maintain and act on this belief

Before coaching begins coach and student should read, understand and sign a 'Coaching Contract' (see Chapter 18). The contract should include a clear statement of the point we are discussing, namely that *the student is responsible for her own performance*. As well as ensuring that the student understands it, the coach might want to re-read it himself from time to time.

Belief 6: Coaching is a process, not a 'quick-fix'

A single coaching session can be an important eye-opener. Normally, however, a student will need more than one session to achieve results. Coaching is often promoted as a brief intervention (e.g. Berg and Szabo, 2005). And it is certainly true that coaches should help their coachees to achieve their goals as quickly as possible. However, it is unwise to expect instant results. Every student will progress at a different rate and a significant improvement may not become apparent until the third, fourth or even final coaching session.

How to develop, maintain and act on this belief

Coaches should remind themselves that success does not happen overnight. They might like to think about how they themselves have achieved goals or overcome obstacles. Did it happen at once? Probably not. Progress is normally gradual and requires patience and persistence.

Belief 7: One of the main aims of coaching is to help the coachee become her own coach

In any coaching programme the coach will be trying to help the student achieve her goal (e.g. to complete a piece of coursework or to improve her performance in Maths). However, there is another aim that is arguably even more important - helping the student to *become her own coach*. Coaching inevitably comes to an end. And the student will not always have somebody to help her. Coaching should therefore equip her with the skills to *help herself* in future. By the end of the programme, she should have learnt how to set goals, identify resources, generate and evaluate options, create action-plans, and more besides.

How to develop, maintain and act on this belief

First, the coach should openly share the tools he is using. For instance, he should explain the 'GROW' model (see Part III) and check that the student understands how to use it ('Do you remember what we do in the 'Options' phase?'). In addition, he should allow the student to take the lead whenever possible. By the final session his input should be minimal. He might even hand over completely to the student and invite her to coach herself. Of course, he can provide assistance if necessary. But he should always remember that he is *helping the student to help herself*. In other words, he needs to think beyond coaching. He may have several sessions with the student. But she has her entire life ahead of her.

Conclusion

In this chapter we have briefly outlined seven essential beliefs that every coach should hold. Obviously these are not the *only* beliefs a coach requires. However they go a long way towards establishing an effective coaching mindset. With these things in mind, we can now turn our attention to tools and techniques, i.e. a coach's *skillset*. This is what we cover in Part II.

Chapter summary

- In order to be effective a coach needs to have certain beliefs about the coachee, himself and the process of coaching.
- The coach needs to believe that (1) the coachee has the potential to make progress, (2) the coachee has more at her disposal than she currently realises, (3) the solutions tend to lie with the coachee not the coach, (4) coaching is about building on success, (5) the coachee is responsible for her own performance, (6) coaching is a process, not a quick fix, and (7) one of the main aims of coaching is to help the coachee become her own coach.
- There are many ways to develop, maintain and act on the above beliefs. For example, coaches should allow students to take the lead in sessions (thus enabling them to become their own coaches).

References

Alexander, G. and Renshaw, B. (2005). *Supercoaching*. London: Random House.

Bandura, A. (1997). *Self-Efficacy: The exercise of control*. New York: W.H. Freeman.

Berg, I.K. and Szabó, P. (2005). *Brief Coaching for Lasting Solutions*. New York: Norton.

Boniwell, I., Kauffman C. and Silberman J. (2014). The Positive Psychology approach to coaching. In E. Cox, T. Bachkirova and D. Clutterbuck (eds), *The complete handbook of coaching* (2nd edn). London: Sage.

Cavanagh, M. (2006). Coaching from a systemic perspective: A complex adaptive approach. In D.R. Stober and A.M. Grant (eds), *Evidence based coaching handbook: Putting best practices to work for your clients*. Hoboken, NJ: John Wiley & Sons.

Crano, W.D. and Mellon, P.M. (1978). Causal influence of teachers' expectations on children's academic performance: a cross-lagged panel analysis. *Journal of Educational Psychology*, 70, 39–49.

Joseph, S. (2014). The person-centred approach to coaching. In E. Cox, T. Bachkirova and D. Clutterbuck (eds), *The complete handbook of coaching* (2nd edn). London: Sage.

Rosenthal, R. and Jacobson, L. (1968). *Pygmalion in the classroom: Teacher expectation and pupils' intellectual development*. New York: Holt, Rinehart, & Winston.

Schunk, D.H. (1989). Self-efficacy and cognitive skill learning. In C. Ames and R. Ames (eds), *Research on motivation in education: Vol. 3. Goals and cognitions*. San Diego: Academic Press.

Stober, D. (2006). Coaching from the humanistic perspective. In D.R. Stober and A.M. Grant (eds), *Evidence based coaching handbook: Putting best practices to work for your clients*. Hoboken, NJ: John Wiley & Sons.

Whitmore, J. (2009). *Coaching for Performance.* (4th edn). London: Nicholas Brealey.

Part II

Core coaching skills

5 Rapport-building, listening and reflecting

In this chapter

- Core coaching skills
- Building rapport with coachees
- The importance of listening
- The value of 'reflecting'.

The coach's skillset

In the last chapter, we examined the mindset that is required for effective coaching. In this chapter and the next three we cover the necessary *skillset*. Although different schools of coaching promote (slightly) different skills, almost all attach great importance to listening, reflecting and questioning. In this book, we also cover rapport-building and affirming. The complete list of skills is therefore as follows:

1. **Rapport-building**
2. **Listening**
3. **Reflecting**
4. **Questioning**
5. **Affirming**

In this chapter, we consider the first three skills, since they are closely related. In the next chapter, we focus on questioning and in the chapter after that we look at 'affirming'.

Rapport-building

In order for coaching to be effective, there must be a certain amount of rapport between coach and coachee. The coachee must be comfortable in the coach's presence and feel that she can speak openly and honestly without fear of judgement (Ives and Cox, 2012). To be clear, there is no need for a 'deep connection'. But most experienced practitioners would agree that 'the foundation of effective coaching is the successful formation of a collaborative relationship' (Stober and Grant, 2006, p. 360). What can the coach do to bring this about? Below are some pointers.

1. Good eye contact

This may seem an obvious point but many people are unaware of it. The coach should make good eye contact with the coachee, *particularly when she is speaking*. However, constant eye contact could make the coachee uncomfortable. The coach may therefore wish to break eye contact occasionally when he himself is speaking.

2. Friendly manner

A coach is not a friend. Nevertheless, it important to be *friendly*. Some commentators argue that too much warmth can be detrimental in coaching (e.g. O'Broin and Palmer, 2010). This may be true but we should also remember that students often see teachers as remote and may feel uneasy in their presence. A friendly manner can help the coachee to relax. This is especially important at the beginning of coaching.

3. Use of humour

Clearly, coach and student need to take coaching seriously. But a touch of humour now and then can be highly effective. It is often a useful way to lighten the mood if a coachee is feeling tense or stressed (Alexander and Renshaw, 2005). It can also encourage a student to speak more freely about her goal and challenges.

4. Informal conversation

A good way to build rapport with the coachee is to talk to her about something other than coaching. The coach could ask the student about her interests or how she spends her leisure time (Dawson and Guare, 2012; O'Connell, Palmer and Williams, 2012). This is actually more than a rapport-building device. It enables the coach to understand the coachee *as a whole*, which can only be a good thing for coaching (Berg and Szabó, 2005).

5. Matching style of communication

A coach can build rapport with a student by adopting a similar mode of expression. For example, if she uses a particular metaphor, he too can use that metaphor. This matching of language and expression (so long as it is done in moderation) often enhances rapport (O'Connell *et al.*, 2012).

6. Showing respect and acceptance

A good coach treats the coachee *as his equal*. There is never a sense of superiority or judgement. Teachers who are used to telling students off will therefore need to learn a new approach. Person-centred counselling espouses the principle of 'unconditional positive regard' (e.g. Rogers, 1957). The same basic idea can be taken to apply in coaching (Stober, 2006).

These are just a few of the ways in which a coach can build rapport with the coachee. However, rapport is rarely immediate. Students will generally be more open with their coaches in the third or fourth session than they are in the first.

We now move on to listening and reflecting, which are also two of the most powerful ways to build rapport. Moreover, they are the primary means by which the coach can understand the student and help her to make progress.

Listening

> *'The most basic of all human needs is the need to understand and be understood. The best way to understand people is to* ***listen to them****.'* (Ralph Nicols - emphasis added)

The importance of listening in coaching cannot be overstated. Greene and Grant (2003) estimate that coaches should spend about 70-80 per cent of their time listening. Moreover, this is *highly focused* listening. The coach should attend as closely as possible not only to what the coachee says but also to how she says it (e.g. Wisker *et al*, 2008). Inexperienced coaches sometimes find this difficult. In fact, it is probably fair to say that *most* people struggle to pay attention in this way. Too often we get lost in in our own thoughts or agenda and lose track of what the other person is saying. Even a trained coach may fall into this trap. For instance, instead of listening to the coachee a coach may be mentally preparing his next question. This severs the connection with the coachee and may result in her feeling that she has not been heard. Fortunately, there are many ways to improve one's listening skills. Here are some of the most effective:

1. Look as well as listen

In listening to the student, the coach should also pay attention to her facial expression and body language. Does she grimace when describing her workload? Does she look excited when describing her goal? These visual clues are extremely important. Listening, therefore, is not just about hearing a person's words. It is about 'receiving everything that person communicates' (Kimsey-House *et al.*, 2011, p. xvii). Ives and Cox (2012) call this '*holistic* listening'.

2. Follow the coachee's train of thought

When a student is speaking, it is very easy for the coach to get lost in his own thoughts. If he believes he already understands the coachee's issue, he may mentally jump ahead to what he considers most important (Stober, 2006). Or he may start to think about a comparable case from his own experience (Kimsey-House *et al.*, 2011). Generally speaking, these mental excursions should be cut short. As far as possible the coach should attempt to follow the *coachee's* train of thought (Whitmore, 2009). What is she getting at? What does she think is going on?

3. Be mindful of distractions

Remaining 100 per cent focused on the student at all times is probably impossible. The key is not to *eliminate* all distractions, but to be aware of them when they occur. This involves noticing irrelevant thoughts, gently letting them go and then refocusing on what the coachee is saying (e.g. Kimsey-House *et al.*, 2011).

4. Pause before responding

Finally, a simple but effective tip. When the student appears to have finished her sentence, the coach should wait for a couple of seconds before responding. This not only enables the student to finish off her thought, but also gives the coach a little more time to process what she has said.

In one sense, listening should be simple: you just listen. And yet many people struggle to do this. What is it that gets in the way? Unfortunately, in student-teacher conversations it may be the teacher's *mindset*. Teachers may fall into the trap of thinking that they know best and that there is not much they can learn from the student. The antidote to this is to rehearse the coaching beliefs from the last chapter. For example, every coach should remember that the student *knows more about her predicament than he does*. He should therefore be *curious* to find out what she thinks. As Grant points out, 'each coaching session is an opportunity for the coach to learn more about coaching *from the coachee*' (Grant, 2016, p. 114).

Reflecting

The next skill we shall consider - *reflecting* - is closely related to listening. Indeed, it is impossible to 'reflect' unless you have listened. Equally, though, the act of reflecting reinforces the act of listening.

When a coach 'reflects,' he tries to *capture the essence of what the student has just said*. Of course, this involves determining what that 'essence' is. But if a coach listens carefully he should normally be able to identify the main point(s) the student is making. He can then reflect this back to the student, using her own words as far as possible:

Student: 'I've got so many tests to revise for - Maths, Biology, French. . .I'm not sure I'll have time to do the reading for my coursework. . .I mean when am I going to do it if I'm revising all the time?'

Coach: *(reflecting)* 'So you've got a lot of tests to revise for and you're not sure you'll have the time to do the reading for your coursework?'

Student: 'Exactly.'

Notice that the coach does not repeat *everything* the student says. He trims away some parts and isolates what he believes to be the key points for the student, namely (i) that she has several tests to revise for and (ii) that she is not sure that she will have the time to do the reading for her coursework. Note too the question mark at the end of the coach's sentence ('for your coursework?'). This gives the student the opportunity to confirm or correct, as appropriate. As Stober (2006, p. 23) notes, coaches should 'maintain a stance of hypothesis, always checking with their [coachees] to ascertain whether they have accurately understood the essence of [their] experience'.

Reflecting serves at least three important purposes (see Stober, 2006):

i It gives the student the opportunity to think about and build on what she has said.
ii It enables the coach to gain a better understanding of the student.
iii It helps to build rapport between coach and student.

i) Giving the student the chance to think about and build on what she has said

Student: *(looking dejected)* 'This term has *not* started well. . .I've missed two deadlines and I completely forgot about a meeting I had yesterday. . .I don't know what's wrong with me. . .I'm not normally like this.'

Coach: *(reflecting)* 'Ok, you've missed two deadlines and you forgot about a meeting. . . but you're not normally like that?'

Student: No, I'm not. Normally I'm pretty organised. . .have everything in my diary. . . I guess it must be the stress of exams.'

Coach: *(reflecting)* 'So normally you're pretty organised and have everything in your diary?'

Student: 'Yeah. I think I need to start using my diary again.'

Notice how the coach helps the student in this example. Rather than offering his own perspective or even asking questions he merely *reflects back what the student is saying*, putting her in a position to build on it. In this case hearing her own words enables her to come to her own conclusion ('I think I need to start using my diary again').

ii) Helping the coach to gain a better understanding of the student

Student: 'I just can't get myself to work. . .I spend so much time on Facebook when I know I should be studying.'

Coach: 'So on the one hand you spend a lot of time on Facebook. On the other hand, you know you should be studying?'

Student: 'Yeah – it's just that work can be so *boring*. I guess Facebook's like my escape or something.'

Coach: 'Facebook is your escape?'

Student: 'Yeah – not just Facebook, though. TV, my phone – anything other than work.'

Coach: 'So when you find work boring, you use things like Facebook, TV and your phone as an escape?'

Student: 'Definitely.'

In the dialogue above it would have been easy for the coach to get the wrong end of the stick. For example, when the student says that she spends 'so much time on Facebook' he might have thought: 'Typical - another teenager who's obsessed with social media.' However, by keeping an open mind and reflecting back the student's words, he allows more of the truth to emerge. It turns out (apparently) that the student is not 'obsessed with social media'. Rather she uses Facebook and other things as an 'escape' from 'boring' work. Reflection in this case enabled the coach to gain a better understanding of the student. More importantly, it probably helped the student to gain a better understanding of herself.

iii) Helping to build rapport between coach and student

Student: *(looking distressed)* 'I know there are exams coming up and I obviously want to do well. . .but giving up hockey is tough. It's the one thing I look *forward* to in the week. But my parents and teachers keep going on about exams. . .'

Coach: *(reflecting)* 'So you want to do well in your exams. But it's tough to give up hockey because it's the one thing you actually look *forward* to?'

Student: *(nodding)* 'Exactly. I wish people would *get* that. . .'

Coach 'I can see how that makes things tough. What solutions have you considered?'

You may recall this scenario from Chapter 2. Note how the coach not only reflects back the two sides of the student's dilemma (her desire to do well in the exams vs. her reluctance to give up something she enjoys) but also *empathises* with the student ('I can see how that makes things tough'). Reflecting should never be mere verbal parroting. The coach should also make an effort to *see* the situation from the student's perspective. Of all the different ways to build rapport, this is arguably the most powerful.

There can be no doubt that 'coachees receive a validation when they hear their own words coming from someone else,' (Bresser and Wilson, 2010, p. 20). They feel heard and understood. And they are able to build on what they have said. Reflecting also allows the coach to enhance his understanding of the student and her situation. But *when* should a coach reflect? Clearly doing so all the time would be both irritating and ineffective. Here are four occasions when reflection is normally helpful:

1. WHEN THE COACH IS NOT SURE THAT HE HAS UNDERSTOOD THE STUDENT.

In this case reflecting allows the coach to check his understanding and prevent misinterpretations ('So you're saying that. . .is that right?'). This also demonstrates to the student that he is making an effort to understand her.

2. WHEN THE STUDENT MENTIONS SOMETHING *POSITIVE*.

When describing a 'problem', the student may inadvertently say something that suggests a solution. Reflecting back one positive remark may be all that the student needs ('So you *did* succeed in . . .').

3. WHEN STUDENT AND COACH ARE AT A CRUCIAL JUNCTURE IN A SESSION.

As we shall see in Part III, there are crucial phases or junctures in every coaching session. At the end of each phase (e.g. 'Goal-setting'), it is a good idea for the coach to reflect back[1] what the student has said or decided on, e.g. 'So your goal for this week is to have. . .'

4. WHEN THE STUDENT IS PARTICULARLY EMPHATIC.

At times the student will express a strong view. Reflecting, in this case, helps the student to feel heard. The coach is showing her that he understands how she feels ('So you *knew* you could have done better in your exams. . .').

This list is clearly not exhaustive. In the chapter on 'Affirming' we consider several other types of reflection. You will also notice examples of 'reflecting' in almost every dialogue in the book. Indeed, alongside questioning, reflecting is the coach's primary mode of communication.

We have now considered three skills - rapport-building, listening and reflecting. These are arguably the first three skills that a coach should develop. However, they are most effective when combined with a fourth - *questioning*. That is what we explore in the next chapter.

Chapter summary

- Three of the most fundamental skills in coaching are rapport-building, listening and reflecting.
- Many things can aid rapport, including good eye contact, a friendly manner, the occasional use of humour, some informal conversation, matching of the coachee's style of communication and showing respect and acceptance.
- Two of the most powerful ways to build rapport are listening closely to the student and reflecting back her thoughts using (largely) her own words.
- Listening is based on looking as well as listening, following the coachee's train of thought, being mindful of distractions and letting the coachee finish her sentences.
- Coaches are unlikely to listen if they believe they know best. They should therefore rehearse the core coaching beliefs (e.g. 'The solutions tend to lie with the coachee, not the coach').
- 'Reflecting' means capturing the essence of what the coachee has just said.
- Reflecting (i) gives the student the chance to think about and build on what she has said, (ii) enables the coach to gain a better understanding of the student, and (iii) helps to build rapport.
- There are many occasions in coaching when reflecting can be helpful. These include times when (i) the coach is not sure that he has understood the student, (ii) the student has mentioned something positive, (iii) a crucial juncture has been reached in a session, or (iv) the student is particularly emphatic about something.

Note

1 Some coaches would call this "summarising" rather than "reflecting".

References

Alexander, G. and Renshaw, B. (2005). *Supercoaching*. London: Random House.

Berg, I.K. and Szabó, P. (2005). *Brief Coaching for Lasting Solutions*. New York: Norton.

Bresser, F. and Wilson, C. (2010). What is coaching? In J. Passmore. (ed.), *Excellence in Coaching: The Industry Guide* (2nd edn). London: Kogan Page.

Dawson, P. and Guare, R. (2012). *Coaching students with executive skill deficits*. New York: Guilford Press.

Grant, A.M. (2016). Solution-focused coaching. In J. Passmore (ed.), *Excellence in Coaching: The Industry Guide* (3rd edn). London: Kogan Page.

Greene, J. and Grant, A.M. (2003). *Solution-focused Coaching: Managing people in a complex world*. Harlow: Pearson Education Limited.

Ives, Y. and Cox, E. (2012). *Goal-focused coaching: Theory and practice*. New York: Routledge.

Kimsey-House, H., Kimsey-House, K., Sandahl, P. and Whitworth, L. (2011). *Co-active coaching: Changing business, transforming lives* (3rd edn). Boston, MA: Nicholas Brealey.

O'Broin, A. and Palmer, S. (2010). Introducing an interpersonal perspective on the coaching relationship. In S. Palmer and A. McDowall (eds), *The coaching relationship: Putting people first*. Hove: Routledge.

O'Connell, B., Palmer, S. and Williams, H. (2012). *Solution Focused Coaching in Practice*. Hove: Routledge.

Rogers, C.R. (1957). The Necessary and Sufficient Conditions of Therapeutic Personality Change. *Journal of Consulting Psychology*, 21, 95-103.

Stober, D. (2006). Coaching from the humanistic perspective. In D.R. Stober and A.M. Grant (eds), *Evidence based coaching handbook: Putting best practices to work for your clients*. Hoboken, NJ: John Wiley & Sons.

Stober, D. and Grant A.M. (2006). Toward a contextual approach to coaching. In D.R. Stober and A.M. Grant (eds), *Evidence based coaching handbook: Putting best practices to work for your clients*. Hoboken, NJ: John Wiley & Sons.

Whitmore, J. (2009). *Coaching for Performance*. (4th edn). London: Nicholas Brealey.

Wisker, G., Exley, K., Antoniou, M. and Ridley, P. (2008). *Working one-to-one with students*. Abingdon: Routledge.,

6 Questioning

In this chapter

- The importance of questions in coaching
- The purposes of questions
- Characteristics of good questions
- Powerful questioning techniques
- Solution-focused questioning.

The importance of questions in coaching

Thought-provoking questions are a hallmark of coaching. In fact, almost all major coaching texts urge coaches to 'ask' rather than 'tell' (e.g. Whitmore, 2009; Greene and Grant, 2003; Starr, 2016). The reason for this is simple. Coaching is - or at least should be - *coachee-led*. Questions put the student in the driving seat.

There are many different purposes that questions may serve. Table 6.1 provides examples.

Coaching involves setting goals, identifying obstacles, devising solutions, planning action and measuring progress. By asking questions - rather than providing 'answers' - the coach can ensure that it is the *student* who does these things: 'What do *you* want to achieve?' 'How could *you* overcome that?' 'What are *you* going to do?'

Table 6.1 The purposes of questions in coaching.

Purpose of question (To help the student. . .)	*Example*
establish her goal	'What do you want to achieve?'
identify obstacles	'What might get in your way?'
think of solutions	'How could you overcome that?'
create an action-plan	'What are you going to do?'
measure progress	'How close are you now to your goal?'

The characteristics of good coaching questions

If you look at the questions in the right-hand column of Table 6.1 you may notice that they have certain things in common. This is not a coincidence. Good coaching questions tend to have the following characteristics:

1 *They are short.*
2 *They are open.*
3 *They are thought-provoking.*
4 *They are genuine.*
5 *They put the onus on the student* (to act, find a solution, etc.).
6 *They stand alone* (i.e. they are followed by silence).

The best way to appreciate the value of these characteristics is to consider each one in turn and contrast it with its opposite.

1. Coaching questions are short

Student: 'I've got a lot of things to do this week. I need to prioritise.'
Question A: 'Ok, thinking about all the different things you have to do, which ones would you say have more overall importance than others?'
Question B: 'What things are most important?'

It should be fairly easy to see that Question B is more effective than Question A. Question A is long-winded. Question B gets straight to the point. Generally speaking, the shorter the question the easier it is to process. The easier it is for a student to process a question, the easier she will find it to answer.

2. Coaching questions are open

Student: 'I can't do any work after school - my brothers are too noisy!'
Question A: 'Have you thought about asking them to be quiet?'
Question B: 'What could you do about that?'

Question A is a *closed* question. Closed questions can be answered with a simple 'yes' or 'no.' Question B is an *open* question. The range of possible answers is theoretically infinite. Closed questions tend to begin with words such as 'Have', 'Can', 'Are', and 'Do'. Open questions tend to begin with words such as 'What' and 'How'. The essential point to note is that closed questions narrow the range of the coachee's thinking whereas open questions expand it. Open questions therefore tend to be more useful than closed ones. As we shall see later in this book, there are one or two occasions when closed questions are effective. By and large, however, coaching questions should be open.

3. Coaching questions are thought-provoking

Student: 'I've told my brothers I need to work but they don't seem to care. I think I just have to face it - I can't work after school. My house is too noisy.'
Question A: 'Why not explain to your brothers how important your work is?'
Question B: 'Imagine you had a big exam tomorrow and you *had* to work after school. What would you do then?'

Good coaching questions provoke thought. They will often get a student thinking in a way *she has not thought before*. This is often the key to making progress. Question A is unlikely to stimulate much new thought. The student has already expressed a lack of faith in her brothers' willingness to co-operate. The coach is therefore going over old ground. Question B, on the other hand, encourages the student to think about her challenge from a new and hypothetical perspective. This may unearth possibilities that she has not yet considered:

Student: 'If I had a big exam tomorrow? Hmm. . .*(student thinks)*. . .In that case, I'd pick up my books and take them to the library. . .or go to my friend's house and work there.'

4. Coaching questions are genuine

Student: 'I'm so *tired* in the mornings. I have no energy for anything.'
Question A: 'What could you make sure you do each night?'
Question B: 'How do you normally find energy?'

When we say that coaching questions should be 'genuine', we mean that '[t]he coach genuinely doesn't know the answer' (McDermott and Jago, 2005, p. 87). Consider Question A. It seems clear that the coach is expecting the student to say 'go to bed early'. His question is therefore a leading one. Compare Question B - 'How do you normally find energy?' Here the coach is actually curious. He genuinely wants to know how the student finds her energy. Perhaps it is by going to bed early. But perhaps not. Perhaps she has her own unique approach. The only way to find out is to ask a genuine question.

5. Coaching questions put the onus on the student (to act, find a solution, etc.)

Student: 'I don't understand 'supply and demand'. My teachers don't explain it properly.'
Question A: 'What should they do differently?'
Question B: 'What could you do to get them to explain it more clearly?'

Coaching encourages students to take responsibility for their own progress. The student's comment here suggests that she may be delegating that responsibility to others ('My teachers don't explain it properly'). Question A is likely to reinforce that approach ('What should *they* do differently?'). On the other hand, good coaching questions - such as Question B - put the onus on the *student* to find a solution: 'What could *you* do to. . .?'

6. Coaching questions stand alone

Student: 'I've got so much on this week. I need to prioritise.'
Question A: 'What's most important to you? I mean, if you had to prioritise your tasks what things would you put first? What can you afford to ignore?'
Question B: 'What's most important to you?' *(followed by silence)*

Question A illustrates a common mistake: continuing to speak after asking a question (e.g. Kimsey-House *et al.*, 2011). This can be especially tempting when the student does not answer immediately. An inexperienced coach may assume that he needs to clarify what he has said or ask an additional question. This may confuse or overwhelm the coachee. For example, if one question is tacked on to another (as in Question A), which one is the student supposed to answer?

Good coaching questions therefore *stand alone*. Consider Question B – 'What's most important to you?' (followed by silence). If the student does not respond immediately that is a *good* thing. It suggests that the question was thought-provoking. Coaches therefore need to ask their questions and then 'hold the silence' (Greene and Grant, 2003, p. 123).

Powerful questioning techniques

Having described the features of good questions, we can now consider a number of powerful techniques. These can be used not only in formal coaching sessions but in any teacher-student interaction.

1. Scaling

Scaling questions ask coachees to rate something (e.g. the amount of progress they have made) on a scale from 0 to 10. They are a key feature of solution-focused coaching (O'Connell, Palmer and Williams, 2012; Greene and Grant, 2003; Berg and Szabó, 2005). To appreciate the value of scaling consider the following:

a. Standard approach

Coach: 'How committed are you to improving your grades?'
Student: 'Fairly committed.'

b. Scaling approach

Coach: 'Suppose 0 is the least committed you can be and 10 is the most. How committed are you to improving your grades on a scale from 0 to 10?'
Student: *(thinks for a second)* '4 maybe'.

It should be clear that the student's answer in (b) is more informative than the answer in (a). 'Fairly committed' is vague. It could mean anything from 'really quite committed' (i.e. high commitment) to 'not that committed' (i.e. low commitment). On the other hand,

Table 6.2 Scaling Questions.

Purpose	*Scaling question*
To measure the student's progress	'Suppose 0 is as far away as possible and 10 is 'goal achieved.' How close are you now to achieving your goal?'
To evaluate the effectiveness of an action-step	'Suppose 0 is 'completely useless' and 10 is 'maximally effective'. How helpful would that be from 0 to 10?'
To measure the student's perceived self-efficacy	'Suppose 0 means 'no chance' and 10 means you're certain you can do it. How confident are you from 0 to 10?'

when the student rates her commitment as '4 maybe' on a scale from 0 to 10, then we get a much clearer picture. It seems fair to say that she is not especially committed to improving her grades. This is highly significant. As we shall see in Chapter 10, without high levels of commitment students are unlikely to achieve their goals. Scaling questions therefore uncover crucial information.

Scaling questions can be used in a variety of contexts. See Table 6.2.

One last point about scaling questions. Rather than saying merely 'On a scale from 0 to 10. . .' it is often a good idea to clarify what the numbers mean (Berg and Szabó, 2005). For example, in the second question in Table 6.2 '0' is said to stand for 'completely useless' and '10' for 'maximally effective.' These signposts can often be helpful.

2. Asking for precision: 'what do you mean exactly?'

Scaling questions are not the only way to achieve precision. Another simple but extremely effective question is: **'when you say X, *what do you mean exactly?*'**

Coach: 'What could you do to improve your grades?'
Student: 'Just be more organised.'
Coach: 'When you say 'be more organised', *what do you mean exactly*?
Student: *(thinks for a moment)* 'Arrange my notes properly, plan when I'm going to study. . . keep all my marked work in one place so I can look over it. . .'

Once again it should be clear that the student's second response is more useful than the first. 'Just be more organised' is too vague. The coach's question invites her to be more specific. Alexander and Renshaw (2005, p. 293) note that 'coachees often use imprecise and generalised language.' Coaches will therefore find it useful to ask: 'When you say X, *what do you mean exactly*?'

3. 'If you were being totally honest. . .'

In coaching we need to be aware of reality. For example, if a student simply isn't motivated, it is better for her to say so. Everyday questions, however, do not always elicit truthful answers (e.g. 'Why haven't you done your homework?'). How can coaches maximise the chances of obtaining honest answers? One option is to preface the question with *'If you were being totally honest'* Compare the 'standard' approach with the 'honest' approach:

The standard approach

Coach: 'What stopped you from meeting the deadline?'
Student: 'I just didn't have time.'

The 'honest' approach

Coach: *'If you were being totally honest*, what stopped you from meeting the deadline?'
Student: *(sighing)* 'I guess I just started it too late.'

In the 'standard' approach the coach asks the sort of question that the student probably hears all the time. She may therefore be giving her default response – 'I just didn't have time.' Note that there is no need to assume that she is *lying*. Rather she may not be thinking about her answer. In the second case, however, the addition of the phrase '*If you were being totally honest*' elicits a more revealing response.

4. 'What else?'

This is arguably the simplest of all techniques. It is also an essential part of the coach's toolkit. A student's first answer to a question may or may not be helpful. But whatever the case she will have more to say. Asking 'what else?' encourages her to dig deeper. It also helps her to put as many ideas on the table as possible:

Coach: 'What could you do to hand in your next essay on time?'
Student: 'Start it earlier I guess.'
Coach: 'Ok, great. What else?'
Student: *(thinks for a second)* 'Plan when I'm going to do each bit.'
Coach: 'So you could start it earlier and plan when you're going to do each bit. What else?'
Student: *(thinks for several seconds)* 'I could do it in the library instead of my bedroom – I'm more focused in the library.'

Notice that in her first answer the student suggests a single option – starting earlier. By asking 'what else?' the coach helps her to identify other possibilities. He also helps her to see that there is more than one way to achieve a goal. This is known as 'pathways thinking', which, according to some psychologists, is positively associated with 'hope' (Snyder, 1994). A 'pathway' is a perceived route to a desired goal. Individuals high in hope are able to generate several different pathways ('To achieve my goal, I could do this. . .or this. . .or this'). The ability to perceive different pathways is especially important when people encounter obstacles – 'If X doesn't work, then I could do Y or Z. . .'

5. Solution-focused questioning

We have already mentioned *solution-focused coaching*. A key feature of solution-focused coaching is its emphasis on 'finding answers' rather than 'untangling problems' (Greene and

Grant, 2003, p. 22). This generally means asking the coachee to think about positives rather than negatives. Unlike the other techniques we have discussed, what we are describing here cannot be reduced to a single type of question. In fact, the solution-focused approach is much more than a questioning technique. It is a full-blown coaching methodology (e.g. Cavanagh and Grant, 2014). When applied specifically to questions, the solution-focused approach encourages students to think about what's *right* rather than what's 'wrong':

- *'When are things **better** for you?'*
- *'How do you do it **at your best?'***
- *'What's **working** for you at the moment?'*
- *'How could you do **more** of that?'*
- *'Imagine you magically had the **solution** – What would it involve?'*
- *'What are your thoughts about that **solution**?'*

No matter how bad things appear to the coachee she must be doing *something* right or else the 'problem' would be even worse! (O'Connell and Palmer, 2008). Similarly, whatever 'problem' the student is experiencing, there will be times when things are not quite so bad. As Berg and Szabó (2005, p. 16) point out: 'No problem exists all the time.' There are always positive *exceptions* (Berg and Szabó, 2005; O'Connell *et al.*, 2012; Greene and Grant, 2003). Solution-focused questions often focus on these exceptions, as illustrated in the following:

Student: *(looking dejected)* 'I really wanna do well in the play but in the last two rehearsals I completely forgot my lines.'
Coach: 'I'm sorry to hear that. When have things been *better* for you?'
Student: 'Well I've acted for years and never had that problem. Even the first two rehearsals were fine. I remembered my lines perfectly. . .'
Coach: 'So the first two rehearsals were fine. What did you do *then* to remember your lines?'
Student: 'I guess I was just more relaxed.'
Coach: 'Ok, so when you were relaxed in the first two rehearsals you remembered your lines perfectly.'
Student: 'Definitely.'
Coach: 'What else do you do *at your best*?'
Student: *(thinks for a second)* 'I just ignore everything else when I go on stage. I try to become the character. Stuff like that.'
Coach: 'So when you're at your best you ignore everything else when you go on stage. And you try to *become* the character?'
Student: *(starting to look and sound more confident)* 'Yeah. And then I have no problem remembering my lines.'
Coach: 'Great. How could you do *more* of that now?'
Student: 'Well I guess I could make sure I do that in the next rehearsal – ignore everything else and become the character.'
Coach: 'How do you feel about that solution?'
Student: *(sounding hopeful)* 'I think it could work.'

Note the coach's questions in this example, e.g. 'When have things been *better* for you?' 'What else do you do *at your best*?' These are classic examples of solution-focused questions. Here they enable the student to see a way forward. Notice, too, how the coach's questions *imply* that things are sometimes better for the student. For example, the coach does not ask: '*Are* things ever better for you?' (to which the student might respond 'no'). Instead he asks '*When* have things been better for you?' This is an important feature of the solution-focused approach. Questions should always be asked in such a way as to imply the existence of 'exceptions', (Guterman and Rudes, 2005).

Evidence suggests that solution-focused questioning is extremely effective with students. In a controlled study, Grant (2012) found that compared to *problem*-focused questions, solution-focused alternatives led to a far greater improvement in students' sense of self-efficacy. They also enhanced positive feelings and led to significantly greater increases in 'goal approach', i.e. how close students felt to achieving their goals. In addition, students who were asked solution-focused questions generated significantly more action-steps than students who were asked about 'problems'.

Final thoughts on questioning

We have covered a lot of material in this chapter. If you are new to coaching you would do well to take one step at a time. First, remember the fundamental aim of *all* coaching questions - to empower the student. Once this point has been grasped, coaches should focus on making their questions short, open, genuine and so on. Perhaps the best way for a coach to improve the quality of his questions is to *record* and *listen* to his coaching. He can then assess the quality of his questions using the criteria in this chapter (i.e. how short was the question? Was it really 'genuine'?).

Chapter summary

- The most effective way to ensure that the student takes the lead is to ask questions rather than suggest answers.
- Questions in coaching serve a range of purposes. These include helping the student to (i) clarify her goals, (ii) identify obstacles, (iii) think of solutions, (iv) plan action, and (v) measure progress.
- Good coaching questions are short, open, thought-provoking, genuine and put the onus on the student to act or find a solution. They also stand alone and are followed by silence.
- Scaling questions ('On a scale from 0 to 10. . .?') enable coaches and students to measure important variables, e.g. the student's commitment, or sense of self-efficacy.
- When students are vague, coaches can help them to be more precise by asking 'When you say X, what do you mean exactly?'

- Coaches can elicit more accurate or truthful answers by prefacing their questions with the phase 'If you were being totally honest. . .'
- Asking 'what else?' encourages the student to add to her first response by suggesting other possibilities. This encourages 'pathways thinking' which is seen as a key component of hope.
- Solution-focused questions encourage students to think about the 'positive' rather than the 'negative', about what 'works' rather than what doesn't. Solution-focused questions have been shown to be more effective than problem-focused questions in enhancing students' perceived self-efficacy, enabling students to generate action-steps and helping them feel closer to achieving their goals.

References

Alexander, G. and Renshaw, B. (2005). *Supercoaching.* London: Random House.

Berg, I.K. and Szabó, P. (2005). *Brief Coaching for Lasting Solutions.* New York: Norton.

Cavanagh, M. and Grant, A.M. (2014). The solution-focused coaching approach to coaching. In E. Cox, T. Bachkirova and D. Clutterbuck (eds), *The complete handbook of coaching* (2nd edn). London: Sage.

Grant, A.M. (2012). Making positive change: A randomised study comparing solution focused vs. problem focused coaching questions. *Journal of Systemic Therapies*, 31, 2, 21–35.

Greene, J. and Grant, A.M. (2003). *Solution-focused Coaching: Managing people in a complex world.* Harlow: Pearson Education Limited.

Guterman, J.T. and Rudes, J. (2005). A solution-focused approach to rational-emotive behaviour therapy: Toward a theoretical integration. *Journal of Rational - Emotive & Cognitive - Behavior Therapy*, 23, 3, 223–244.

Kimsey-House, H., Kimsey-House, K., Sandahl, P. and Whitworth, L. (2011). *Co-active coaching: Changing business, transforming lives* (3rd edn). Boston, MA: Nicholas Brealey.

McDermott, I. and Jago, W. (2005). *The Coaching Bible: The Essential Handbook.* London: Piatkus.

O'Connell, B. and Palmer, S. (2008). *Solution-focused coaching.* In S. Palmer and A. Whybrow (eds), *Handbook of coaching psychology: A guide for practitioners*. London: Routledge.

O'Connell, B., Palmer, S. and Williams, H. (2012). *Solution Focused Coaching in Practice*. Hove: Routledge.

Snyder, C. (1994). *The psychology of hope: You can get there from here.* New York: Free Press.

Starr, J. (2016). *The coaching manual* (4th edn). Harlow, England: Pearson.

Whitmore, J. (2009). *Coaching for Performance.* (4th edn). London: Nicholas Brealey.

7 Affirming

In this chapter

- The importance of affirming
- Affirming progress, action and effort
- Reminding coachees of their commitment
- Affirming positive exceptions
- Affirming the coachee's contributions to sessions
- Should coaches affirm intelligence or ability?

The importance of affirming

Many books on coaching emphasise the value of *affirming*. Of course, terminology differs from text to text. Greene and Grant (2003, p. 23) say that the role of the coach is to 'praise, compliment and acknowledge'. McDermott and Jago (2005) say that it is to 'champion' and 'encourage' whilst Berg and Szabó (2005, p. 17) believe the coach should 'give compliments'. Finally, according to Dawson and Guare (2012, p. 26) the coach's role is to 'highlight the positive'. In this chapter, we shall speak of 'affirming'.

There are many things that a coach could affirm. Consider the following:

- Affirming *aptitude*: 'You're obviously very good at this!'
- Affirming *capability*: 'You can definitely do this!'
- Affirming *effort*: 'You're clearly working hard!'
- Affirming *commitment*: 'It's great you're so committed.'
- Affirming *progress*: 'Look how far you've come!'
- Affirming *success*: 'Well done – you've achieved your goal!'

Exactly what the coach should affirm depends on the student and context. Moreover, whether the coach should affirm *all* of the above is actually a point of debate. As we shall discover, some researchers have expressed concerns about certain types of affirmation.

But why bother to affirm at all? According to Bandura (1997), one of the four main sources of a person's perceived self-efficacy is verbal or social persuasion (e.g. 'You can do this'). A student is more likely to have faith in herself if the people around her provide appropriate encouragement. Those people will typically include parents and teachers (Dweck, 1999). But they also include coaches. Grant (2006) notes that one of the coach's main roles is to help the coachee develop a sense of self-efficacy. Fortunately, this can often be quite straightforward. Schunk (1983) found that simply telling children that they could attain their goal enhanced their sense of self-efficacy.

In this chapter, we shall focus on the concept of *affirming*. 'Affirming' means making positive, encouraging comments about a student's commitment, potential, progress and achievement. This should leave that student feeling confident and empowered. It should also promote tangible success. Students with high perceived self-efficacy engage more readily, work more diligently, show greater persistence and achieve higher levels of academic performance (Schunk and Pajares, 2002).

Affirming progress

Every coaching session offers the coach an opportunity to affirm the student's **progress**. As explained in Chapter 13, at the beginning of each session (except the first) the coach finds out how the coachee got on with her proximal goal and how close she now is to her *ultimate* goal. Consider Saima. Saima's ultimate goal is to have reached the point where she can hold a five minute conversation in French about her hobbies. Her fourth coaching session begins as follows:

Coach: *(stating Saima's last proximal goal)* 'So your goal for last week was to have held a two minute conversation with your teacher using the advanced vocabulary from Module 3.'

Saima: 'Yeah.'

Coach: 'How did you get on with that?'

Saima: 'I made quite a few mistakes but I did speak for two minutes. . .and I used a lot of the vocabulary.'

Coach: 'That's great Saima.'

Saima: *(lacking conviction)* 'I guess so.'

Coach: 'Let's think about how far you've come since the first session. What level were you at when we first started coaching?'

Saima: *(laughs)* 'I could barely string a sentence together – at least not in French!'

Coach: 'Ok, so three weeks ago you could barely string a sentence together. And now you've held a two minute conversation – in French – using a lot of the advanced vocabulary.'

Saima: *(sounding more convinced)* 'I guess that's pretty good.'

Coach: 'It sounds great to me. You're clearly making progress.'

Saima: *(smiling)* 'Thank you.'

In this example Saima tells the coach how she got on with her most recent proximal goal. The coach not only celebrates her achievement ('That's great, Saima') but highlights her *progress* ('so three weeks ago. . .and. . .now'). Perceived self-efficacy is normally enhanced when a student is aware of herself progressing towards her goal and becoming more skilful (Schunk and Rice, 1991). Perceptions of goal progress are also positively linked to students' subjective well-being (Brunstein, 1993).

Notice how the coach emphasises not how far Saima still has to go (e.g. 'You're three minutes away from your goal') but rather how far she has *come* ('You've now held a two minute conversation'). This is the right way to affirm progress. Framing performance as a gain - 'You're 40 per cent of the way there' - is much more likely to enhance a student's perceived self-efficacy than framing it as a shortfall - 'You're 60 per cent off' (Bandura, 1997). Unfortunately, students will often take the latter perspective, i.e. focus on what they *haven't* achieved or on how far they still have to go. When affirming progress, therefore, the coach should always recast things in terms of how far she has come.

Affirming the student's *actions*

Unfortunately, there may be times when the perception of progress does little or nothing to enhance a student's sense of self-efficacy. For example, if students attribute their success to luck or the ease of the task or some other factor over which they have no control, then they may feel no more confident of their own abilities (Schunk, 1996). The dialogue with Saima could have been very different:

Coach: 'How did you get on with your goal for last week?'
Saima: 'I made quite a few mistakes but I did manage to speak for two minutes. . .and I used a lot of the vocabulary.'
Coach: 'That's great Saima.'
Saima: 'Not really - it was just luck.'
Coach: 'What do you mean exactly?'
Saima: 'I got asked the right questions. If I tried it again I probably wouldn't manage.'

In this scenario Saima is aware of her success but her sense of self-efficacy is unaffected ('If I tried it again I probably wouldn't manage.') The reason for this is that she is attributing her success to luck, a factor over which she has little or no control. The coach needs to help Saima to see how *she herself* brought about the result. Of course, luck may have been a factor. But it cannot have been the only factor. Saima too must have played a part:

Coach: 'So you got asked the right questions, which was lucky.'
Saima: 'Yeah.'
Coach: 'Tell me, if you'd been asked those same questions three weeks ago, how would you have managed?'
Saima: *(thinks for a second)* 'I would probably have messed it up.'
Coach: 'So how did you manage so well this time?'
Saima: 'I guess I'm at a higher level now. . .'
Coach: 'What have you *done* to reach that level?'

Saima: 'I guess I've studied pretty hard. . .practised with my mum.'

Coach: 'Great. What else did you do to be able to speak for two mins?'

Saima: *(thinks for a moment)* 'I learnt all the advanced vocabulary. . .and how to use it in a conversation.'

Coach: 'How did you do that?'

Saima: 'I put the words into different categories and then learnt about five a day until I knew them all.'

Coach: *(affirming action)* 'Ok, so if you'd been asked those questions two weeks ago you would have struggled. But since then you've studied hard, practised with your mum, put all the words into different categories and then learnt five a day until you knew them all. As a result, you managed to hold a two minute conversation with your teacher, using the advanced vocabulary.'

Saima: 'Yeah.'

Coach: 'So was it *all* down to luck?'

Saima: 'No, I suppose I did quite a lot myself.'

Coach: *(affirming action)* 'I think that's clear. You went away, worked hard, used effective strategies and improved your level.'

Saima: *(sounding more confident)* 'Yeah, I guess I did.'

In this extract, the coach asks Saima what she *did* to achieve her goal (e.g. 'How did you do that?') This directs her attention away from factors over which she has no control (e.g. the teacher's choice of questions) and towards her own behaviour. The coach then affirms the steps she took ('You went away, worked hard, used effective strategies and improved your level'). He also affirms effort: 'But since then you've studied hard' and 'You. . .worked hard.' Crucially, whereas 'luck' attributions tend to have a negative impact on a student's sense of self-efficacy, '[s]tudents who attribute success to a combination of ability, effort and strategy use should feel efficacious about learning and remain motivated to work diligently' (Schunk, 1996, p. 10). This is good news for coachees. Research shows that coaching *does* in fact lead to an increased tendency to attribute success to internal factors, such as the use of particular strategies (Moen and Skaalvik, 2009).

Affirming commitment

We now reach our first caveat. We saw earlier that affirming progress can enhance a student's sense of self-efficacy. However, if the coach is not careful, it can also undermine her commitment. Research shows that when students focus *only* on their progress they may engage in behaviour that is inconsistent with their goals (Fishbach and Dhar, 2005). For example, if Saima perceives that she has improved her French, she may be tempted to rest on her laurels or act in a way that will not help her French. For example, she might choose to watch TV instead of revising the next part of her vocabulary list.

Does this mean that coaches shouldn't affirm progress? No, it does not. Coaches *should* affirm progress for the reasons already explained. Helping a student to see how far she has come is an essential part of coaching. The key is simply to prevent her from *dwelling* on that progress and forgetting her ultimate goal. Coaches should therefore take a two-step approach:

Step 1: Affirm the coachee's *progress*

Step 2: Remind her of her *commitment to her goal*[1]

We have already seen how the coach affirms progress (i.e. Step 1). The next step is to remind the student of her commitment to her goal:

Coach: 'So you've obviously made great progress. And we've just seen that you brought that about yourself.'
Saima: *(still smiling)* 'Yeah, I guess I did.'
Coach: 'Now that you've done that, what makes you want to *keep* working on your goal?'
Saima: *(thinks for a moment)* 'Well my oral is coming up and I need to speak for five minutes. . .so I've got to keep working.'
Coach: 'How important is it to you to do well on that oral?'
Saima: '*Very* important.'
Coach: 'So you're happy about your progress – which is great. But you also know that you have to keep working so that you can do well on your oral. And your oral is very important to you.'
Saima: 'Definitely. That's my ultimate goal.'
Coach: 'Ok, suppose 0 means you feel no commitment at all, and 10 means you're '100 per cent committed.' On a scale from 0 to 10, how committed are you to your ultimate goal?'
Saima: '9.'
Coach: 'And how confident are you that you can achieve it?'
Saima: 'At least 8.'
Coach: 'That's great. The fact that you're confident *and* committed is really going to help you.'

In the example above the coach has not only reinforced Saima's sense of self-efficacy. He has also helped her to remember her commitment. The combination of high perceived self-efficacy and high commitment bodes extremely well for Saima's progress.

Affirming positive 'exceptions'

In Chapter 6, we saw how *solution-focused* questioning focuses a student's attention on success rather than failure, on what's 'working' rather than what's not. Affirming can serve a similar purpose. For example, if a student asserts that she 'always' fails at some task, the coach can affirm the exceptions:

Coach: 'So your goal for this week is be on time for all of your meetings and extra sessions.'
Evelyn: 'Yeah, but I doubt I'll be able to do it.'
Coach: 'Suppose 0 means you think you have no chance and 10 means you're certain you can do it. How confident are you that you can achieve your goal on a scale from 0 to 10?'

Evelyn: 'Maybe 3. I'm always late.'

Coach: 'When *do* you turn up on time?'

Evelyn: *(thinks for a moment)* 'I was on time for my drama meeting. . .and the science clinics.'

Coach: 'How did you manage that?'

Evelyn: *(thinks for a moment)* 'I put a post-it note in my locker.'

Coach: 'What else did you do?'

Evelyn: 'I listened to the bell and went straight to the room. . .normally I keep chatting with my friends.'

Coach: *(affirming the 'exceptions')* 'Ok, so you *do* have success when it comes to punctuality. You were on time for your drama meeting last week, and for the science clinics. You got yourself there by putting a post-it in your locker and by going straight to the room when you heard the bell.'

Evelyn: 'Yeah.'

Coach: 'With that in mind, from 0 to 10, how confident are you now that you can achieve this week's goal?'

Evelyn: *(sounding more confident)* 'About 7.'

In this example, Evelyn's goal is to improve her punctuality but she is initially pessimistic about her chances. She says to her coach that she is 'always late.' Solution-focused coaches, however, know that no 'problem' exists all the time (Berg and Szabó, 2005; Greene and Grant, 2003; see also Chapter 6). There are always positive *exceptions*. The coach first asks about these exceptions: 'When *do* you turn up on time?' He then makes a point of affirming them: 'so you *do* have success when it comes to punctuality. You were on time for. . .' Affirming exceptions is a powerful way of enhancing a student's sense of self-efficacy.

Affirming the coachee's contributions to a session

As we have already seen, the beginning of each session provides an excellent opportunity to affirm the student's progress. However, the *end* of a session is also a good time for affirming. In this case, the coach can affirm the student's contributions to the session (O'Connell, Palmer and Williams, 2012):

Coach: 'You've been extremely focused today, Evelyn. You made a real effort to think about what you're doing and how it relates to your goal.'

Evelyn: 'I tried to, yeah.'

Coach: 'It's impressive. You also did a great job of working out what you do when you *are* on time – responding to the bell, using post-it notes. . .'

Evelyn: 'Thank you.'

Coach: 'You noticed that you're already doing quite a lot *right*. But you also realised that you've got to do *more* of it if you want to achieve your goal.'

Evelyn: 'Definitely.'

Praising Evelyn for her contributions to the session not only leaves her feeling good but also helps her to see that *she* is the driving force in coaching. Remember, however, that affirming progress alone may encourage self-defeating behaviour. This is why the coach ends the session by reminding Evelyn of her commitment to her ultimate goal: 'But you also realised that you've got to do *more* of it if you want to achieve your goal.'

Should coaches affirm intelligence or ability?

Before we end this chapter, we need to say something about affirming *ability* or *intelligence* - an issue that we have so far deliberately ignored. It is not uncommon for teachers to tell students that they have 'natural ability' for a subject or that they are blessed with great 'intelligence.' Should coaches provide this sort of affirmation? The issue is contentious. On the one hand, there are those who point out that praising students for their ability or intelligence can have several adverse effects (e.g. Mueller and Dweck, 1998; Dweck, 1999). Students who are praised in this way may (a) develop a 'fixed mindset', (b) shy away from tasks that could expose a lack of ability, and (c) see failures as a sign of personal inadequacy, i.e. low ability or low intelligence as opposed to, say, low effort. On the other hand, research also shows that affirming ability (e.g. 'You're good at this!') can bolster students' perceived self-efficacy and have a positive effect on performance (Schunk, 1996). In short, the evidence is mixed. What is a coach to do?

The view taken here is that coaches should generally encourage coachees to focus 'on those things over which the latter feel they have control and [which they believe] are subject to change, i.e. effort and skills, not aptitude.' (Ives and Cox, 2012, p. 33). Coaching is ultimately about action, i.e. *doing* what is required to achieve one's goals. A student may feel that there is very little she can do about 'natural ability'. On the other hand, commitment, effort, strategy and action - these are largely under her control. She can, for example, make more or less effort and adopt this or that strategy. Affirming effort and action is therefore generally more helpful than affirming aptitude or intelligence. Of course, this is not to disparage the research on praise for ability. As already noted, affirming ability ('You're good at this!') can boost a student's sense of self-efficacy (e.g. Schunk, 1996). However, if a coach does decide to affirm a student's natural ability, he should help the student to see that her success depends on a *number* of factors (including effort and strategy), not on ability alone. The student may also come to see that ability itself can be improved through hard work.

Chapter summary

- Affirming means making positive, encouraging statements about the coachee's progress, effort, action, commitment and so on.
- Affirming is an important way to boost the coachee's sense of self-efficacy. Students with high levels of perceived self-efficacy work harder, are more engaged, show greater persistence and achieve higher levels of performance.
- Coaches should affirm the student's progress at the beginning of each session. Perceptions of progress enhance students' perceived self-efficacy and are linked to subjective well-being.

- When a coach affirms action, he highlights what the student did to bring about success. He can also affirm the effort she made to achieve her goal. Students who attribute their progress to factors they control (e.g. effort, action, strategy) are more likely to feel a sense of self-efficacy than students who attribute their success to luck.
- Once coaches have affirmed progress, they should then affirm commitment. If a student focuses exclusively on progress she may engage in behaviour that is detrimental to her goal. Reminding her of her commitment helps her to stay on track.
- When students talk about 'problems', solution-focused coaches affirm 'exceptions'. This means highlighting the occasions when things go *right*.
- The coach should affirm the student's contributions to each session. This helps the student to see that she is the driving force in coaching.
- Affirming aptitude or ability ('You're good at this!') can enhance perceived self-efficacy and improve performance. However, ability praise may also have negative effects, such as encouraging a fixed mindset.
- It is generally better for coaches to affirm things over which students have control, e.g. effort, commitment, and choice of strategy.

Note

1 I would like to thank Professor Ayelet Fishbach for helping me to develop this approach.

References

Bandura, A. (1997). *Self-Efficacy: The exercise of control*. New York: W.H. Freeman.
Berg, I.K. and Szabó, P. (2005). *Brief Coaching for Lasting Solutions*. New York: Norton.
Brunstein, J. (1993). Personal goals and subjective well-being: A longitudinal study. *Journal of Personality and Social Psychology*, 65, 1061-1070.
Dawson, P. and Guare, R. (2012). *Coaching students with executive skill deficits*. New York: Guilford Press.
Dweck, C. (1999). Caution—Praise can be dangerous. *American Educator*, 23, 1, 4-9.
Fishbach, A. and Dhar, R. (2005). Goals as excuses or guides: The liberating effect of perceived goal progress on choice. *Journal of Consumer Research*, 32, 370-377.
Grant, A. (2006). An integrative goal-focused approach to executive coaching. In D.R. Stober and A.M. Grant (eds), *Evidence based coaching handbook: Putting best practices to work for your clients*. Hoboken, NJ: John Wiley & Sons.
Greene, J. and Grant, A.M. (2003). *Solution-focused Coaching: Managing people in a complex world*. Harlow: Pearson Education Limited.
Ives, Y. and Cox, E. (2012). *Goal-focused coaching: Theory and practice*. New York: Routledge.
McDermott, I. and Jago, W. (2005). *The Coaching Bible: The Essential Handbook*. London: Piatkus.
Moen, F. and Skaalvik, E. (2009). The effect from executive coaching on performance psychology. *International Journal of Evidence based Coaching and Mentoring* 7, 31-49.
Mueller, C.M., and Dweck, C. (1998). Intelligence Praise Can Undermine Motivation and Performance. *Journal of Personality and Social Psychology*, 75, 33-52.
O'Connell, B., Palmer, S. and Williams, H. (2012). *Solution Focused Coaching in Practice*. Hove: Routledge.
Schunk, D.H. (1983). Goal difficulty and attainment information: Effects on children's achievement behaviors. *Human Learning*, 2, 107-117.

Schunk, D.H. (1996). Attributions and the development of self-regulatory competence. Paper presented at the annual conference of the American Educational Research Association.

Schunk, D.H. and Pajares, F. (2002). The development of academic self-efficacy. In A. Wigfield and J. Eccles (eds), *Development of achievement motivation*. San Diego: Academic Press.

Schunk, D.H. and Rice, J.M. (1991). Learning goals and progress feedback during reading comprehension instruction. *Journal of Reading Behavior*, 23, 351-364.

Part III

Coaching sessions and coaching programmes

8 The 'GROW' model

In this chapter

- Introduction to the 'GROW' model
- Ultimate Goals and Proximal Goals
- Coaching with GROW
- Assessing the student's progress.

The 'GROW' model

Coaching sessions are underpinned by a coaching *model*. As Grant (2011, p. 118) notes, session structures or models 'act as a guide for the coach, helping the coach and coachee stay focused on relevant issues and preventing the coaching session [from] drifting off into conversation that has no clear purpose or goal'.

The best known model in coaching is GROW, which was originally devised by Graham Alexander (see Alexander and Renshaw, 2005) and promoted by John Whitmore (Whitmore, 2009).[1] The GROW model is clear, elegant and can be applied to almost any goal or challenge a student may have. In addition, although other models exist, GROW is one of the simplest to learn and is therefore ideal for anyone new to coaching.

Each letter of 'GROW' stands for a key phase in the coaching process:

G = **G**oal

R = **R**eality

O = **O**ptions

W = **W**ill (or **W**ay forward)

Table 8.1 provides a brief summary of each phase:

Table 8.1 The phases of 'GROW'.

Phase	*What happens?*
Goal	• The coach helps the student **set a goal.** The first goal to set will be her *ultimate goal*, i.e. what she wants to achieve *by the end of coaching.* • At the beginning of each session she will set a (new) *proximal goal*, i.e. what she wants to achieve *by the next session.*
Reality	• Coach and student explore the student's '*reality*', i.e. her current situation: how much of her goal has she already achieved? What is helping her to achieve it? What obstacles are standing in her way?
Options	• The coach helps the student to *generate options*, i.e. ways of getting from where she is now (Reality) to where she wants to be (Goal). • With the help of her coach the student then *evaluates her options* in terms of effectiveness and feasibility.
Will	• Finally, the coach helps the student to what she *will* do to achieve her goal, i.e. to decide on the *way forward.* This normally means turning some of her 'options' into action-steps.

Table 8.1 outlines each phase of the GROW model. However, we can summarise the process even more simply. GROW essentially revolves around the following questions:

1 What do you want to achieve? **(Goal)**
2 What are things like for you *now*? **(Reality)**
3 What *could* you do to achieve your goal? **(Options)**
4 What *will* you do to achieve your goal? **(Will)**

As you may have gathered, coaching typically begins with 'G' (goal-setting) and ends with 'W' ('Will'). However, there is nothing to prevent the coach and student from revisiting an earlier phase. For example, while exploring her options (O) a student may realise that she needs to go back and adjust her goal (G).

Table 8.1 presents GROW in the abstract. It may be easier to understand the process with a concrete example - see Table 8.2. Assume that the student in question has already set herself the following *ultimate goal* (to be achieved by the final coaching session).

Ultimate Goal

'To have produced a high-quality draft of my entire EPQ[2] essay.'

Table 8.2 illustrates how GROW would apply in this student's second session. If you are new to coaching or new to GROW then Table 8.2 will repay close examination. Note that the column labelled 'Specifics' does not include everything that is said in each phase of GROW. Rather the student/coach comments should be taken as excerpts from a more detailed discussion.

Table 8.2 A specific case of GROW.

Phase	*What happens?*	*Specifics*	
GOAL	The student sets her first *proximal goal.*	**Coach:** **Student:**	'What do you want to have achieved by next week?' 'I want to have *sorted out the title for my EPQ.*'
REALITY	Coach and student explore the student's *present situation*	**Coach:** **Student:**	'How far have you got in sorting out the title?' 'It's almost there. But I need to improve the wording.'
OPTIONS	**Generation:** The coach helps the student to *generate* options: How could she achieve her goal? **Evaluation:** The coach helps the student *evaluate* the options she has come up with.	**Coach:** **Student:** **Coach:** **Student:**	'What could you do to improve the wording of your title? 'I could compare it with my friends' titles. Or ask my English teacher.' 'How helpful would it be to compare it with your friends' titles?' 'Probably not that helpful. It's better to run it by my English teacher.'
WILL	The coach helps the student decide what she ***will*** do to achieve her (proximal) goal.	**Coach:** **Student:**	'So what will you do to sort out your title?' 'I'll show it to my English teacher and use her feedback to improve it.'

Table 8.2 should make it easier to see how GROW works in practice. Do not worry if some points are still unclear. In the next few chapters we examine every aspect of the model in minute detail.

How to interpret the 'Goal'

Although other models have been developed, GROW is still the most widely used model in coaching. However, not all coaches apply it in the same way. Perhaps most importantly, coaches differ in their understanding of the 'goal'. For some it is the goal *for the session* (e.g. Alexander, 2016). But it can also be understood as the coachee's goal *for the future* (see Ives and Cox, 2012). These are both valid approaches and can even be combined (Whitmore, 2009; Berg and Szabó, 2005). Table 8.3 outlines and clarifies *three* different ways of understanding the 'G' in the GROW model.

In this part of the book (Part III), students set *ultimate goals* and *proximal goals*, but not session goals. Remember that we are focusing not on isolated coaching sessions but on larger coaching programmes. As we saw in Chapter 2, the point of a coaching programme is to help a student achieve a desired *ultimate goal* (e.g. to have completed an EPQ) by means of successive *proximal goals* (e.g. to have sorted out the title).

Table 8.3 Three different ways to understand 'goal'.

TYPE OF GOAL	*COACH'S QUESTION (example)*	*STUDENT'S ANSWER (example)*
Ultimate goal *(a goal for the coaching programme as a whole)*	'What do you want to have achieved *by the end of coaching?*'	'I want *to have produced a high-quality draft of my entire EPQ essay.*'
Proximal goal *(a goal for the interval between sessions)*	'What do you want to have achieved *before our next session?*'	'I want *to have sorted out the title for my EPQ.*'
Session goal *(a goal for a particular coaching session)*	'What do you want to have achieved *by the end of this session?*'	'I want *to know how to fix my EPQ title.*'

GROW, feedback and the coaching process

One of the great advantages of GROW is its simplicity. As we have seen, there are only four phases: (1) Goal-setting, (2) Reality, (3) Options, and (4) Will. However, this simplicity comes at a price. The four letters of 'GROW' leave out a key step: *monitoring the student's progress*. We have said that the point of a coaching programme is to help the student achieve her ultimate goal by means of successive proximal goals. In each coaching session (after the first), it is important to find out what the student has done and how much progress she has made, i.e.

1 *Did the student carry out her action-steps?*
2 *Did she achieve her last proximal goal?*
3 *How close is she now to her ultimate goal?*

The value of performance and progress *feedback* was highlighted in Chapter 3. Some commentators have therefore suggested that 'GROW' should be augmented. For example, Grant (2011) proposes a 'RE-GROW' model in which 'R' and 'E' stand for 'review' and 'evaluate'. This expanded memory-aid may be helpful for some coaches. However, to keep things simple we shall continue to refer to 'GROW' and simply include an additional step – *performance and progress feedback*. This step is carried out before **G** in every session apart from the first. Figure 8.1 should make this clear. 'S' stands for 'student'.

The five boxes at the top of Figure 8.1 represent what happens in each coaching session. Note that the last phase of every session is **W** – the student decides what she *will* do *before the next session*. At the beginning of the next session, she and her coach find out how she got on and assess her progress. First the coach will ask: 'Did you carry out your action-steps?' Then he will find out (i) whether she achieved her proximal goal (e.g. sorting out the title for her EPQ), and (ii) how close she is now to her *ultimate* goal (e.g. producing a high-quality draft of her entire EPQ essay).

After this feedback phase, the coach and student go back into GROW. That is, the student will set a *new* proximal *goal* (e.g. to write the introduction to her EPQ essay). Then she

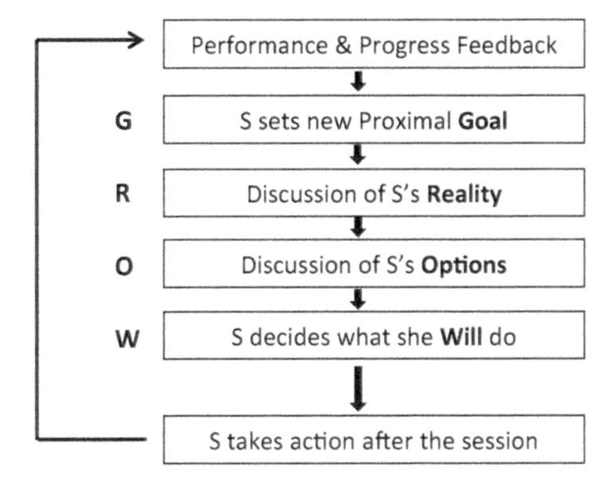

Figure 8.1 GROW and the coaching process.

and her coach will discuss the relevant *reality* (e.g. how much of that introduction she has already written) and so on.

The process in Figure 8.1 repeats itself until the student achieves her ultimate goal or until coaching comes to an end. It is a good idea to study Figure 8.1 carefully before moving on to the next chapter. You should be able to see not only how the GROW model fits in but also how the whole coaching process unfolds.

In the next chapter, we focus on the first phase of GROW - Goal-setting. As noted in chapter 2, goal-setting is the foundation of all effective coaching.

Chapter summary

- A model such as GROW gives structure to the session. GROW is the most popular model in coaching.
- 'G' stands for 'Goal,' 'R' for 'Reality,' 'O' for 'Options' and 'W' for 'Will' or 'Way Forward'.
- The 'G' in 'GROW' can stand for an ultimate goal, proximal goal or session goal. In this book 'G' stands for either the student's ultimate goal or a relevant proximal goal.
- At the beginning of each session (apart from the first), the student and coach will engage in an additional phase: Performance and Progress Feedback. This will involve finding out (i) whether the student carried out her action-steps, (ii) to what extent she achieved her proximal goal and (iii) how close she is now to her ultimate goal.

Notes

1 Although there is still some dispute as to who actually created the GROW model. Some credit Graham Alexander; others John Whitmore (see Bresser and Wilson, 2016).
2 'EPQ' stands for 'Extended Project Qualification'. This qualification is taken by some students in the UK and is equivalent to half an A level.

References

Alexander, G. (2016). Behavioural coaching: the GROW model. In J. Passmore, (ed.), *Excellence in coaching: The Industry Guide* (3rd edn). London: Kogan Page.
Alexander, G. and Renshaw, B. (2005). *Supercoaching.* London: Random House.
Berg, I.K. and Szabó, P. (2005). *Brief Coaching for Lasting Solutions.* New York: Norton.
Bresser, F. and Wilson, C. (2016). What is coaching? In J. Passmore (ed.), *Excellence in Coaching: The Industry Guide* (3rd edn). London: Kogan Page.
Grant, A. (2011). Is it time to REGROW the GROW model? Issues related to teaching coaching session structures. *The Coaching Psychologist,* 7, 2, 118–126.
Ives, Y. and Cox, E. (2012). *Goal-focused coaching: Theory and practice.* New York: Routledge.
Whitmore, J. (2009). *Coaching for Performance.* (4th edn). London: Nicholas Brealey.

9 Goals and goal-setting (G)

In this chapter

- The importance of setting goals
- SMART goal-setting
- Ultimate goal setting vs. proximal goal setting
- Outcome goals, performance goals and learning goals.

The importance of goal-setting

The first phase of GROW is *Goal-setting*. Students who have asked for coaching will normally know what they want to work on, e.g. time management or revision. However, this is not enough. The coach needs to help the student establish a *clear goal*. A goal is a specific outcome that the student wants to achieve by a certain date, e.g. '*to have completed my EPQ by 21 October*,' or '*to have learnt how to use the present subjunctive by next week*.'

As we saw in Chapter 3, an immense amount of research has been conducted on goal-setting. The results are unequivocal: setting specific, challenging goals enhances performance. People who set such goals accomplish and learn more than those who set no goals at all or vague goals such as 'to do their best' (Locke and Latham, 1990, 2013) or 'to learn as much as possible' (Rothkopf and Billington, 1979). In addition, students who set goals achieve better grades and manage their workloads more effectively than students who do not set goals (Morisano *et al*., 2010).

What makes goals so effective? For one thing, they are motivational (West, Ebner and Hastings, 2013). If a student has committed herself to a desirable goal then she is likely to devote time and energy to achieving it. Moreover, she will be driven not only by the anticipated satisfaction of achieving the goal but also by *dis*-satisfaction if she is currently falling short of it (Bandura and Cervone, 1983). Research also shows that specific, challenging goals lead to greater persistence in studying and increase the amount that students learn (LaPorte and Nath, 1976). In addition, goals draw people's attention towards what is relevant and away from what is irrelevant (Locke and Latham, 2002). For example, Rothkopf and Billington (1979) found that when students had specific learning goals for a piece of prose they spent more time looking at goal-relevant passages and less time looking at irrelevant material.

We can see, then, that having a goal makes a world of difference. Ives and Cox (2012, p. 35) therefore argue that 'the key skill of the coach is crafting and constructing the goal.' This is a view we shall adopt, with one significant amendment: the key skill of the coach is *helping the student* to craft and construct the goal. In our approach, it is the student - not the coach - who sets the goal. This is in keeping with the coachee-led ethos. It is also supported by research. For although goals assigned by others (e.g. by a teacher or coach) can be just as effective in raising performance (Locke and Latham, 2013), *self*-set goals do more to enhance students' perceived self-efficacy (Schunk, 1985). In addition, when students are low in achievement motivation, self-set goals do a better job of helping them to improve their performance (Horn and Murphy, 1985).

Goal-setting with Zara

As previous chapters have made clear, we need to distinguish between the student's *ultimate* goal (what she wants to achieve *by the end of coaching*) and any *proximal* goal (what she wants to achieve *by the next session*). In this chapter, we cover both ultimate and proximal goal-setting. You will be pleased to hear that the process is basically the same in both cases.

Imagine that it is the first session of a six-session programme. A coach is about to help a student - Zara - set her *ultimate goal*. There are two stages in this process:

1 **The Exploratory stage**
2 **The 'SMART' stage**

Before we get to these, however, we need to introduce Zara.

> **Zara** is a 17-year-old student in the Lower Sixth of an independent school in the UK. Last year she struggled to complete assignments on time, leaving them to the last minute and rushing her work. This year she has sought coaching in order to improve her performance in this area.

The exploratory stage

The first thing to realise is that simply asking the student 'What is your goal?' will almost certainly not work. Coachees rarely turn up to coaching with perfectly formed goals (Rogers, 2012). Before a concrete goal can be set, therefore, the student will need to think in broad terms about what she wants. In order to help her, the coach might ask questions such as:

- 'What's most important to you?'
- 'How do you see your future?'
- 'What would make school more rewarding?'
- 'What led you to coaching?'
- 'What would you like to get out of this year?'

Some of these questions - particularly the first two - may seem rather abstract or open-ended. In fact, that is the point. This is the *exploratory* stage. The student needs to be given the chance to consider various possible futures and to identify those that she finds most desirable (see Morisano *et al.*, 2010). Open-ended questions are therefore useful at this stage:

Coach: 'What would you like to get out of this year?'
Zara: 'I wanna stop leaving things to the last minute. . .Especially big things like coursework or my EPQ.'
Coach: 'What do you want to do instead?'
Zara: 'Plan things properly. Do them on time.'
Coach: 'What's so important to you about that?'
Zara: 'I'll get better grades.'
Coach: 'So instead of leaving things to the last minute you want to plan them properly and do them in good time because that will help you get better grades?'
Zara: 'Exactly.'
Coach: 'You also said that that's especially important if it's a big thing like coursework or your EPQ.'
Zara: 'Definitely - those are the things that count.'

In this exploratory stage, the coach encourages Zara to think about what *matters* to her. Ultimately, this will help her to set a goal that is aligned with her core values. Goals that are aligned with a person's values are more likely to be engaging and to inspire genuine effort (Grant, 2006). Having gone through the exploratory stage, Zara and her coach can now move on to the actual business of goal-setting.

'SMART' goal-setting

One of the most effective ways of setting goals is to use the criteria in the acronym **'SMART'** (e.g. O'Connell, Palmer and Williams 2012). A 'SMART' goal is:

- **S**pecific
- **M**easurable
- **A**chievable
- **R**elevant/**R**ewarding
- **T**ime-bound

With help from her coach Zara will go through each of the criteria and refine her goal.

Ensuring that the goal is SPECIFIC (S)

A *specific* goal is one that states clearly and precisely what the student wants to achieve. Without help from a coach, students may set goals that are simply too vague to be workable (e.g. Travers, 2013).

Coach: 'Let's see if you can set a specific goal based on what you've said.'
Zara: 'Ok.'
Coach: 'We've got six sessions together over the next six weeks. What exactly would you like to have achieved by the end of the programme?'
Zara: 'To have done my work *properly*.'
Coach: 'When you say your 'work', what do you mean exactly?'
Zara: 'The big projects.'
Coach: 'Which big projects would that be?'
Zara: 'Well the only one I have in the next six weeks is my English coursework.'
Coach: 'So what would your goal be?'
Zara: 'To have. . .completed my English coursework properly by the end of coaching.'
Coach: 'What do you mean by 'properly'?'
Zara: 'By working on it bit by bit. . .each week. . .not leaving it to the last minute.'
Coach: 'So by the end of coaching you want to have completed your English coursework, having worked on it bit by bit each week?'
Zara: 'Yes.'

When asked to state her goal, Zara's first answer is: 'To have done my work *properly*.' Note how the coach picks up on the lack of clarity in the phrases 'my work' and '*properly*'. In both cases he asks Zara to explain what she means. Similarly, when she says 'big projects' he encourages her to make clear exactly which project(s) she has in mind. In short the coach helps the student to ensure that her goal is *specific*. Research has shown time and again that goals that are specific lead to enhanced performance (see especially Locke and Latham, 1990, 2013).

Ensuring that progress and achievement are MEASURABLE (M)

Having made the goal specific, coach and student must ensure that progress and achievement are *measurable* (e.g. Kimsey-House *et al.*, 2011). We saw in Chapter 3 that as well as having goals people need regular performance and progress feedback, i.e. knowledge of how they are doing in relation to their goals. Regularly measuring progress helps the student to stay on track. In addition, awareness of progress enhances perceived self-efficacy. Finally, coach and student must have some means of determining whether she has actually achieved her goal (Berg and Szabó, 2005):

Coach: 'So your goal is to have completed your English coursework by the end of coaching, having worked on it bit by bit each week.'
Zara: 'Yes.'

Coach: 'How are we going to measure your progress towards that?'

Zara: *(thinks for a moment)* 'Well I guess we could see what I've done each week. . .'

Coach: 'What do you mean exactly?'

Zara: 'Well like for the first week I could do the reading and in the second week the introduction. . .'

Coach: 'So you'd set yourself one thing to do each week and we would see how you got on with it?'

Zara: 'Yeah.'

Coach: 'Ok. Let's imagine it's the end of the programme. How will we know whether you've actually completed your English coursework the way you planned?'

Zara: *(thinks for a second)* 'I could bring it to the session. All finished.'

Coach: 'How will we know whether you completed it bit-by-bit rather than rushing it at the last minute?'

Zara: *(thinks for a moment)* 'Well you'll know what bits I've done each week cos I'll tell you in each session.'

Coach: 'So we'll measure your progress each week by checking whether you've done the bit you set yourself. And at the end of the programme we'll know whether you've achieved your goal because you'll bring the finished coursework to the session. *(Zara nods)*. And we'll know that you've done it bit-by-bit because you'll be telling me each week about the bit you've done?'

Zara: 'Sounds good to me.'

Ensuring that the goal is ACHIEVABLE but challenging: (A)

Once coach and student know how they will measure progress and achievement, they must then consider how *achievable* the goal is. There are actually two key points here. The first is that the student must have the knowledge, skills and ability to attain her goal. There is no sense in setting a goal that is beyond her reach. The second point, however, is that the goal should not be *too* easy to achieve. Rather it should be achievable yet *challenging*. Research has demonstrated that ***challenging*** goals inspire greater motivation and lead to better performance than goals that are easy to achieve (e.g. Locke and Latham, 1990). Coach and student therefore need to strike the right balance. See Figure 9.1.

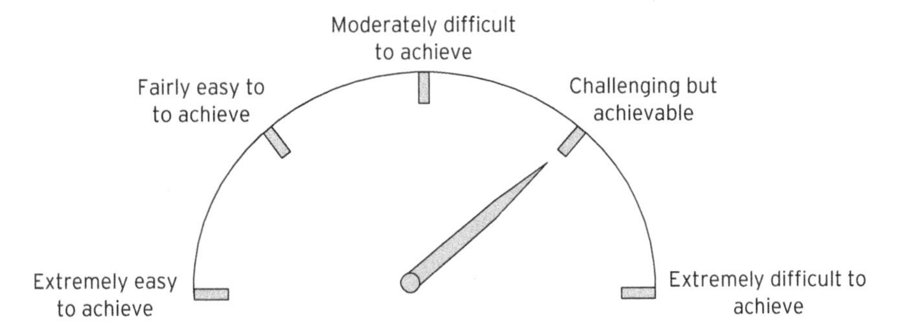

Figure 9.1 Setting a challenging but achievable goal.

Coach: 'So by the end of this programme you want to have completed your English coursework, having worked on it bit by bit each week.'

Zara: 'Yep.'

Coach: 'Ok, how easy will that be to achieve?'

Zara: *(thinks for a moment)* 'Definitely not easy. Last year I missed loads of deadlines.'

Coach: 'Ok, so what reasons are there to think that you *can* achieve it?'

Zara: 'English is one of my best subjects. I know the texts really well. Plus I'm motivated. If I break it down into bits I think I can do it.'

Coach: 'Ok, imagine a scale from 0 to 10. 0 means "no challenge at all" and 10 is the biggest challenge you could have.'

Zara: 'Ok'

Coach: 'On a scale from 0 to 10, how much of a challenge will it be to achieve this goal?'

Zara: *(thinks for a while)* '5 or 6.'

Coach: 'So challenging but achievable?'

Student: 'Yeah, I'd definitely say that.'

Note how the coach uses a scaling question to help Zara ensure that her goal is both challenging and achievable. He also asks her to identify *reasons* for thinking that she can achieve the goal. The key, as we have said, is to strike the right balance. If the goal is *too* easy to achieve, then she is unlikely to be motivated. Research indicates that individuals work harder for more challenging goals (West *et al.*, 2013). On the other hand, if the goal is too *difficult* to achieve she will probably also lose motivation. People tend to give up when they consider their goal unrealistically demanding (Bandura, 1991).

What should coach and student do if the student does not (currently) have what it takes to achieve her goal? One option is to consider setting a *learning goal* rather than a *performance* (or outcome) *goal*. We discuss learning, performance and outcome goals later on, so nothing will be said about them here. Suffice it to say that a learning goal for Zara might be: *'To have discovered a practical way to break down my coursework into manageable weekly steps.'*

Ensuring that the goal is RELEVANT/REWARDING (R)

Once it has been established that the goal is challenging but achievable, the next step is to ensure that it is *relevant* and *rewarding*. The goal must *mean* something to the student. Travers (2013) records the following piece of advice (offered by a student): 'Bear in mind that successful goals can only be developed on things which are of importance or relevance to you. It is no good writing a theoretically perfect goal if you feel no commitment or motivation to achieve it' and 'Really think about your goals. They need to be the right ones in order to gain commitment, think about areas that you really believe you'll benefit and improve in' (Travers, 2013, p. 616).

As this student realises, goal-setting requires *commitment*. If people are not really committed to their goals, then they are very unlikely to take action (Locke and Latham, 1990, 2013). Commitment depends on (i) believing that a goal is achievable and (ii) perceiving it as important or desirable (Locke and Latham, 2013; Morisano, 2013). We have already covered the first of these conditions (under the 'Achievable' criterion). Let's see how Zara and her coach handle the second.

Coach: 'So your ultimate goal is to have completed your English coursework on time by the end of the programme, having worked on it bit by bit each week.'

Zara: 'Yeah.'

Coach: 'Imagine that it's the end of the programme and you've achieved your goal. You worked on your coursework bit by bit each week. And you've now completed it on time so it's ready to hand in. (*pauses*) How do you feel?'

Zara: *(smiling)* 'Really good. Proud too.'

Coach: 'Great. And what will achieving this goal actually *do* for you?'

Zara: 'I'll avoid the stress and panic of doing everything at the last minute.'

Coach: 'What else?'

Zara: *(thinks for a moment)* 'It will help me do well on the coursework, so I can get a good grade.'

Coach: 'What about the impact on your life in general?'

Zara: *(thinks for a moment)* 'I'll probably get on better with my parents. They've been nagging me about my work. And I'll probably be able to enjoy the rest of my life more because I won't be feeling guilty about my coursework.'

Coach: 'Ok, let's summarise. When you achieve this goal, you'll feel really good and proud. You'll have avoided the stress and panic of rushing it at the last minute. You'll also have helped yourself to do *well* on the coursework and get a good grade. You'll probably get on better with your parents. And you'll be able to enjoy the rest of your life more because you won't be feeling guilty about your coursework.'

Zara: *(looking very content)* 'Yeah.'

Coach: 'When you think about all that, how rewarding will it be to achieve your goal on a scale from 0 to 10?'

Zara: *(speaking confidently)* '10, for sure.'

Zara's responses in the above extract are sufficiently encouraging. However, there are times when it can be helpful to invite the student to think about the consequences of *not* working towards her goal (e.g. Greene and Grant, 2003):

Coach: 'Alright, let's think about what might happen if you *don't* bother with this goal. What will happen if you *don't* work on your coursework bit by bit each week?'

Zara: *(thinks for a moment)* 'My workload will start to pile up. . .and *(starting to frown)* I'll get more and more stressed. . .and there'll be a mad rush to do it at the last minute.'

Coach: 'And what will happen if you *don't* complete it on time?'

Zara: *(looking upset)* 'I'll get in trouble with my teachers. . .and probably get a bad grade . . .and my parents will give me grief.'

Coach: 'How would you feel then?'

Zara: 'Really disappointed. Especially cos I'll know I could've done it if I'd just made an effort.'

Coach: 'When you bear that in mind, how important is it to you to achieve your goal? On a scale from 0 to 10?'

Zara: '10.'

In some cases students may be motivated to act when they reflect on the benefits of doing so (e.g. the possibility of a good grade). However, students are often *more* motivated to act when they think about the consequences of *not* doing so (e.g. the danger of a *bad* grade). Experience tells us that negative outcomes tend to have greater *urgency* or *potency* than their positive counterparts (Rozin and Royzman, 2001). In addition, the seminal work of Kahneman and Tversky has taught us about *loss aversion*, i.e. the fact that 'we are driven more strongly to avoid losses than to achieve gains' (Kahneman, 2012, p. 302; see also Tversky and Kahneman, 1991). Consider two questions:

(a) *What good things will happen if you do work for your goal?*
(b) *What bad things will happen if you don't work for your goal?*

When students are stirred more by (b) than they are by (a), loss aversion may well be at work (Kahneman, personal communication).

Ensuring that the goal is TIME-BOUND (T)

Finally, the coach and student must ensure that the goal is *time-bound*. This simply means that there must be a date by which she is to achieve it. Without a deadline, students may lack motivation. Similarly, if the deadline lies too far in the future, then people feel little or no reason to act *now* (Bandura, 1997).

In our example, the deadline for Zara's ultimate goal has effectively been set. Remember that the coach began by asking her what she wanted to achieve *by the end of coaching*. Since we are assuming that Zara's programme is composed of six weekly sessions the deadline for the goal should be clear. However, coach and student need to make it explicit:

Coach: 'We just need to check the deadline for your goal.'

Zara: 'Ok, sure.'

Coach: 'So your ultimate goal is to have completed your English coursework on time by the end of the programme, having worked on it bit by bit each week.'

Zara: 'Yes.'

Coach: 'As you know, we have six sessions together and the date of the last session will be 21 October. So what we're saying is that your goal is to have completed your English coursework by 21 October. How does that sound?'

Zara: *(thinks for a moment)* 'It'll be tough but I reckon I can do it.'

Coach: 'Ok.'

Zara and the coach have now reached the end of SMART. At this point Zara would write down her goal on her coaching form (see Appendix C) and the coach would ensure that they both have a copy of it:

Box 9.1 Zara's ultimate goal.

Ultimate goal

'To have completed my English coursework by 21 October, having worked on it bit-by-bit each week.'

The coach should now carry out one final check on the student's commitment. You may think that Zara and her coach have already covered commitment when dealing with the 'R' (Relevant and Rewarding) criterion. However, it is important to address the issue once more. After all, this is the goal that Zara will be working on for the next six sessions. Unless she is fully committed, that time will be wasted. To measure her commitment to her ultimate goal the coach need only ask one more scaling question:

> *'On a scale from 0 to 10, how committed are you to achieving this goal?'*

Zara's answer should be '8' or higher. We shall assume that this is the case.

Proximal goal setting

Why are proximal goals necessary?

Proximal goals are a means of 'making complex tasks easier through subdivision into more manageable units' (Bandura, 1991, p. 101). A coach can help a student achieve a challenging ultimate goal (e.g. to have completed a piece of coursework in six weeks) by breaking it down into simpler weekly tasks. These proximal goals will also sustain motivation. As Bandura notes, '[p]roximal subgoals mobilise self-influences and *direct what one does in the here and now*. Distal goals alone are too far removed in time to provide effective incentives and guides for present action,' (Bandura, 1997, p. 134, italics added). In addition, proximal goals are an important way of developing students' perceived self-efficacy (e.g. Bandura and Schunk, 1981). Consider the following comment from a student:

> 'Instead of setting myself one large challenge to complete in a given time frame, which feels impossible and therefore de-motivates me, I set myself mini-goals to complete, and each time I complete a goal it fills me with a sense of achievement which in turn encourages me to complete the next goal.' (Travers, Morisano and Locke 2015, p. 14).

However, proximal goals not only enhance motivation and self-efficacy. They also raise achievement. Students who set proximal goals in addition to ultimate (or 'distal') goals attain higher levels of performance – both academically and otherwise – than students who set ultimate goals alone (Morgan, 1985; Latham and Seijts, 1999; Latham and Brown, 2006).

In short, the evidence suggests overwhelmingly that coaches should help students set proximal as well as ultimate goals. And in our approach they do.

The proximal goal-setting process

Proximal goal-setting is like ultimate goal-setting, in miniature. First the coach begins by asking the student to think about what's important in broad terms (the 'exploratory' stage). Then he helps her to set a SMART goal. The only difference is that in the case of *proximal* goal-setting the SMART goal is what the student wants to achieve *by the beginning of the next session.* Imagine that it is Zara's second session. With the help of her coach she is about to set her first proximal goal.[1]

The exploratory stage

Coach: 'So we know your ultimate goal is to have completed your English coursework by 21 October, working on it bit by bit each week.'

Zara: 'Yes.'

Coach: 'With that in mind, what's most important *this week*?'

Zara: *(thinks for a moment)* 'I need to have some sort of plan. . .Like how many sections I'm going to have. . .what things I want to cover.'

SMART goal-setting

Having explored what's most important, Zara will turn her ideas into a 'SMART' proximal goal. This is confirmed at the end of the session:

Coach: 'So let's summarise. What's your goal for this week?'

Zara: *(reading her 'SMART' goal)* 'To have constructed an overall plan for my coursework, breaking it down into sections and listing the main points I want to cover.'

Coach: 'Great. And how are we going to measure progress?'

Zara: 'I'm gonna bring the plan to our next session.'

Coach: 'Excellent. On a scale from 0 to 10 how committed are you to achieving that goal?'

Zara: 'Definitely a good 9.'

In the student's coaching form (Appendix C) the expression 'This week's goal' is used instead of 'proximal goal'. Part of Zara's form would therefore look like this:

Box 9.2 Zara's first proximal goal.

This week's goal

To have constructed an overall plan for my coursework, breaking it down into sections and listing the main points I want to cover in each section.

Outcome goals, performance goals and learning goals

Since goal-setting theory first emerged, most studies have focused on *performance* or *outcome* goals (Locke and Latham, 1990; Seijts, Latham and Woodwark, 2013). However, there is now a growing body of research on a different type of goal, namely the *learning goal*. Table 9.1 below should clarify the differences between performance, outcome and learning goals. Bear in mind that in coaching these goals would have deadlines:

Table 9.1 Outcome, performance and learning goals.

TYPE OF GOAL	*EXAMPLE*
Outcome goal	'To get an A on my Maths test.'
Performance goal	'To have completed 15 questions in my "Quadratic Equations" booklet.'
Learning goal	'To have learnt how to use the quadratic formula to solve equations.'

Outcome goals and performance goals

Outcome goals specify results, e.g. 'To get an A on my Maths test.' *Performance* goals state what a student wants to have done, e.g. 'To have completed 15 questions. . .' Performance goals are related to outcome goals. For example, in order to get an A on a test (an outcome goal), a student might need to answer at least 80 per cent of the questions (a performance goal). It should be noted that many goal-setting experts - including Locke and Latham - do not distinguish between a performance goal and an outcome goal (Latham, personal communication).

Learning goals

As noted, many experts see no need for separate 'performance' and 'outcome' goal categories. However, all researchers are agreed that performance/outcome goals must be distinguished from learning goals. A learning goal concerns the *knowledge* that a student wants to acquire, the *strategies* she would like to discover or the *skills* she wishes to develop. Consider the example from Table 9.1: '*To have learnt how to use the quadratic formula to solve equations*.' Here are some other examples of learning goals:

- *To have learnt how to make a basic spreadsheet in Microsoft Excel.*
- *To have identified three practical strategies to improve the quality of my essays.*
- *To have found out how to set up a student society.*

Whereas a performance or outcome goal stresses the end result, learning goals focus on the knowledge or skills that *facilitate attainment* of that result (Seijts and Latham, 2012). When should learning goals be set, rather than performance goals? The issue is discussed in detail in Appendix B. However, the main point is simple: if students (currently) lack the knowledge or skills to perform a task, then a learning goal should be set instead of a performance goal. However, if students already *have* the required knowledge and skills, then a performance goal may make more sense.

The ultimate goal set by Zara in our example is a good example of a performance goal: *'To have completed my English coursework by October 21st, having worked on it bit-by-bit each week.'* It seems safe to assume that Zara has the knowledge, skills and ability to achieve this. Recall that she said that (i) English was one of her best subjects, (ii) she knew the texts well, and (iii) she believed she could complete the coursework on time if it was broken down into weekly tasks. Her performance goal therefore seems appropriate.

On the other hand, suppose that Zara had not only struggled with English but had never successfully produced an extended piece of writing. In this case, a challenging performance goal would probably not be appropriate. In such a situation the coach could have helped Zara to set an ultimate *learning* goal instead, such as: *'To have learnt how to break down a 3000 word essay into manageable weekly steps.'*

Bear in mind that *proximal* goals - like ultimate goals - can be of either the 'learning' or 'performance' variety. In our example, Zara's first proximal goal was *'To have constructed an overall plan for my coursework, breaking it down into sections and listing the main points I want to cover in each section.'* This is a performance goal. But she could just as well have set herself a proximal *learning* goal such as: *'To have identified and understood the criteria for a top grade.'* Finally, note that the SMART criteria apply to every goal that a student sets. This includes learning goals, which must also be specific, measurable, achievable (but challenging), relevant/rewarding, and time-bound.

Final thoughts on the 'G' phase

In this chapter, we have covered the goal-setting phase in considerable detail. Remember that goal-setting is the cornerstone of coaching. If the student does not set her goals effectively, then she is unlikely to make much progress. On the other hand (as the saying goes), a goal well set is half achieved. It therefore pays to be meticulous.

There is more good news. Although it may take some time for a student to set her ultimate goal, setting weekly proximal goals is often straightforward. By the third or fourth session the coach may only need to ask: *'What do you want to have done* ***by next week****?'* Once the student has provided an answer, she and her coach will ensure that it is 'SMART' before moving on to 'Reality' - the second phase of GROW and the subject of the next chapter.

Chapter summary

- At the beginning of coaching the student sets her ultimate goal, i.e. what she wants to achieve *by the end of coaching*. At the beginning of each session (apart from the first), she sets a proximal goal, i.e. what she wants to achieve *by the next session*.
- Ultimate and proximal goals should always be 'SMART,' i.e. Specific, Measurable, Achievable (but challenging), Rewarding/Relevant and Time-bound.

- Students can set either performance goals or learning goals. Students may set performance goals if they are confident that they have the knowledge and skills to achieve them. If students (currently) lack these things, then they should set learning goals instead.
- There are two basic stages in the goal-setting process – the 'exploratory' stage and the 'SMART' phase. These two stages apply to both ultimate and proximal goal setting.

Note

1 Why doesn't Zara set her first proximal goal immediately after her *ultimate* goal (i.e. in the first session)? One reason is time. This issue is covered in detail in Chapter 13.

References

Bandura, A. (1991). Self-regulation of motivation through anticipatory and self-reactive mechanisms. In R.A. Dienstbier (ed.), *Nebraska symposium on motivation: Perspectives on motivation*. Lincoln, NE: University of Nebraska Press.

Bandura, A. (1997). *Self-Efficacy: The exercise of control*. New York, NY: W.H. Freeman.

Bandura, A. and Cervone, D. (1983). Self-evaluative and self-efficacy mechanisms governing the motivational effects of goal systems. *Journal of Personality and Social Psychology*, 45, 1017–1028.

Bandura, A. and Schunk, D.H. (1981). Cultivating competence, self-efficacy, and intrinsic interest through proximal self-motivation. *Journal of Personality and Social Psychology*, 41, 586–598.

Berg, I.K. and Szabó, P. (2005). *Brief Coaching for Lasting Solutions*. New York: Norton.

Grant, A. (2006). An integrative goal-focused approach to executive coaching. In D.R. Stober and A.M. Grant (eds). *Evidence Based Coaching Handbook: Putting Best Practices to Work for Your Clients*. Hoboken, NJ: John Wiley & Sons.

Greene, J. and Grant, A.M. (2003). *Solution-focused Coaching: Managing people in a complex world*. Harlow: Pearson Education Limited.

Horn Jr, H.L. and Murphy, M.D. (1985). Low need achievers' performance: The positive impact of a self-determined goal. *Personality and Social Psychology Bulletin*, 11, 275–285.

Ives, Y. and Cox, E. (2012). *Goal-focused coaching: Theory and practice*. New York: Routledge.

Kahneman, D. (2012). *Thinking, Fast and Slow*. London: Penguin.

Kimsey-House, H., Kimsey-House, K., Sandahl, P. and Whitworth, L. (2011). *Co-active coaching: Changing business, transforming lives* (3rd edn). Boston, MA: Nicholas Brealey.

LaPorte, R.E. and Nath, R. (1976). Role of performance goals in prose learning. *Journal of Educational Psychology*, 68, 260–264.

Latham, G.P. and Brown, T.C. (2006). The Effect of Learning vs. Outcome Goals on Self-Efficacy, Satisfaction and Performance in an MBA Program. *Applied Psychology: An International Review*, 55, 606–623.

Latham, G.P. and Seijts, G.H. (1999). The effects of proximal and distal goals on performance on a moderately complex task. *Journal of Organizational Behavior*, 20, 421–429.

Locke, E.A. and Latham, G.P. (1990). *A theory of goal setting and task performance*. Englewood Cliffs, NJ: Prentice Hall.

Locke, E. and Latham, G.P. (2002). Building a practically useful theory of goal setting and task motivation: A 35-year odyssey. *American Psychologist*, 57, 705–717.

Locke, E.A and Latham, G. (2013). *New Developments in Goal Setting and Task Performance*. New York: Routledge.

Morgan, M. (1985). Self-monitoring of attained subgoals in a private study. *Journal of Educational Psychology*, 77, 623–630.

Morisano, D. (2013). Goal setting in the academic arena. In E.A. Locke and G.P. Latham (eds). *New developments in goal and task performance*. New York: Routledge.

Morisano, D., Hirsh, J.B, Peterson, J.B., Pihl, R.O. and Shore, B.M. (2010). Setting, elaborating, and reflecting on personal goals improves academic performance. *Journal of Applied Psychology*, 95, 255-264.

O'Connell, B., Palmer, S. and Williams, H. (2012). *Solution Focused Coaching in Practice*. Hove: Routledge.

Rogers, J. (2012). *Coaching Skills: A Handbook*. Maidenhead: Open University Press.

Rothkopf, E. and Billington, M. (1979). Goal-guided learning from text: Inferring a descriptive processing model from inspection times and eye movements. *Journal of Educational Psychology*, 71, 592-608.

Rozin, P. and Royzman, E. (2001). Negativity bias, negativity dominance, and contagion. *Personality and Social Psychology Review*, 5, 296-320.

Schunk, D.H. (1985). Participation in goal setting: Effects on self-efficacy and skills of learning disabled children. *Journal of Special Education*, 19, 307-317.

Seijts, G. and Latham, G. (2012). Knowing when to set learning versus performance goals. *Organizational Dynamics*, 41, 1-6.

Seijts, G.H., Latham, G.P. and Woodwark, M. (2013). Learning goals: A qualitative and quantitative review. In E.A. Locke and G.P. Latham (eds), *New developments in goal setting and task performance*. New York: Routledge.

Travers, C. (2013). Using Goal Setting Theory to Promote Personal Development. In E.A. Locke and G.P. Latham (eds). *New developments in goal and task performance*. New York: Routledge.

Travers, C., Morisano, D. and Locke, E.A. (2015). Growth goals and academic achievement: A qualitative study. *British Journal of Educational Psychology*, 85, 224-241.

Tversky, A. and Kahneman, D. (1991). Loss aversion in riskless choice: A reference dependent model. *Quarterly Journal of Economics*, 106, 4, 1039-61.

West, R.L., Ebner, N.C. and Hastings, E.C. (2013). Linking goals and aging: Experimental and life-span approaches. In E.A. Locke and G.P. Latham (eds). *New developments in goal and task performance*. New York: Routledge.

10 Reality (R)

In this chapter

- The importance of the 'Reality' phase
- Taking a solution-focused approach
- Asking about obstacles and mental contrasting
- Performance-interfering thoughts (PITs)
- Performance-enhancing thoughts (PETs).

The importance of the 'Reality' phase

After the student has set her goal ('ultimate' in the first session, 'proximal' in any other), she and the coach need to consider her **reality**. This is the second phase of the GROW model. Unfortunately, it is often overlooked. Inexperienced coaches tend to jump from goal-setting ('What do you want to achieve?') to options ('How could you achieve it?'). This is too hasty. Coaches should take the time to explore the student's current situation, i.e. what things are like for her *now*. In fact, quite often 'the options for finding a solution become clearer as a direct consequence of having invested in the Reality phase' (Alexander and Renshaw, 2005, p. 242).

But what does it mean to 'invest in the Reality phase'? There are many possible areas to address. The following are arguably the most important:

1. *How much of the goal has the student* ***already achieved?***
2. *What is currently* ***helping*** *her to achieve it?*
3. *What* ***obstacles*** *are standing in her way?*
4. *What* ***resources*** *does she have at her disposal?*

Each of the above points can be usefully explored. Taken together they provide a powerful springboard for the student's progress. It is not surprising, therefore, that for the inventor of the GROW model – Graham Alexander – 'the bulk of time in coaching is spent at the Reality phase' (Alexander and Renshaw, 2005, p. 239).

You may recall from Chapter 4 that coaching is about *building on success*. In our approach, therefore, the Reality phase begins with two *solution-focused* questions: 'How much of the goal have you *already achieved*?' and 'What is currently *helping* you to achieve it?' The fourth question in our list - enquiring about resources - also reflects a solution-focused mentality. But what about question 3? Should we really ask about *obstacles* if we are being solution-focused? We address this issue later on.

The Reality phase in action

Let's return to our student Zara. Recall that her ultimate goal was to have completed her English coursework by 21 October, having worked on it bit by bit each week. We shall now assume that Zara is in her second coaching session. She has just set her first proximal goal, which is as follows:

> **Box 10.1 Zara's first proximal goal.**
>
> **Proximal goal**
>
> 'To have constructed an overall plan for my coursework, breaking it down into sections and listing the main points I want to cover.'

Zara and her coach can now enter the 'Reality' phase of GROW.

1. How much of the goal has the student already achieved?

Coach: *(reading from Zara's coaching form)* 'So your goal for this week is to have constructed an overall plan for your coursework, breaking it down into sections and listing the main points you want cover?'

Zara: 'Yeah.'

Coach: 'Let's see how much you've already achieved. Suppose "10" means you *have* the overall plan and "0" means you're as far away as you could possibly be. Where are you now from 0 to 10?'

Zara: *(thinks for a moment)* 'I'd say about 3.'

Coach: 'What makes it 3 rather than 0?'

Zara: 'Well I've got an idea of the points I want to cover. . .'

In the dialogue above the coach uses a scaling question to find out how much of the (proximal) goal Zara has already achieved. Once she has provided a number - '3' - the coach asks her: *'What makes it a 3 rather than a 0?'* Together these questions help Zara to see that she has already made some progress. She is not starting from '0'. This should be encouraging.

2. What is currently helping the student to achieve her goal?

We have seen that Zara is starting from a '3' not a '0'. This implies that she must be doing something right. The coach should therefore help Zara to see what is *working* for her, i.e. what has she done to get herself to a 3? And what else is she is doing that is helping her to achieve her goal?

Coach: 'So you've already managed to get yourself to a 3. What have you done to get that far?'
Zara: *(thinks for a moment)* 'I guess I've been paying more attention in class. . .especially when my teacher talks about coursework.'
Coach: 'That's great. What else are you doing that's helping you construct your plan?'
Zara: *(thinks again)* 'I've been looking at the notes my teacher gave us. . .that gives me ideas about what to include.'
Coach: *(reflecting)* 'So you've been paying more attention in class, especially when your teacher talks about the coursework. And you've also been looking at your teacher's notes, which gives you ideas about what to include in your coursework.'
Zara: 'Yeah.'
Coach: 'What else are you doing that's helping you?'
Zara: *(thinks hard)* 'Well I've talked to my friends about it. . .but that hasn't really helped.'

We said in Chapter 1 that one of the benefits of coaching is that it raises *awareness*. In particular, coaching helps students to see *how they are* helping (or hindering) themselves in pursuit of their goals. In the dialogue above the coach encourages Zara to think about what she has been doing to construct her coursework plan. First, he helps her to see what she has done to get to a '3'. Then he helps her to identify any other actions that are proving helpful. It can be extremely heartening for students to realise that they are already taking effective action, even without the help of a coach. Indeed, helping a student to see how she is helping herself is a powerful way of enhancing her sense of self-efficacy.

Of course, not everything the student is doing will be productive. For example, Zara notes that talking to her friends about her coursework has not been useful. This is valuable information. The 'Reality' phase of coaching is not only about helping students to see what is 'working'. It is also about helping them identify what is *not* working. This dual awareness enables coachees to do more of the former and less of the latter (e.g. Jackson and McKergow, 2007).

3. What obstacles are standing in her way?

So far we have been strictly *solution-focused* in our approach, asking the student (1) how much of her goal she has already achieved and (2) what is *helping* her to achieve it. However, our third question is about obstacles. Solution-focused texts generally urge coaches to eschew talk of 'barriers' or 'obstacles' and focus instead on 'what's working' (e.g. Jackson and McKergow, 2007; Ratner and Yusuf, 2015). It might be argued, for instance, that talking about obstacles will make students feel stuck.

On the other hand, traditional approaches to coaching *do* involve looking at obstacles (e.g. Alexander and Renshaw, 2005; Dunbar, 2009; Starr, 2016). And there is empirical evidence to support this. In Chapter 3, we briefly discussed *mental contrasting*, i.e. thinking first about what one wants to achieve and then about the obstacles in one's way. Merely focusing on the goal or outcome 'may obscure the fact that achieving the desired future requires exerting substantial effort, overcoming hindrances, and resisting temptations' (Gollwitzer *et al.*, 2011, p. 404). On the other hand, students who think not only about the desired outcome but also about *the obstacles in their way* tend to feel greater commitment and achieve higher levels of academic performance (Gollwitzer *et al.*, 2011).[1] In addition, research suggests that when students take the time to think about what might prevent them from achieving their goals they become clearer about potential pitfalls and plan more effectively as a result (e.g. Adriaanse *et al.*, 2010). Most importantly, they have more success than students who do *not* consider what might hold them back.

Overall, then, it seems to be a good idea to pay attention to obstacles. But note that this focus is temporary. We are not abandoning the solution-focused approach. As will be clear a little later, the final stage of 'Reality' involves asking about *resources*. Moreover, in the next phase of 'GROW' - 'Options' - the coach will help Zara to think of ways to *overcome* any obstacles she identified in 'Reality'. And in the final phase - 'Will' - he will help her to construct helpful 'if. . .then' plans, i.e. *'if obstacle X occurs, then I will do Y to overcome it.'* There is therefore little risk of her feeling stuck.

In the dialogue below the coach helps Zara identify obstacles through *mental contrasting*:

Coach: 'So your goal for this week is to have constructed an overall plan for your coursework. And we know how much of that you've achieved and what's been helping you to achieve it.'

Zara: 'Yep.'

Coach: 'Imagine, for a moment, that you've achieved your goal - you've got your overall coursework plan. Close your eyes, if it helps. *(Zara closes her eyes)*. What is the best thing about having this plan?'

Zara: 'It makes it much, much easier to do the coursework. Having a plan makes me way more confident about how I'm gonna do it. . .'

Coach: *(waiting for a moment)* 'So those are the benefits of achieving the goal. *(Zara nods.)* Ok, what could *stop* you from achieving that?'

Zara: 'Well, I could just put it off.'

Coach: 'Ok really imagine putting it off. (*Zara closes eyes.*) What you're imagining right now - that could stop you from achieving your goal?'

Zara: *(Zara opens her eyes)* 'Yeah. To be honest, I *have* been putting it off. . .I don't think it'll be that hard when I get going but when I think about the hassle of starting I just avoid it.'

Coach 'So on the one hand you don't think it'll be that hard when you get going. On the other hand, when you think about the "hassle" of starting you tend to put it off?'

Zara: 'Yeah, getting started is a hassle.'

Table 10.1 From PITs to PETs.

Performance-interfering thoughts ('PITs')	*Performance-enhancing thoughts ('PETs')*

Adapted from Centre for Coaching (2014)

Consider the 'mental contrasting.' Zara first described and imagined the benefits of achieving her goal. Then she described and imagined the *obstacle* in her way. As Oettingen (1999, p. 317) says: '[t]his mental contrasting transforms the desired future into a future that needs to be attained and the impeding reality into a reality that needs to be changed.'

It is helpful to see Zara's obstacle - the 'hassle of starting' - in cognitive behavioural terms. You may recall from Chapter 2 that cognitive behavioural coaching (CBC) encourages coachees to identify performance-interfering thoughts - **PITs**. It also helps them to develop performance-*enhancing* thoughts - **PETs** (e.g. Palmer and Szymanska, 2008). Simple two-column forms can be used to help students identify their PITs and counter them with PETs. See Table 10.1 (also Appendix E).

In this book, we are taking a cognitive-behavioural approach to coaching. 'Reality' therefore includes not only what a student is *doing* to achieve her goal, but also how she is *thinking* about it, and, crucially, whether that thinking is helping her. We shall assume that Zara has been given a PITs-PETs form (Table 10.1; Appendix E), which she will be filling out as she goes through the GROW model. Her coach now draws attention to her thoughts:

Coach: 'So you've mentioned a way of thinking there. You sometimes have the thought "Getting started is a hassle"?'
Zara: 'Yeah.'
Coach: 'To what extent does that thought help you do your coursework plan?'
Zara: *(thinks for a moment)* 'I guess it doesn't help at all.'
Coach: 'What makes you say that?'
Zara: 'Well when I think like that I just put it off.'
Coach: 'Have you got your PITs-PETs form?
Zara: 'Yep.'
Coach: 'In what column would you put "Getting started is a hassle"?'
Zara: 'PITs. Shall I write that in?'
Coach: 'Absolutely - it's your form.'

Zara's form now looks like Table 10.2.

Remember, however, that in the solution-focused approach *no problem exists all the time* (e.g. Berg and Szabó, 2005). Zara may well sometimes think 'getting started is a hassle'. But her reality is multifaceted. At other times, she will have different thoughts, some of which will be more helpful:

Table 10.2 'PITs to PETs' table with a 'PIT' filled in.

Performance-interfering thoughts ('PITs')	*Performance-enhancing thoughts ('PETs')*
Getting started is a hassle.	

Adapted from Centre for Coaching (2014)

Coach: 'When *do* you feel motivated to start your plan?'

Zara: *(thinks for a moment)* 'When I think about what it's for.'

Coach: 'And what *is* it for?'

Zara: 'Well I need the plan to do the coursework. And I wanna do this coursework properly.'

Coach: 'So you need the plan to do your coursework, which is something you want to do properly *(Zara nods)*. And when you think about that, you feel motivated to start?

Zara: 'Definitely.'

Coach: 'What about the "hassle" of starting?'

Zara: 'I just need to get on with it.'

Coach: 'So you *can* put up with the hassle?'

Zara: 'Yeah, if I remember why I'm doing it. Plus it's OK when I get going.'

Coach: 'You've now come up with a lot of *different* thoughts. You said that you need the plan to do your coursework; that you want to do your coursework properly; that you can put up with the hassle if you remember why you're doing it; and that it's actually OK when you get going.'

Zara: *(looking slightly surprised)* 'Yeah. When you say all that, it feels different.'

Coach: 'Interesting. Let's see how you could use those thoughts to respond to that PIT *(pointing to "Getting started is a hassle")*. What would be a good response?'

Zara: 'It's OK when I get going. . .I *need* this plan for my coursework. . .so just get *on* with it!'

Coach: 'With those thoughts in mind, how do you feel about starting the plan?'

Zara: 'More motivated – I wanna get on with it.'

Coach: 'So where would you write those thoughts?'

Zara: 'In the PETs column.'

In the extract above the coach helps Zara to come up with 'performance-*enhancing* thoughts' (PETs) to counter her 'performance-interfering thoughts' (PITs). First, he helps Zara get into a determined, goal-directed state of mind: *'When* ***do*** *you feel motivated to start your plan?'* Then he elicits the thoughts that she has in this state of mind. Finally, after reflecting back those thoughts, he invites Zara to fill in her form.

Perhaps the most important thing to note about this process is that the coach did not tell Zara what to think. That would be *his* 'reality,' not hers. Instead he helped Zara tap into her own motivation and find her own performance-enhancing thoughts. She is more likely to be persuaded by these 'PETs' than by any of his admonitions.

Table 10.3 Countering 'PITs' with 'PETs'.

Performance-interfering thoughts ('PITs')	*Performance-enhancing thoughts ('PETs')*
Getting started is a hassle.	It's OK when I get going. I need the plan for my coursework Just get *on* with it!

Adapted from Centre for Coaching (2014)

4. What resources she has at her disposal

The last step in the reality phase is to establish what *resources* the coachee has at her disposal (Whitmore, 2009; Alexander and Renshaw, 2005):

Coach: 'So by next week you want to have constructed an overall plan for your coursework. We also know what you've done so far, what's helping you achieve your goal and what could hold you back.'
Zara: 'Yep.'
Coach: 'What *resources* do you have that could help you achieve your goal?'
Zara: 'What do you mean?'
Coach: 'What could help you construct your plan?'
Zara: 'I've got my teacher's notes.'
Coach: 'Ok, what else?'
Zara: *(thinks for a moment)* 'I've also got the assessment criteria. . .and examiners' reports for last year's coursework. . .'
Coach: 'Great. Let's think about people – who could help you construct your overall plan?'
Zara: 'Well I've already asked my teacher and I don't think she's allowed to give us any more help.'
Coach: 'Ok, who else could be helpful?'
Zara: *(thinks for while)* 'I've got a friend in the year above, Grace. . .she did well on her coursework. She might be able to help.'
Coach 'Great. So you've got your teacher's notes, the assessment criteria and examiners' reports for last year's coursework. You've also got a friend in the year above who could possibly help you too.'
Zara: *(looking optimistic)* 'Yeah.'

Before helping Zara to identify possible action-steps (the 'Options' phase of GROW), the coach helps her to become aware of anything she has that could help her to achieve her goal. This should also include relevant *personal strengths*. Raising awareness of internal as well as external resources can be a powerful way to enhance a coachee's sense of self efficacy (e.g. O'Connell, Palmer and Williams, 2012):

Coach: 'So we've talked about people and things that might be helpful. What *skills* or *qualities* do you have that could make it easier for you to construct your plan?'

Zara: *(thinks for a second)* 'Well I'm not good at starting plans, but when I *do* get started, I'm normally pretty good.'

Coach: 'In what way are you pretty good?'

Zara: 'I stick to it until it's done.'

Coach: 'So when you get started on work like this, you stick to it until it's done.'

Zara: 'Most of the time, yeah.'

In the extracts above the coach has helped Zara to identify both external and internal resources. Zara should now be feeling motivated and empowered. This is an excellent time to enter the 'Options' phase of GROW. As we shall see in the next chapter, 'Options' involves thinking about what the student can *do* to achieve her proximal goal.

Chapter summary

- Four key areas to address in the 'Reality' phase of GROW are: (i) how much of the goal the student has already achieved, (ii) what is helping her to achieve it, (iii) what obstacles are standing in her way, (iv) what resources she has at her disposal.
- Much of 'Reality' is solution-focused. However, asking about obstacles can also be effective, particularly in the context of 'mental contrasting'.
- A student's 'Reality' will have both a behavioural and a cognitive dimension. The coach can find out about any 'performance-interfering thoughts' (PITs) the student is having and help her to find 'performance-enhancing thoughts' (PETs) instead.
- By the end of the 'Reality' phase the student should be feeling confident and empowered. This is an excellent time to think about 'Options'.

Note

1 There is one important qualification – 'mental contrasting' enhances commitment *only if students have expectations of success*, i.e. believe that they can overcome the obstacles and achieve their goals (Oettingen, Park and Schnetter, 2001).

References

Adriaanse, M.A., Oettingen, G., Gollwitzer, P.M., Hennes, E.P., de Ridder, D.T.D. and de Wit, J.B.F. (2010). When planning is not enough: Breaking unhealthy snacking habits with mental contrasting and implementation intentions (MCII). *European Journal of Experimental Social Psychology*, 40, 1277–1293.

Alexander, G. and Renshaw, B. (2005). *Supercoaching*. London: Random House.

Berg, I.K. and Szabó, P. (2005). *Brief Coaching for Lasting Solutions*. New York: Norton.

Centre for Coaching (2014). Primary Certificate in Performance Coaching Training Manual. Course held by Centre for Coaching, London, on the 15–16 July 2014.

Dunbar, A. (2009). *Essential life coaching skills*. Abingdon: Routledge.

Gollwitzer, A., Oettingen, G., Kirby, T., Duckworth, A. and Mayer, D. (2011). Mental contrasting facilitates academic performance in school children. *Motivation and Emotion*, 35, 403–412.

Jackson, P.Z. and McKergow, M. (2007). *The solutions focus: Making coaching & change SIMPLE* (2nd edn). London: Nicholas Brealey.

O'Connell, B., Palmer, S. and Williams, H. (2012). *Solution Focused Coaching in Practice*. Hove: Routledge.
Oettingen, G. (1999). Free fantasies about the future and the emergence of developmental goals. In J. Brandtstädter, and R.M. Lerner (eds), *Action and self-development: Theory and research through the life span*. Thousand Oaks/CA: Sage.
Oettingen, G., Pak, H. and Schnetter, K. (2001). Self-regulation of goal setting: Turning free fantasies about the future into binding goals. *Journal of Personality and Social Psychology*, 80, 736-753.
Palmer, S. and Szymanska, K. (2008). Cognitive behavioural coaching: An integrative approach. In S. Palmer and A. Whybrow (eds), *Handbook of coaching psychology: A guide for practitioners*. London: Routledge.
Ratner, H. and Yusuf, D. (2015). *Brief Coaching with Children and Young People: A solution focused approach*. London: Routledge.
Starr, J. (2016). *The coaching manual* (4th edn). Harlow, England: Pearson.
Whitmore, J. (2009). *Coaching for Performance*. (4th edn). London: Nicholas Brealey.

11 Options (O)

In this chapter

- Bridging the gap between 'Reality' and 'Goal'
- Helping the student to generate options
- Knowing when and how to make suggestions
- Helping the student to evaluate her options.

The 'Options' phase – a bridge from 'Reality' to 'Goal'

We are now in the third phase of GROW – 'Options'. The purpose of this phase is to help Zara think of ways to bridge the gap between her 'Reality' and her 'Goal.' Figure 11.1 should make this clear:

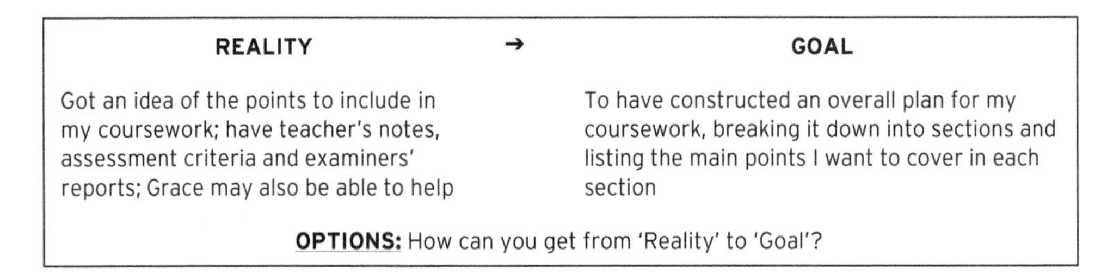

Figure 11.1 Getting from 'Reality' to 'Goal' via 'Options'.

It can be helpful for Zara to *see* something like Figure 11.1 or even to write it out for herself. This should make it easier for her to come up with options. The 'Options' phase itself is divided into two halves. The first half is devoted to the *generation* of options. The second is spent on their *evaluation*. These processes should be kept separate.

Generation of options

In order to help the student generate options, the coach can simply do the following:

i *Remind the student of her 'Reality'* (e.g. how much of her goal she has already achieved; what resources she has at her disposal etc.).

ii *Remind the student of her 'Goal'.*

iii *Ask the student how she can get from 'Reality' to 'Goal'.*

We shall assume that the coach has drawn out a version of Figure 11.1. Zara can now see her 'Reality' and 'Goal' and think about how to get from one to the other:

Coach: *(pointing to 'Reality' in Figure 11.1)* 'So you've already got an idea of the points you want to include in your coursework. And you have your teacher's notes, the assessment criteria and examiners' reports for last year. You've also got your friend Grace who could help you.'

Zara: 'Yeah.'

Coach: *(pointing to 'Goal' in Figure 11.1)* 'And your goal for this week is to have constructed an overall plan for my coursework, breaking it down into sections and listing the main points I want to cover in each section.'

Zara: 'Yep.'

Coach: 'Ok, bearing that in mind, how could you get from here *(pointing to "Reality")* to here *(pointing to "Goal")*?'

Zara: 'Hmm. . .maybe I could check the assessment criteria and see what areas I need to cover.'

The process of 'options generation' has now begun. The coach will write down each of Zara's suggestions, beginning in this case with '*check assessment criteria to see what areas I need to cover.*' His aim is to help Zara come up with as many ideas as possible:

Coach: 'Ok, what else could you do to construct your overall plan?

Zara: *(looks again at Figure 11.1)* 'I could ask Grace where to put my points. . .maybe ask my dad too.'

Coach: *(writes down Zara's last ideas)* 'Great, what else could you do?'

Zara: 'I could use my teacher's notes to edit my plan. . .'

Coach: *(writes down Zara's last idea)* 'Ok great. What could you do *right after this session?*'

Zara: 'Right after this session? Mmm. . .I could. . .go to the library and write down the points I want to include in my coursework.'

Coach: *(writing down Zara's last idea)* 'This is great, Zara. You're coming up with lots of options.'

In helping the student generate options the coach's approach is straightforward. He simply asks the student what she could do to achieve her proximal goal, i.e. construct her coursework plan. When she suggests a possibility, he makes a note of it and then asks: '*What else?*' Normally he would continue to do this until the student has run out of ideas. It is always a good idea to ask the student: '*What could you do right after this session?*' Securing immediate action helps to prevent procrastination.

So far, the coach has dealt with the *practical* side of Zara's proximal goal. It is now time for him to ask how she could overcome the psychological obstacle she mentioned in the 'Reality' phase:

Coach: 'Let's go back to your PITs and PETs. You realised earlier that you sometimes think it's a 'hassle' to get started and then want to put it off.'
Zara: 'Yeah.'
Coach: 'What could you do to get over that?'
Zara: 'I could remind myself of the PETs.'
Coach: 'When exactly?'
Zara: 'If I start thinking it's a hassle. . .'
Coach: 'So if you start thinking it's a "hassle" to get started, then you would remind yourself of your PETs?'
Zara: 'Yeah.'
Coach: 'What else could you do?'
Zara: 'Just get started!'

The coach has now helped Zara to think of ways to overcome the obstacle she mentioned in 'Reality', i.e. the thought of the 'hassle' of getting started. In the final phase of coaching ('Will'), he will help her turn these ideas into an 'if. . .then' plan, e.g.

> *'**If** I start thinking it's a "hassle", **then** I will remind myself of my PETs. . .'*

Knowing when to make suggestions

When I am training people in coaching, one of the most frequently asked questions is: '*Can the coach make suggestions?*' You might assume that the answer is 'no'. After all, coaching is about helping the student find her *own* solutions. Some commentators therefore argue that the coach should refrain from making suggestions in the 'Options' phase' (e.g. Wisker *et al.*, 2008).

On the other hand, it can be argued that effective coaching 'involves the active and collaborative participation of *both* the coach *and* the coachee' (Kimsey-House *et al.*, 2011, italics added). This is closer to the approach of this book. We assume that coaching is indeed a collaboration between coach and student. However, the student should be taking the lead. That is, the vast majority of options should be proposed by the student not the coach. If the coach believes that he has a useful idea, he should do the following:

1 First, elicit as many options as possible from the student.
2 When the student has run out of ideas, ask permission to offer a suggestion.
3 Offer the suggestion (if the student grants permission).
4 Make it clear to the student that she is free to reject the suggestion.

Let's see how this works in practice:

Coach: 'What else could you do to construct your overall plan?'
Zara: *(thinks for a while)* 'I really don't know. That's everything I can think of.'

Coach: 'Ok, would it be ok if I make a suggestion? You can ignore it completely if you don't like it. . .'
Zara: 'Sure.'
Coach: 'I was just thinking about the examiners' reports you mentioned. I wonder if they could be helpful.'
Zara: 'Oh yeah, I forgot about them.'
Coach: 'How could you use them to construct your plan?'
Zara: 'Well I can make sure my plan includes everything they say is important.'
Coach: *(writing down Zara's last idea)* 'Great.'

In the dialogue above the coach asks permission to make a suggestion. He then leaves it to Zara to turn that suggestion into a possible action-step. This ensures that the process is 'coachee-led'. However, as already noted, before making any suggestions of his own the coach should do everything he can to elicit ideas from the student. As we have seen, the most basic way to do this is to ask:

i '*What could you do to* [statement of student's goal]?'
followed by
ii '*What else?*'

Eventually, however, this will draw a blank ('I don't know'). For more advanced methods of eliciting options see Appendix A. Finally, remember that the purpose of the 'Options Generation' stage is to leave the coachee with a large number of options to choose from (Whitmore, 2009; Alexander and Renshaw, 2005). How many options should she have? It is impossible to lay down any hard and fast rules. When I am coaching I normally keep going until the student has proposed at least half a dozen options. But it depends on the goal we are working on. If a coach is not sure whether the student has enough options, there is a simple solution: ask the student. If she is satisfied with the list, then she can move on to evaluation.

Evaluation of options

There are two criteria on which options should be judged: *effectiveness* and *feasibility*. By 'effectiveness' we mean: 'To what extent would this option *help the student achieve her goal*?' By 'feasibility' we mean: 'To what extent will the student *be able to carry this out*?' An option may be high in effectiveness (i.e. it would help her to achieve her goal), but low in feasibility (i.e. she would struggle to carry it out) and vice versa. Remember that the coach wrote down each option Zara suggested. In fact, he has been using a form which now looks like Table 11.1.

Helping Zara *evaluate* her options is now a straightforward matter. The coach will simply read through the list of options and ask Zara to give each one a score for 'effectiveness' and a score for 'feasibility':

Coach: 'Ok let's consider each of your options. The first one you suggested was to check the assessment criteria to see what areas you need to cover.'
Zara: 'Yeah.'

Table 11.1 Zara's Options form.

Options	*Effectiveness*	*Feasibility*
1 Check assessment criteria to see what areas I need to cover		
2 Ask Grace where to put my points		
3 Ask Dad where to put my points		
4 Use my teacher's notes to edit my plan		
5 Go to the library and write down the points I want to include in my coursework		
6 Read 'PETs' and just get started (if it seems like a 'hassle')		
7 Read examiners' reports and make sure my plan includes everything they say is important		

Coach: 'Ok, imagine a scale from 0 to 10. 0 is "completely useless" and 10 is as effective as anything can be.'

Zara: 'Ok.'

Coach: *(pointing at option 1)* 'From 0 to 10, how effective would that be in helping you construct your coursework plan?'

Zara: 'Probably an 8. The assessment criteria are pretty important. . .'

Coach: *(writes down '8' for effectiveness)* 'Great. Now imagine another scale from 0 to 10. 0 means it's impossible for you to do and 10 means it's the easiest thing in the world.'

Zara: 'Ok.'

Coach: 'From 0 to 10, how easy would it be for you to check the assessment criteria and see what areas you need to cover?'

Zara: '9. I've got the criteria in my folder so I just have to read through them.'

Coach: *(writes down '9' for feasibility).* 'Great. Let's look at the second option. . .'

In order to help Zara determine the effectiveness and feasibility of each option the coach uses two scaling questions ('From 0 to 10'). Notice too that he explicitly links the option to Zara's *proximal goal*. He does not ask merely 'how effective would that be?' but rather 'how effective would that be *in helping you construct your coursework plan*?' It is important for Zara to have her goal in mind as she evaluates each option.

The end of the 'Options' phase

Imagine that it is now the end of the 'Options' phase. Zara has evaluated each of her ideas in terms of effectiveness and feasibility. The completed options form is presented in Table 11.2 on the following page.

Final thoughts on 'Options'

Two last points should be made about 'Options'. The first point is that this phase – perhaps more than any other – requires the coach to be *non-judgemental*. Coachees must 'feel safe enough to express their thoughts without inhibition or fear of judgement from the coach'

Table 11.2 Zara's Options form completed.

Options	*Effectiveness*	*Feasibility*
1 Check assessment criteria to see what areas I need to cover	8	9
2 Ask Grace where to put my points	6	7
3 Ask Dad where to put my points	5	7
4 Use my teacher's notes to edit my plan	8	9
5 Go to the library and write down the points I want to include in my coursework	10	9
6 Read 'PETs' and just get started (if it seems like a 'hassle')	10	9
7 Read examiners' reports and make sure plan includes everything they say is important	10	9

(Whitmore, 2009, p. 79). Zara should be encouraged to suggest whatever options she likes. No matter how unsuitable they appear, the coach should write them down, without expressing any negative opinions.

The second point concerns the wider benefits of 'options generation'. On one level the purpose of this stage is simply to help the student achieve her goal. However, on another level, 'options generation' also serves to give the student more *hope*. When a hopeful person finds that one route is blocked, 'he or she is able to search for and find other pathways to the goal and maintain a sense of agency' (Kauffman, 2006, p. 229). By continuing to ask the student 'what else could you do?' the coach helps her to see that there is more than one way to achieve her goal. Options generation encourages 'pathways thinking' which is a key component of hope (Kauffman, 2006). This may be one of the reasons why coaching has been shown to increase students' levels of hope (Green, Grant and Rynsaardt, 2007). The benefits of having high levels of hope are well documented and include better physical health, higher academic functioning and greater ability to face and overcome obstacles (Snyder, 2000; Kauffman, 2006).

We are now ready to enter the final phase of the GROW model – 'Will'. As we shall see in the next chapter, this involves helping the student turn her options into *action-steps*.

Chapter summary

- The purpose of the 'Options' phase is to help the student get from where she is now ('Reality') to where she wants to be (her 'Goal).
- The Options phase is divided into two separate stages: (1) Generation, and (2) Evaluation.
- When helping a student to generate options the coach's basic approach is to ask 'What could you do to [statement of student's goal]?' followed by 'What else?'
- The coach should elicit as many options as possible from the student before offering to make a suggestion. He should also make it clear that the student is entirely free to reject his suggestion.

(continued)

(continued)

- Once the student is satisfied that she has generated enough options, she and the coach begin evaluation. The coach asks the student to rate each of her options - on a scale from 0 to 10 - in terms of effectiveness and feasibility.
- By the end of the Options phase the student should have a list of possible steps she could take to achieve her proximal (or ultimate) goal. Next to each option there should be two scores - one for effectiveness and the other for feasibility.
- The process of generating options can help to enhance a student's level of hope. The more 'pathways' a student perceives, the more optimistic she is likely to feel.

References

Alexander, G. and Renshaw, B. (2005). *Supercoaching*. London: Random House.

Green, S., Grant, A. and Rynsaardt, J. (2007). Evidence-based life coaching for senior high school students: Building hardiness and hope. *International Coaching Psychology Review*, 2, 24-32.

Kauffman, C. (2006). Positive psychology: The science at the heart of coaching. In D.R. Stober and A.M. Grant (eds), *Evidence based coaching handbook: Putting best practices to work for your clients*. Hoboken, NJ: John Wiley & Sons.

Kimsey-House, H., Kimsey-House, K., Sandahl, P. and Whitworth, L. (2011). *Co-active coaching: Changing business, transforming lives* (3rd edn). Boston, MA: Nicholas Brealey.

Snyder, C. (2000). *Handbook of hope: Theory, measures, and applications*. San Diego, CA: Academic Press.

Whitmore, J. (2009). *Coaching for Performance*. (4th edn). London: Nicholas Brealey.

Wisker, G., Exley, K., Antoniou, M. and Ridley, P. (2008). *Working one-to-one with students*. Abingdon: Routledge.

12 Will (W)

In this chapter

- The importance of the 'Will' phase
- Turning options into action-steps
- The written Action-plan
- Identifying and overcoming obstacles
- 'If. . .then' implementation intentions
- Checking commitment.

The importance of the 'Will' phase

Let's remind ourselves where we are in coaching. First, Zara set herself a proximal goal (G). Then she and her coach explored her reality (R). After that Zara generated and evaluated several options (O). And now she has reached the final phase of GROW – **'Will'.**

The main purpose of the 'Will' phase is simple: to prepare the student to *take action*. In more eloquent terms, this phase involves 'the construction of an action plan to meet a requirement that has been clearly specified, on ground that has been thoroughly surveyed. . .using the widest possible choice of building materials' (Whitmore, 2009, p. 85). In one sense, the 'Will' phase of GROW is the most important. Zara will get nowhere at all unless she takes action. In fact, the most important part of any coaching programme is what the student does *outside* coaching sessions. If a student is new to coaching, the coach might want to highlight this point:

Coach: 'So you've set yourself a goal for this week and you've got a list of options.'
Zara: 'Yep.'
Coach: 'What will happen if you stop here?'
Zara: 'You mean if I don't do anything with the list?'
Coach: 'Exactly. What will happen if you don't do anything with the list?'
Zara: 'Nothing I guess.'
Coach: 'Ok, so what do you need to do now?'
Zara: 'Decide what I'm going to do.'

Coach: 'And then?'
Zara: *(smiling)* 'Actually do it.'

In the dialogue above the coach's questions are almost leading ones. Leading questions are normally to be avoided in coaching (see Chapter 6). In this case, however, they can perhaps be accepted since they help Zara to grasp a key point.

Turning options into action-steps

At the end of the 'Options' phase Zara had in front of her the following list:

Table 12.1 Zara's completed Options form.

Option	*Effectiveness*	*Feasibility*
1 Check assessment criteria to see what areas I need to cover	8	9
2 Ask Grace where to put my points	6	7
3 Ask Dad where to put my points	5	7
4 Use my teacher's notes to edit my plan	8	9
5 Go to the library and write down the points I want to include in my coursework	10	9
6 Read 'PETs' and just get started (if it seems like a 'hassle')	10	9
7 Read examiners' reports and make sure my plan includes everything they say is important	10	9

The beauty of Table 12.1 is that it makes it easy for the student to decide what to do. As Whitmore (2009, p. 82) notes, '[o]nce a comprehensive list [of options] has been generated, the *will* phase of coaching may just be a simple matter of selecting the best of the bunch.' Nevertheless, a step-by-step guide may be helpful:

Step 1: Ask the student to identify her preferred options.

Step 2: Ask her for precise action-steps and get her to enter these into her Action-plan.

Step 3: Help her to identify and overcome any obstacles to her action-steps.

Each of the above steps is fairly simple and the whole process unfolds in a highly intuitive manner.

Step 1: Ask the student to identify her preferred options

Here the coach need only point to the list and ask 'What options appeal to you?' or 'What options stand out for you?' (Alexander and Renshaw, 2005, p. 256).

Coach: *(pointing to Table 12.1)* 'When you look at the list, which options stand out for you?'
Student: 'Number 1. . .4. . .5. . .6 and 7.'
Coach: *(circling the options)* 'Great.'

Often students will simply pick the options to which they gave the highest ratings for effectiveness and feasibility. This is certainly a sensible approach. However, students may also have their own reasons for choosing some options rather than others. If time permits, it can therefore be helpful to ask the coachee to explain her selection (Alexander and Renshaw, 2005). This will help her to adopt a more thoughtful approach to decision-making. Whatever the case, it is essential that the student should be allowed to *make her own choices*.

Step 2: Ask her for precise action-steps and get her to enter these into her action-plan.

After Zara has identified the options that appeal to her, the coach should ask her what exactly she is going to do. There is a world of difference between 'What *could* you do?' and 'What *will* you do?' (e.g. Whitmore, 2009). It is time to focus on the latter. Zara should leave the session with a clear plan of action that specifies precisely what steps she will take to achieve her proximal goal. In order to help her, the coach will do the following:

- i Ask her what she is going to do and *when* and *where* she is going to do it.
- ii Jot down her plan in rough.
- iii Ask her to look over the rough plan and to make any necessary amendments (e.g. to change the date of a particular step)
- iv Invite her to enter each step into her *action-Plan* table (see Table 12.2).

Note that it should be the *student* (not the coach) who fills in the final Action-Plan. She needs to take ownership of the process. Writing down her own action-steps should help to enhance her commitment (Greene and Grant, 2003).

The beginning of Step 2 might go like this:

Coach: 'So the options that appeal to you are 1, 4, 5, 6 and 7.'
Zara: 'Yeah.'
Coach: 'Ok, let's turn them into action-steps. What *exactly* are you going to do?'

Table 12.2 Action-Plan Template.

	Time and date	*Action*	*Place*
1	When it is	Then I will	In ....
2	When it is	Then I will	In ....
3	When it is	Then I will	In ....

Zara: 'Well I'll probably do 5 first. . .go to the library and write down the points I want to include.'

Coach: 'When will you do that?'

Zara: 'I can do it right after this session. . .11:15.'

Coach: 'Where in the library will you do it?'

Zara: *(thinks for a second)* 'In the quiet section upstairs by the ICT room.'

Coach: 'So when it is 11:15am today, then you'll go to the library and write down all the points for your coursework in the quiet section upstairs by the ICT room.'

Zara: 'Exactly.'

Coach: *(writing down the step in rough)* 'Great. What are you going to do next?'

Note how the coach asks Zara to describe the action she is going to take *in minute detail*. This is a key feature of the 'Will' phase. One of the advantages of this detail is that it enables the coachee to visualise exactly what she is going to do and foresee potential obstacles (Peterson, 2006). In addition, as we saw in Chapter 3, research shows that students who are asked to specify where and when they will perform a task are much more likely to take action than students who are not asked to be specific about their plans (Gollwitzer and Brandstatter, 1997). This is why coaches should ask questions such as:

1 ***What*** *are you going to do?*
2 ***When*** *are you going to do it?*
3 ***Where*** *are you going to do it?*
  and, if appropriate:
4 ***How*** *are you going to do it?*

After the coach has elicited answers to these questions and helped Zara to formulate her first action-step, he then asks her to describe the second: 'What are you going to do next?' Remember that her action-steps are not yet cast in stone. In our example, the coach is jotting down Zara's steps *in rough*. This means that the order can be changed and details can be amended.

However, once Zara has looked over what the coach has written and confirmed the action-steps, she will fill out her own Action-plan. See Table 12.3 on p. 111.

Zara's first action step would read as follows:

> ***When*** *it is 11:15am today,* **then** *I will go to the library and write down the points I want to include in my coursework in the quiet section by the ICT room.*

The crucial feature is the 'when. . .then' wording. In most published research 'if' is used instead of 'when,' i.e. '*If* it is. . .*then* I will. . .' and the resulting plan is known as an *implementation intention*. The pioneer in this area is Peter Gollwitzer, whose work was mentioned in Chapter 3. Gollwitzer points out that when we are referring to a point in time it is more natural to use 'when' than 'if,' i.e. '*When* it is 11:15am. . .' (Gollwitzer, personal communication).

Table 12.3 Zara's completed action-plan.

Time and date	*Action*	*Place*
When it is *11:15am today (5 September)*	Then I will *go to the library and write down the points I want to include in my coursework*	In *the quiet section by ICT room*
When it is *9pm on Tues 6 September*	Then I will *go to my desk, take out assessment criteria and check what I need to cover*	In *my bedroom*
When it is *2pm on Wed 7 September*	Then I will *go to the library and use my teacher's notes to edit my plan*	In *the quiet section by ICT room*
When it is *4pm on Fri 9 September*	Then I will *go to the library, read examiners' reports and make sure my plan includes everything they say is important*	In *the quiet section by ICT room*

In 'if/when. . .then' plans, the 'if/when' part highlights the *critical cue* (in this case an opportunity to act – 11:15am), and the 'then' part specifies the *goal-directed response* (e.g. going to the library and writing down points for one's coursework). Gollwitzer and his colleagues have found that these plans enable people to act in the moment without needing to think about what to do. The critical cue automatically triggers the behaviour. As Gollwitzer puts it, implementation intentions 'delegate the control of goal-directed responses to anticipated situational cues, which (when actually encountered) elicit these responses automatically' (Gollwitzer, 1999, p. 493). In other words, when Zara's watch indicates 11:15am she may find herself walking to the library without a moment's hesitation.

Is it really necessary to use the 'when. . .then' format for action-steps? Couldn't Zara just make a note of what she is going to do as well as when and where she is going to do it? She could, and this sort of planning would be effective. However, recent research has shown that the 'implementation intention' format makes it even more likely that students will take action (Pakpour *et al.*, 2016).

Step 3: Help the student identify and overcome any obstacles to her action-steps

Once the student has filled out her Action-plan, the coach's job is to help her identify potential obstacles and think of ways to overcome them.

Coach: 'Let's think about what might stop you from taking each step.'

Zara: 'Ok.'

Coach: *(pointing to Zara's first step)* 'What could stop you from going to the library today at 11:15 and doing that?'

Zara: 'If I start thinking it's a hassle. . .I might want to put it off.'

Coach: 'How can you get over that hurdle?'

Zara: 'Remind myself of my PETs and just get on with it!'

Coach: 'So if you catch yourself thinking it's a "hassle", then you'll remind yourself of your PETs and just get on with it?'
Zara: *(sounding determined)* 'Yeah.'

You will recall from Chapter 10 that in reflecting on her own thinking Zara identified both performance-interfering thoughts (PITs) and performance-enhancing thoughts (PETs). Her PITs – PETs form looked like this:

Table 12.4 Zara's PITs and PETs.

Performance-interfering thoughts (PITs)	*Performance-enhancing thoughts (PETs)*
Getting started is a hassle.	It's ok when I get going. I need the plan for my coursework Just get <u>on</u> with it!

Adapted from Centre for Coaching (2014)

Zara has realised that one obstacle to carrying out her first action-step (i.e. going to the library after the session) is the thought that it is a 'hassle'. However, she also came up with a more helpful way of thinking (see the PETs column). The coach would now help her to construct an 'if. . .then' plan using her PETs. Consider two possibilities:

(i) *'If I catch myself thinking it's a "hassle," then I'll remind myself that* ***it's ok when I get going*** *and* ***just get on with it****!'*
(ii) *'If I catch myself thinking it's a "hassle," then I'll remind myself that* ***I need the plan for my coursework*** *and* ***just get on with it****!'*

These are further examples of *implementation intentions*. In this case the critical cue in the 'if' half is an anticipated obstacle and the 'then' half specifies what Zara will do to *overcome* that obstacle. Not all obstacles, however, require 'if. . .then' plans. In some cases, the student can simply change part of the action-step:

Coach: 'Ok, what could stop you from doing the *second* thing in your plan?'
Zara: 'I guess I could be pretty tired by 9pm. . .'
Coach: 'What could you do about that?'
Zara: *(thinks for a moment)* 'I could do it before dinner instead.'
Coach: 'What time would that be?'
Zara: '6pm.'
Coach: 'How effective would that be?'
Zara: 'Very. . .I'll have much more energy at 6 than at 9.'
Coach: 'Great. Would you like to change the time in your Action-Plan?'
Zara: 'Yep.' (*Zara crosses out '9pm' and writes '6pm.'*)

The coach would now go through Zara's remaining action-steps in Table 12.3. For each one he will ask *'What could stop you from doing that?'* and then *'How could you overcome that hurdle?'* Once all potential obstacles have been dealt with, the coach can wrap up the 'Will' phase and bring the session to an end.

Wrapping up the 'Will' phase - checking commitment

Two final steps can be helpful in the 'Will' phase. First, the coach may wish to remind the student of the link between her Action-plan, proximal goal, and ultimate goal:

Coach: 'When you've done all these steps, what will you have?'
Zara: 'My overall plan.'
Coach: 'And what will that do for you?'
Zara: 'It'll make it much easier to do the coursework.'
Coach: 'So, when you do these action-steps you'll have your plan. And having that plan will make it much easier to do your coursework.'
Zara: 'Yep.'

Here the coach helps Zara to remember the bigger picture. That is, rather than getting her to focus on the action-steps themselves he encourages her to think about *why* she is undertaking them, i.e. how they are connected to her ultimate goal (e.g. Dawson and Guare, 2012). Asking people to consider *why* they engage in action (as opposed to *how* they engage in it) activates a certain type of thinking, which some researchers call 'high level construal' (e.g. Trope and Liberman, 2010). Research shows that when students reflect on *why* they do what they do (i.e. think about high-level goals), they experience less desire for immediate gratification, less inclination to give in to temptations, greater physical endurance and stronger intentions to exert self-control (Fujita *et al.*, 2006). Focusing on the 'instrumentality' of a course of action - i.e. why one engages in it - also enhances students' motivation to *pursue* that course of action (Fishbach and Choi, 2012).

The layout of the student's coaching form also encourages 'high-level construal'. Have a look at Appendix C. Note the upward arrows - from 'Action-Plan' to 'This Week's Goal' to 'Ultimate Goal' and finally to 'Benefits' (and 'Costs'). All of this should help the student to see the bigger picture, which should enhance and maintain her motivation.

The final step in wrapping up the 'Way Forward' phase is to check the student's *commitment* to each individual step. A simple scaling question will suffice:

'On a scale from 0 to 10, how committed are you to taking this step?'

Whitmore notes that when the answer is less than 8, coachees seldom follow through (Whitmore, 2009). If a student rates her commitment to a particular step as 7 or less, the coach should ask her: 'What could you do to make it an 8 or higher?' To raise her commitment she might need to modify the action-step. For example, rather than reading yet another article (commitment = 6), she might decide to listen to a podcast (commitment = 9).

If you look at Appendix C, the last sentence underneath the student's Action plan is:

'I confirm that I will carry out these action-steps before our next session.'

If Zara is committed to each step in her plan, the coach can invite her to sign it. Evidence suggests that signing a 'behavioural contract' makes people more likely to follow through and take action (Neale *et al.*, 1990).

Final thoughts on the 'Will phase'

Before we bring this chapter to a close and conclude our exposition of the GROW model, a few crucial points need to be reiterated. The first is that the student should have a *written copy* of her Action-plan to take away with her (Whitmore, 2009). The coach too should have a copy of this plan. As noted earlier, it can be helpful to make a photocopy of the Action-plan (e.g. Dawson and Guare, 2012). Alternatively, the student (or coach) could take a photo of the plan using a tablet or smartphone.

In addition, the student should be encouraged to do something immediately. In our example Zara's first step was to go to the library *right after the session.* This should help her to avoid procrastination and build momentum. Many commentators therefore argue that 'coaching should aim to secure practical action as soon as possible' (Ives and Cox, 2012, p. 44; see also Berg and Szabó, 2005).

Finally, coaches should not allow students to be vague about their action-steps. For example, if a student says she is going to start her essay 'this weekend' then it is the coach's responsibility to ask '*when* exactly this weekend?' She may not like being precise. But it is for her own good. If she is reluctant to be specific about when (or where) she will take action, the coach should draw her attention to the research that has been done on action-planning and implementation intentions, all of which demonstrates the importance of being precise. Whatever the case, '[i]t is up to the coach to tie the coachee down to exact timings. The coachee may wriggle, but a good coach will not let [her] off the hook,' (Whitmore, 2009, p. 86).

And with that we come to the end of the GROW model. In the last four chapters, we have seen how a coach can help a student set a goal (G), assess her reality (R), generate and evaluate options (O) and finally decide what she will do (W). However, some questions remain. Is there really time to go through GROW in every session? How long should each phase of GROW last? And do all sessions have the same structure? These questions are answered in the next chapter.

Chapter summary

- The 'Will' phase of GROW is in many ways the most important. Students need to understand that coaching will have no effect whatsoever unless they take action.
- Helping the student decide what she will do may be as simple as asking her to select from her 'options'.
- The student must state precisely what she is going to do as well as when and where she is going to do it. The coach initially writes down her plan in rough. The student then checks each step and fills in her Action-Plan.
- Action-plans make use of implementation intentions ('when. . .then'). Research shows that these are extremely effective in bringing about action.

- The coach also helps the student to identify potential obstacles and think of ways to overcome them. The student may need to construct an 'If. . .then' plan.
- The coach can help the student remember and rehearse her 'performance-enhancing thoughts' (PETs).
- The coach can encourage 'high-level construal', i.e. help the student to see *why* she is carrying out her action-steps and how they are linked to her proximal and ultimate goal.
- The coach should check the student's commitment to each action-step using a scaling question ('On a scale from 0 to 10, how committed are you to. . .?').
- Both student and coach should have a copy of the student's Action-plan.

References

Alexander, G. and Renshaw, B. (2005). *Supercoaching.* London: Random House.

Berg, I.K. and Szabó, P. (2005). *Brief Coaching for Lasting Solutions.* New York: Norton.

Centre for Coaching (2014). Primary Certificate in Performance Coaching Training Manual. Course held by Centre for Coaching, London, on the 15-16 July 2014.

Dawson, P. and Guare, R. (2012). *Coaching students with executive skill deficits.* New York: Guilford Press.

Fishbach, A. and Choi, J. (2012). When thinking about goals undermines goal pursuit. *Organizational Behavior and Human Decision Processes*, 118, 99-107.

Fujita, K., Trope, Y., Liberman, N. and Levin-Sagi, M. (2006). Construal levels and self-control. *Journal of Personality and Social Psychology*, 90, 351-367.

Gollwitzer, P.M. (1999). Implementation intentions: Strong effects of simple plans. *American Psychologist*, 54, 493-503.

Gollwitzer, P. and V. Brandstatter (1997). Implementation intentions and effective goal pursuit. *Journal of Personality and Social Psychology*, 73, 1, 186-199.

Greene, J. and Grant, A.M. (2003). *Solution-focused Coaching: Managing people in a complex world.* Harlow: Pearson Education Limited.

Ives, Y. and Cox, E. (2012). *Goal-focused coaching: Theory and practice.* New York: Routledge.

Neale, A.V., Singleton, S.P., Dupuis, M.H. and Hess, J.W. (1990). The use of behavioral contracting to increase exercise activity. *American Journal of Health Promotion.* 4, 6, 441-447.

Pakpour, A.H., Gholami, M., Gellert, P., Yekaninejad, M.S., Dombrowski, S.U. and Webb, T.L. (2016). The effects of two planning interventions on the oral health behavior of Iranian adolescents: A cluster randomized controlled trial. *Annals of Behavioral Medicine*, 1-10.

Peterson, D.B. (2006). People are complex and the world is messy: A behaviour-based approach to executive coaching In D.R. Stober and A.M. Grant (eds), *Evidence Based Coaching Handbook: Putting Best Practices to Work for Your Clients.* Hoboken, NJ: John Wiley & Sons.

Trope, Y. and Liberman, N. (2010). Construal-level theory of psychological distance. *Psychological Review*, 117, 440-463.

Whitmore, J. (2009). *Coaching for Performance.* (4th edn). London: Nicholas Brealey.

13 A coaching programme

In this chapter

- Before the first session
- The first session
- Subsequent sessions
- The final session
- GROW vs. 'GROW-lite'
- Tailoring sessions to the student's needs.

Before the first session

In order to save time a few steps should be taken *before* the first session. Most importantly, students should be given a copy of the '*Coaching Contract*'. This contract is discussed fully in Chapter 18. It explains what coaching entails and what coach and student can expect from each other. The student should be encouraged to read this carefully before the first session and make a note of anything that is unclear. She should also be encouraged to think about what she wants to address in coaching. The following introductory email might be helpful:

Box 13.1 An introductory email sent to a prospective coachee.

Dear [name of student],

I hope you are looking forward to coaching. In order to get the most out of the programme, please read through the attached 'Coaching Contract', which tells you what you can expect from coaching.

After you have read the contract, think about *what you want to work on in coaching.* Please jot down your answers to the following questions and bring them to your first session:

(i) **What issue or area would you like to work on?** *(e.g. managing your workload, preparing for exams)*
(ii) **What would you like to have achieved by the end of coaching?** *(e.g. to have a better work-life balance, to feel more confident about exams)*

If the student has read the introductory email and answered the questions, then the first coaching session will be much easier to conduct.

The first session

In the first session, the coach will normally have to carry out some preliminary steps, e.g. welcoming the student, answering questions about coaching, signing the contract and so on. Once these steps have been completed, the coach will help the student to set her *ultimate goal* for the programme. As we saw in Chapter 9, coach and student need to be extremely thorough in this process. After the contracting and ultimate goal-setting phase, there may not be much time left in the session. It is for this reason that *the full version of GROW is not used in the first session.* Instead the coach uses a pared-down version, which we shall call *GROW-lite.* Table 13.1 presents the phases of the first session. We are assuming that coach and student have 30 minutes together.

We have said that in the first session coach and student will be using not GROW but GROW-*lite.* As you can see from Table 13.1, apart from the Goal-setting phase (which makes up the bulk of the session) the phases of GROW-lite are very short. 'Reality', 'Options' and 'Will' take no more than two or three minutes each. These timings are not meant to be rigid. But note that in the first session coach and student spend far less time in the last three phases of GROW than they do in any subsequent session. This should be a relief for both of them. After the rigours of ultimate goal-setting (see Chapter 9), the rest of the first session will be a lighter introduction to coaching.

Table 13.1 The first coaching session

	Phase	*Duration*	
1	**Contracting**	5 mins	
2	**Goal-setting**	17 mins	'GROW-Lite'
3	**Reality**	3 mins	'GROW-Lite'
4	**Options**	2 mins	'GROW-Lite'
5	**Will**	3 mins	'GROW-Lite'

Phase 1: Contracting

The contracting process is covered in Chapter 18. It involves discussing and agreeing on the terms and conditions of coaching. At the end of this phase, coach and student will sign the Coaching Contract (see Appendix D) The coach will then supply the student with the necessary materials, i.e. coaching forms (Appendix C) and PITs-PETs tables (Appendix E).

Phase 2: Goal-setting

The student now sets her *ultimate goal*, i.e. what she wants to have achieved *by the end of coaching*. We explored this process in Chapter 9. Of all the phases in 'GROW-lite' ultimate goal-setting is by far the lengthiest and most involved. You may recall from Chapter 9 that Zara's ultimate goal for coaching was:

> *'To have completed my English coursework by October 21st, having worked on it bit-by-bit each week.'*

Zara would write the above in the 'Ultimate Goal' box in her coaching form (Appendix C).

Phase 3: Reality

Once the student has set her ultimate goal, she and her coach will *briefly* explore reality. Note that this means reality *in relation to her ultimate goal*. This phase takes only two or three minutes:

(i) Finding out what the student has already achieved

Coach: 'How much of your English coursework have you already done?'
Zara: 'I've got a few notes and written a few lines in rough.'

(ii) Finding out what is helping the student to achieve her goal

Coach: 'What's *helping* you to complete your coursework?'
Zara: 'My teacher's notes are pretty helpful. . .and I guess I'm pretty motivated.'

(iii) Identifying potential obstacles (through mental contrasting)

Coach: 'Imagine you've completed your coursework on time. What would the best thing about that?'
Zara: *(eyes closed)* 'I'll feel really proud of myself and probably get a good grade.'
Coach: 'Ok. Now what could *stop* you from completing your coursework on time?'
Zara: 'Being disorganised - my sheets are all over the place.'

(iv) Uncovering useful resources

Coach: 'What *resources* do you have that could help you complete your coursework?'
Zara: 'Er. . .teacher's notes, a few study aids. . .the assessment criteria, I think.'

Phase 4: Options

The 'Options' phase in the first session is even shorter than 'Reality'. The coach will ask the student for *one small but significant step* she can take to make progress towards her goal. He will also ask her what she could to overcome the obstacle she identified in 'Reality'. This may become a second step. However, it may also be combined with the first:

Coach: 'What small but useful step could you take before our next session?'
Zara: 'I could find all my sheets and resources.'
Coach: *(jotting down the option)* 'Ok. You said that the one thing that could stop you from achieving your goal is being disorganised. What could you do about that?'
Zara: 'I could organise all my sheets in one folder.'

The action Zara is proposing here may seem trivial. However, note two things. First, it may help her to overcome what she identified as the biggest obstacle to achieving her goal - being disorganised. Second, one small but significant action often leads to another. Berg and Szabó (2005) compare a coachee's initial action to a snowball rolling down a hill. Although it may not be much to begin with, it quickly gathers pace, becoming more and more substantial.

Phase 5: Will

The 'Will' phase in GROW-lite follows naturally from 'Options'. The coach helps the student to determine her action step(s), using the 'When. . .then' format:

Coach: 'So what will you actually do before our next session?'
Zara: 'I'll find all my sheets and organise them in one folder.'
Coach: 'When will you do that?'
Zara: 'I can do it today - at the beginning of break.'
Coach: 'Where will you do it?'
Zara: 'In my form room.'
Coach: 'Ok, would you like to write that down in your Action-plan table?'
Zara: 'Sure.'

Zara would now write her action-step in the action-plan table at the bottom of her coaching form (see Appendix C), i.e.

> *When it is the beginning of break, then I will find all my sheets and organise them in one folder in my form room.*

In the first session, the 'action plan' constructed in the 'Will' phase may consist of a single step. As already noted, the purpose of GROW-lite is to ease the student into coaching. Coaches should therefore 'have coachees take small, easily achievable steps that build in time to overall stretching goals, rather than overwhelm them with large initial actions'

Table 13.2 Subsequent coaching sessions.

	Phase	Duration
1	**Feedback**	3 mins
2	**Goal-setting**	2 mins
3	**Reality**	7 mins
4	**Options**	10 mins
5	**Will**	8 mins

(Grant, 2016, p. 121). These easily achievable action-steps can be seen as 'quick wins' that give the coachee an early taste of success and enhance her sense of self-efficacy (Ives and Cox, 2012).

Subsequent sessions

The agenda for subsequent sessions is presented in Table 13.2. Notice (i) that the first phase is now *feedback*, and (ii) that GROW has replaced GROW-lite. Once again, we are assuming that the session is 30 minutes long.

Phase 1: Feedback

The importance of performance and progress feedback was emphasised in Chapter 3. In this phase, the coach will ask three main questions:

1 *Did you carry out your* ***action-steps****?*
2 *On a scale from 0 to 10, to what extent did you achieve* ***last week's goal****?*
3 *On a scale from 0 to 10, how close are you now to your* ***ultimate goal****?*

If it is the student's *second* session then she will not have set a proximal goal. In this case, question 2 can be omitted. From the second session onwards, she will be setting herself weekly proximal goals, in which case the second question is essential. Two additional questions are often helpful in the Feedback phase:

(i) *'What did you* ***learn*** *that could help you in future?'*
(ii) *'What will you do* ***differently*** *from now on?'*

These questions can be asked *after* the three main questions. But they are often naturally woven into the discussion:

Coach: 'So your action-step was to find all your resources and organise them in one folder.'
Zara: 'Yep.'
Coach: 'Did you do that?'
Zara: 'Yeah, I did. But it took longer than I thought. . .the sheets were everywhere.'
Coach: 'So what did you learn that could help you in future?'

Zara: 'That I need to put everything in one place straightaway.'

Coach: 'Great. Let's think about where you are in relation to your ultimate goal.'

Zara: 'Ok.'

Coach: 'Your ultimate goal is to have completed your English coursework by 21 October, having worked on it bit-by-bit each week. *(Zara nods).* If "0" is as far away as you could possibly be, and "10" is "goal achieved", how close are you now from 0 to 10?'

Zara: *(thinks for a moment)* 'Maybe 1 and a half. . .'

Coach: 'So you've already made a bit of progress.'

Zara: 'Yeah, a little bit. . .but I need to be more focused.'

Coach: 'When you say "more focused" what do you mean exactly?'

Zara: 'Like listen more in class.'

Coach: 'So what will you do differently from now on?'

Zara: *(thinks for a second)* 'I'll pay more attention if my teacher's talking about coursework. . .and take notes.'

Coach: 'How could you turn that into an "if. . .then" plan?'

Zara: '*If* my teacher. . .starts talking about coursework, *then*. . .I will. . .pay more attention and start taking notes.'

Coach: 'That sounds like a good plan. Shall we think about your goal for this week?'

Zara: 'Sure.'

As you can see from the above, the Feedback phase need not take long. But it is a crucial aspect of coaching. We have made the point elsewhere that most of the *real* work in coaching takes place in the coachee's day-to-day life (Berg and Szabó, 2005). It is therefore essential to find out what the coachee has done *between sessions* (Palmer and Szymanska, 2008). In addition, the student needs to see how *well* she has done (performance feedback) and find out how much progress she has made towards her ultimate goal (progress feedback). This will enable her to (i) adjust her approach (if necessary) and (ii) feel confident that she is on the right path.

Phases 2-5: GROW

In all sessions, apart from the first and last, phases 2-5 are the phases of GROW. Note that from the second session onwards, the goal ('G') is a *proximal* goal, i.e. something the student wants to achieve *by the next session*. We covered the phases of GROW in Chapters 9-12 so there is no need to discuss them here. It may however be useful to compare GROW (used from the second session onwards) with GROW-lite (used in the first session). 'C' stands for 'Coach' and 'S' for 'Student':

As you can see from Tables 13.3a and 13.3b, the Goal phase of 'GROW-lite' is actually much *longer* than the corresponding phase in GROW (which takes place in subsequent sessions). The reason for this is that the 'Goal' in the first session is the student's *ultimate* goal, which may take a while to establish. However, the remaining phases - R, O and W - are a great deal shorter than they are in subsequent sessions. Hence the name 'GROW-lite.'

Table 13.3a and Table 13.3b GROW-lite (first session) vs. GROW (subsequent sessions).

	FIRST SESSION: GROW-lite			*SUBSEQUENT SESSIONS: GROW*	
G	S sets *ultimate goal* for coaching programme	**(17 mins)**	**G**	S sets *proximal goal* - to be achieved by next session	**(2 mins)**
R	C & S briefly discuss S's reality in relation to *ultimate* goal	**(3 mins)**	**R**	C & S discuss S's reality in relation to *proximal* goal	**(7 mins)**
O	S thinks of 1-2 small things she could do before next session	**(2 mins)**	**O**	S thinks of and evaluates many ways to achieve *proximal* goal	**(10 mins)**
W	S decides what she will do before next session	**(3 mins)**	**W**	S constructs a multi-step Action-Plan	**(8 mins)**

The final session

Table 13.4 presents one possible way to structure the final coaching session:

Table 13.4 The final session.

	Phase	*Duration*
1	**Feedback**	4 mins
2	**Celebrate achievements**	10 mins
3	**Plan for the future**	10 mins
4	**Student's thoughts**	5 mins
5	**Thanks and Goodbye**	1 min

As before, we are assuming that the session lasts 30 minutes. Each phase is summarised below.

Phase 1: Feedback

As always, the coach will ask the three main 'Feedback' questions:

1 *Did you carry out your **action-steps**?*
2 *On a scale from 0 to 10, to what extent did you achieve **last week's goal**?*
3 *On a scale from 0 to 10, how close are you now to your **ultimate goal**?*

Since this is the final coaching session, achievement of the student's last *proximal* goal should also signal achievement of her *ultimate* goal:

Coach: *(having gone through each action-step)* 'So you carried out all the steps.'
Zara: 'Yes.'
Coach: 'Great. Your goal for last week was (*reading Zara's coaching form*) to have edited your coursework using your teacher's comments. On a scale from 0 to 10, to what extent did you achieve that?'
Zara: '9. I made a lot of edits. And I used most of my teacher's comments.'

Coach: 'Excellent. Your ultimate goal for coaching was *(reading from Zara's form)* to have completed your English coursework by 21 October, having worked on it bit-by-bit each week.'

Zara: 'Yep.'

Coach: 'On a scale from 0 to 10, to what extent have you achieved that?'

Zara: *(looking proud)* '10. I've got it here if you wanna see it.'

Coach: 'That's fantastic Zara. I'd love to see it.' *(Zara hands the coach her completed coursework.)*

Phase 2: Celebrate achievements

By the end of coaching the student may or may not have achieved her ultimate goal. Whatever the case, it is essential for her to leave coaching with a sense of what she has accomplished.

To this end, the coach will ask her what she has achieved and how she has achieved it, what skills she has improved and what good habits she has developed. He can also invite her to consider where she is now in comparison to where she was at the start of coaching:

Coach: 'Let's think about all your achievements. What were things like for you before coaching?'

Zara: *(smiling)* 'A mess.'

Coach: 'In what way?'

Zara: 'My notes were everywhere. . .couldn't get stuff in on time. . .left things to the last minute.'

Coach: 'And what are things like for you now?'

Zara: 'A lot better.'

Coach: 'In what way?'

Zara: 'I've organised my notes. . .not just for English but for other subjects too.'

Coach: 'Great. What else are you doing better?'

Zara: 'I'm better at motivating myself to start work.'

Coach: 'How are you doing that?'

Zara: 'Well like when I start thinking "eugh. . .it's a hassle" then I think about *why* I'm doing it and just tell myself to get *on* with it.'

Coach: 'That sounds very helpful. So to summarise, before coaching you felt that things were a bit of a mess. Over the last 6 weeks you've organised your notes – not just for English but also for other subjects. And you've been motivating yourself to start work. If you find yourself thinking it's a "hassle" then you focus on why you're doing it and tell yourself to get on with it. *(Zara nods).* What has all that enabled you to achieve?'

Zara: 'I got my coursework done on time. And I'll probably get a better grade now. And I'm actually doing better in my other subjects too.'

Coach: 'Fantastic. What does it say about you that you've managed to do all this?'

Zara: *(thinks for a moment)* 'That I'm pretty determined. . .and that I can do it if I put my mind to it.'

Coach: 'When you say "it" what do you mean exactly?'
Zara: 'Work on projects bit-by-bit, plan assignments. . .get things done on time.'

Notice that the coach puts the onus on Zara to identify her own achievements. He then reflects back her thoughts, occasionally providing affirmation. He could also point out any achievements or successes that *he* has perceived. However, it may be better to postpone this until the final phase of the session.

Phase 3: Plan for the future

Coaching inevitably comes to an end. Clearly the coach will want the student to maintain her success *beyond* the last session. He can help her to do this by asking her the questions that are normally part of the 'Feedback' phase:

(i) *'What did you **learn** that could help you in future?'*
(ii) *'What will you do **differently** from now on?'*

He could also ask: *'How are you going to maintain your success?'*

Coach: 'If you think about the whole coaching programme over the last 6 weeks, what have you *learnt* that could help you in the future?'
Zara: *(thinks for a moment)* 'That I need to organise all my notes from the beginning.'
Coach: 'Ok. What else?'
Zara: *(thinks for a few seconds)* 'That it's not actually that hard to get started. . .if I focus on the goal I'm working for.'
Coach: 'Great. So what are you going to do differently from now on?'
Zara: 'Organise all my notes straightaway. . .And set myself goals – big goals for the whole term and then small weekly goals.'
Coach: 'Suppose you succeed at those things. What would be the best thing about that?'
Zara: *(thinks for a moment)* 'I'll probably get better grades and feel more proud.'
Coach: 'Imagine that for a moment. You're getting better grades and feeling more proud.'
Zara: *(eyes closed)* 'Ok.'
Coach: 'What could *stop* you from achieving that?'
Zara: 'If I start thinking work is a hassle.'
Coach: 'Ok, really imagine that for a moment *(pauses)*. How could you overcome that?'
Zara: 'I could use those PITs-PETs tables. . .'
Coach: 'Great. Let's see if you can make an "if. . .then" plan.'
Zara: *(thinks for a second)* '*If* I start thinking work is a hassle, *then*. . .I will. . .do a PITs-PETs table. . .'
Coach: 'Anything else?'
Zara: 'and. . .just get going.'
Coach: 'So your plan is: "*If* I start thinking work is a hassle, *then* I will do a PITs-PETs table and just get going".' (*Zara nods*)

You may recall from Chapter 4 that one of the main aims of coaching is *to help the coachee become her own coach* (e.g. Williams, Edgerton and Palmer, 2014). Resources such as the coaching form (Appendix C) and PITs-PETs tables (Appendix E) can be used by the student well after coaching. Moreover, by the final session she should be fairly adept at using them.

Notice, too, how the coach helps Zara plan for the future. You may have spotted the recurrence of mental contrasting and 'if. . .then' plans. In the case of mental contrasting, the coach first asked Zara to imagine the rewards of success – 'What would be the best thing about that?' Then he invited her to think about what might get in her way. Assuming that she believes she can overcome the obstacles and achieve her goals, this mental contrasting should enhance her commitment (e.g. Oettingen, 1999). Immediately after the mental contrasting, the coach encouraged Zara to form an 'if. . .then' plan to overcome the obstacle. Consider another 'if. . .then' plan that she could have come up with:

> *'**If** I am set a big assignment, **then** I will break it down into small weekly goals.'*

It is the coach's job to ensure that the Zara writes down her 'if. . .then' plans in a place where she is likely to see them (e.g. her diary).

Phase 4: Student's thoughts

In the fourth phase of the final session, the coach will ask the student for her thoughts on the programme. What has she found helpful? What has she enjoyed? What improvements would she suggest? However, the coach should not expect too much from the student. She will normally need time to think about these questions and may find it easier to answer them later on a questionnaire. For now, therefore, the coach should be satisfied with brief comments:

Coach: 'What have you found most useful about coaching?'
Zara: 'Just breaking things down every week. . .and having an action-plan.'
Coach: 'Great. What else?'
Zara: 'Thinking about what could stop me from doing things. . .and then coming up with ways to get over that.'
Coach: 'That's good to hear. What, in your opinion, could have been even better?'
Zara: 'Er. . .Maybe if we'd had a bit more time in some sessions.'

Phase 5: Thanks and Goodbye

The last phase of the final session involves thanking the student for her participation and saying goodbye. The coach should praise the student for her contributions throughout coaching. He should also offer to 'check in' with her in two to three weeks and then perhaps once more after a month:

Coach: 'It's been a pleasure to work with you, Zara. You've been really committed throughout the programme and I think you've made excellent progress.'
Zara: 'Thank you.'

Coach: 'You came up with loads of ideas in every session, thought about your goals very carefully and dealt with those PITs really well.'

Zara: 'Thanks. I tried pretty hard.'

Coach: 'I know - and it paid off. If you like, I can send you an email in a couple of weeks to see how you're getting on?'

Zara: 'Yeah, that'd be nice.'

Coach: 'Great. So that's the end of our coaching.'

Zara: 'Ok, thank you for all your help.'

Coach: 'You're very welcome.'

Tailoring the sessions to the student's needs

We have now explored the structure of each and every coaching session, from the first to the last. However, it is important to remember that the structure is *never set in stone*. The various tables in this chapter are meant to be guidelines, not straitjackets. If a given structure does not appear to suit a particular student, then the coach should feel free to adapt it. As Grant (2011, p. 122) notes, '[t]he primary driver should be the *needs of the coachee*' (italics added).

Having read Part III, you may also be wondering whether coaching sessions really have to be as thorough and involved as the example with Zara. The chapters on GROW may have given you the impression that coaches must explore every nook and cranny with their coachees. This is not the case. Some students will require less than others. And some tasks are simpler than others. There will certainly be occasions when thoroughness and attention to detail are necessary. But there will also be times when students whizz through the phases of GROW with very little required from the coach. Many commentators therefore refer to 'Occam's razor' or the principle of parsimony (e.g. Jackson and McKergow, 2007; Palmer and Szymanska, 2008). This means cutting out unnecessary steps and doing the *least* that is required to help a given student. If you are new to coaching it is a good idea to begin with the structures provided in this chapter. But always pay attention to the student. If it seems clear that she does not need 30 minutes each week, then you may wish to shorten the sessions. Similarly, if she finds working through the full GROW model too laborious, experiment with 'GROW-lite' instead. Sessions should always be tailored to the student's needs. And no two students are the same.

Chapter summary

- Before the first session the coachee should be sent an introductory email including the Coaching Contract.
- The structure of the first session is as follows: (1) Contracting, (2) (Ultimate) Goal-setting, (3) Reality, (4) Options, and (5) Will. In the first session GROW is replaced by 'GROW-lite'.

- 'GROW-lite' is a pared-down version of GROW. Whilst the first phase - Goal-setting - is longer than in GROW, the remaining phases are much shorter.
- The structure of subsequent sessions is as follows: (1) Feedback, (2) (Proximal) Goal-setting, (3) Reality, (4) Options and (5) Will. GROW now replaces GROW-lite.
- The Feedback stage involves asking the student (i) whether she carried out her action-steps, (ii) how much of her proximal goal she achieved, and (iii) how close she is now to her ultimate goal. Two other questions are often useful: '*What did you learn that could help you in future?*' and '*What will you do differently from now on?*'
- One possible way to structure the final session is as follows: (1) Feedback, (2) Celebrate achievements, (3) Plan for the future, (4) Student's thoughts and (5) Thanks & Goodbye.
- In planning for the future, the student should be encouraged to form 'if. . .then' plans. 'Mental contrasting' can also be used to enhance her commitment.
- The student should be reminded of the various resources that coaching has offered her (e.g. Goal-sheets, Action-plans, PITs-PETs forms etc.).
- The structure of a coaching session is not set in stone. Coaches should adhere to the principle of parsimony, i.e. do the *least* that is required to help the student make progress. It is also important to tailor the session to the student's needs.

References

Berg, I.K. and Szabó, P. (2005). *Brief Coaching for Lasting Solutions*. New York: Norton.
Grant, A. (2011). Is it time to REGROW the GROW model? Issues related to teaching coaching session structures. *The Coaching Psychologist*, 7, 2, 118-126.
Grant, A.M. (2016). Solution-focused coaching. In J. Passmore (ed.), *Excellence in Coaching: The Industry Guide* (3rd edn). London: Kogan Page.
Ives, Y. and Cox, E. (2012). *Goal-focused coaching: Theory and practice*. New York: Routledge.
Jackson, P.Z. and McKergow, M. (2007). *The solutions focus: Making coaching & change SIMPLE* (2nd edn). London: Nicholas Brealey.
Oettingen, G. (1999). Free fantasies about the future and the emergence of developmental goals. In J. Brandtstädter and R.M. Lerner (eds), *Action and self-development: Theory and research through the life span*. Thousand Oaks/CA: Sage.
Palmer, S. and Szymanska, K. (2008). Cognitive behavioural coaching: An integrative approach. In S. Palmer and A. Whybrow (eds), *Handbook of coaching psychology: A guide for practitioners*. London: Routledge.
Williams, H., Edgerton, N. and Palmer, S. (2014). Cognitive behavioural coaching. In E. Cox, T. Bachkirova and D. Clutterbuck (eds), *The Complete handbook of Coaching* (2nd edn). London: Sage.

Part IV

Emotional obstacles

14 Understanding emotional obstacles

In this chapter

- Emotional obstacles in coaching
- When is it appropriate for coaches to deal with emotions?
- The ABC model of emotional disturbance.

Why do coaches need to bother with students' emotions?

So far in this book we have focused largely (but not exclusively) on behavioural coaching. That is, we have been concerned with what students *do* to achieve their goals. Sometimes this is enough. If a student can achieve her goals by creating and following a simple action-plan, then there is no need for psychological coaching (Williams, Edgerton and Palmer, 2014).

Sometimes, however, a purely behavioural approach is not enough. As every teacher knows, students become anxious, dejected, envious and so on. These negative emotions (e.g. dejection) can make it difficult for students to achieve their goals. Consider three examples.

Example 1

Saima, who we met in Chapter 7, is keen to improve her French. Her ultimate goal is to hold a 5 minute conversation (in French) about her hobbies. Unfortunately, she struggled to do this in her practice oral and now feels rather dejected.[1] At the beginning of her third coaching session she calls herself *'hopeless'* (citing her *'awful'* performance) and says she no longer believes she can achieve her goal.

Example 2

Rachel is a 15-year-old student whose ultimate goal is to have revised effectively for her English mock exam. However, in order to do this Rachel needs to read Thomas Hardy's *Tess of the D'Urbervilles* – a 'boring' novel that she just *'can't bear'* (her words). Whenever Rachel begins to read it, she quickly becomes angry and gives up. In her second coaching session she says: 'I can't revise if I have to read this book!'

Example 3

Abby is an 18-year-old student who is determined to improve her work-life balance. For each week of coaching her proximal goal is to have completed all of her work *by no later than 8pm*. However, from week 4 onwards there are several big tests to prepare for. Abby is feeling anxious since she believes she *'mustn't'* get a bad mark. She is inclined to revise beyond 8pm and therefore doubts whether she will achieve her coaching goal.

Saima, Rachel and Abby are struggling to overcome what we shall call *emotional obstacles*. For Saima the emotion is dejection; for Rachel it is anger; and for Abby it is anxiety. It should be clear from the descriptions above that unless they overcome their emotional obstacles, Saima, Rachel and Abby are unlikely to achieve their goals. Recall that the coach's primary objective is to *help the coachee to achieve her goal*. It therefore follows that he should help her overcome any obstacles in the way.

Or does it? Should coaches really deal with emotions? Isn't that the role of a counsellor or therapist? We touched on these issues in Chapter 1. However, we now need to revisit the matter.

When is it appropriate for coaches to deal with emotions?

Consider Saima, Rachel and Abby. We described their challenges as **emotional obstacles**. As noted in Chapter 1, an emotional obstacle is not an emotional *disorder*. When Saima feels 'dejected' after a practice oral, it does not follow that she is clinically depressed. If Rachel becomes frustrated and says she 'can't bear' 'Measure for Measure,' this doesn't necessarily mean that she needs to see a specialist in anger management. Finally, when Abby is worried about an upcoming test, we don't need to assume that she is suffering from an anxiety disorder. In fact, we shall assume that Saima, Rachel and Abby are experiencing what *every* student experiences at one point or another.

Teachers and adults are no different. We all run into emotional obstacles. They are simply part of life. As Neenan (2008) points out, it would be ludicrous to suggest that people need counselling or therapy as soon as they experience or display a negative emotion. Students often *do* feel anxious about tests, angry about work, or dejected about results. Nor are they immediately referred to the school counsellor. Sometimes they overcome these obstacles on their own. At other times, a teacher or friend might help. And coaches too may be of assistance.

There are limits, however. Sadly, for some students negative emotions are more than mere 'obstacles'. Overwhelming stress, *pathological*[2] anxiety, clinical depression - these things are known to affect a certain percentage of students. And for such issues counselling or therapy is certainly an appropriate (and perhaps necessary) intervention.

We therefore need to draw a distinction between everyday emotional obstacles and more serious mental health issues. Whilst the former may be addressed by an appropriately trained coach, the latter should be handled only by counsellors, therapists and other mental health professionals. How can coaches tell the difference? Fortunately, education professionals are normally given at least a modicum of training in recognising mental health issues in students. Although coaches cannot be expected to be mental health diagnosticians, it is useful for them to be aware of the symptoms of common mood and anxiety disorders (Cavanagh, 2005). These are covered by Buckley and Buckley (2006) and Dikel (2014).

However, distinguishing between everyday emotional obstacles on the one hand and mental health issues on the other is only part of the story. From the fact that a student is facing an 'emotional obstacle' (rather than a mental health issue), it does not necessarily follow that the coach should intervene. A number of other criteria need to be met. The following are inspired by Dryden (2011). If the answer to all of these questions is 'Yes', then a coaching intervention is appropriate:

1 ***Does the student's issue appear to be an everyday 'emotional obstacle' (rather than a mental health issue)?***
It is not always possible to declare with certainty that a person is mentally 'healthy'. Buckley and Buckley (2006, p. 13) say that 'the best that will be achieved by any professional is 'no signs of psychological dysfunction are evident'.'
2 ***Is the 'obstacle' preventing the student from achieving her goals?***
As noted in Chapter 1, coaching does not deal with emotional issues *per se*. That is the role of the counselling or therapy (Dryden, 2011). But if a negative emotion is *preventing the student from achieving her coaching goals*, then it does fall within the coach's remit, provided the other conditions are met.
3 ***Does the student actually need any help to overcome the obstacle?***
It is a general rule in coaching that we do not do for coachees what coachees can do for themselves. For example, if Saima believes she can get over her dejection easily enough on her own, then there is no need for the coach to intervene. On the other hand, if she is struggling to motivate herself[3] (after her 'awful' performance), then the coach may offer to help.
4 ***Does the student want the coach's help in overcoming the obstacle?***
Even if a student needs a little help, she may not want it in coaching. Coaches should always ask permission to intervene. Saima's coach could say: *'We could look at this in coaching or I could leave it to you. What would you prefer?'*
5 ***Is the coach sufficiently well-trained to help the student with the obstacle?***
In order to help students overcome emotional obstacles coaches will often need more than the foundational skills described in Part II. Of course, coaches might be able to help by offering the sort of encouragement that friends and family often provide (*'Don't worry, Saima. It's just a practice oral. You'll do better in the real thing'*). But this may not be very effective. In the rest of Part IV we will be introducing a much more powerful approach used in cognitive behavioural coaching (CBC). Coaches who wish to use this approach should seek additional CBC training (Williams *et al.*, 2014).

In the examples from now on, we shall assume that the answer is 'Yes' to all of the above. That is, we shall assume that (i) the student's issue appears to be an everyday emotional obstacle (not a mental health issue); (ii) the obstacle is preventing her from achieving her coaching goal(s); (iii) the student needs a little help to overcome the obstacle; (iv) the student *wants* the coach's help; and (v) the coach has had sufficient training in the relevant approach (which in this book is CBC).

The ABC model of emotional disturbance

It is now time to introduce the *ABC* model. Originally developed by Albert Ellis - the founder of Rational Emotive Behaviour Therapy (REBT) - the ABC model is now widely used in cognitive behavioural coaching - CBC (e.g. Williams *et al.*, 2014; Neenan, 2016). In my experience, it also tends to make a great deal of sense to students and teachers alike:

- *A* stands for the *aspect* of the situation about which the student is most angry, anxious, dejected, etc.
- *B* stands for her *beliefs* about that aspect.
- *C* stands for the *consequences* of her beliefs (i.e. the resulting *emotion* and *behaviour*[4]).

To illustrate this model, let's first consider Saima. Table 14.1 lays out the ABCs of her emotional obstacle:

Table 14.1 Saima's ABCs.

A *Aspect of the situation*	**B** *Beliefs about 'A'*	**C** *Consequences*
'I messed up.'	• 'It's *awful* (that I messed up).' • 'I'm *hopeless* (for messing up).'	• Feeling of dejection (*emotional consequence*) • Inclination to give up on French (*behavioural consequence*)

Situation: Saima comes out of her practice oral exam in French.

Let's examine each part of the model. Following her practice oral Saima feels *dejected*. This feeling of dejection is an emotional consequence and therefore falls under *C*. The other C is behavioural - Saima is now inclined to give up on French, i.e. to stop studying.

Next, we need to ask: '*What does Saima feel most dejected about?*' Saima tells her coach that it's the fact that she 'messed up'. This is the *aspect* of the situation about which she is most dejected, i.e. *A* in the model. 'A' is sometimes known as the 'Adversity', 'Activating Event' or '*Critical* A'. The word 'critical' highlights the subjective importance of this aspect to the coachee.

Now comes the most important part of the model - *B*, i.e. beliefs. The key insight in cognitive behavioural coaching was articulated by the Stoic philosopher Epictetus almost 2000 years ago:

> *Humans are disturbed not by things, but by the* ***views*** *they take about things.*

In terms of the ABC model we can say that students are disturbed not by aspects of situations – A – but by the *beliefs* they *hold* about those aspects – B. It is the B that largely determines C.

Look closely at Table 14.1. You may think that Saima's awareness that she 'messed up' *made* her feel dejected, i.e. that A led to C. However, this is not the case. Many other students may think that they 'messed up' *without* feeling dejected. Some may be a little disappointed. Others may be totally indifferent.

But if A (thinking that one has 'messed up') doesn't automatically lead to C (dejection) then what does? Answer: the student's *evaluation* of A, i.e. her *beliefs* at B. Consider Saima's beliefs: 'It's *awful* (that I messed up)', and 'I'm *hopeless* (for messing up)'. Given these extreme beliefs, it is hardly surprising that Saima feels dejected.

Consider another example. Recall that our third student – Abby – was anxious about getting a bad mark on a test. Abby's ABCs are presented below:

Table 14.2 Abby's ABCs.

A *Aspect of the situation*	*B* *Beliefs about 'A'*	*C* *Consequences*
'I might get a bad mark.'	• 'I *mustn't* get a bad mark.' • 'It would be *awful* if I got a bad mark!'	• Feeling of anxiety (*emotional consequence*) • Abby keeps revising until 11pm (*behavioural consequence*)

Situation: Abby is revising for a test.

We can see from Table 14.2 that Abby's emotional *C* was anxiety. Behaviourally, the consequence was that she kept revising until 11pm. When asked about the *A* – i.e. the aspect of the situation about which she is most anxious – she says 'I might get a bad mark'. However, as before, *A* does not *on its own* lead to *C*. Many students are aware that they 'might get a bad mark'. Not all of them are anxious or work until 11pm. The crucial component, therefore, is *B* – Abby's beliefs: 'I *mustn't* get a bad mark,' and 'It would be *awful* if I got a bad mark!' It shouldn't be too difficult to see the link between these beliefs and Abby's anxiety.

Focusing on the Bs – rigid and extreme beliefs

You should now be able to see that it is largely a student's *beliefs* that leave that student feeling dejected, anxious or whatever it is. In terms of the ABC model we call this the 'B-C connection':

Box 14.1 The 'B-C connection.'

The 'B-C connection'

Negative **emotions** at '**C**' stem largely from **beliefs** at '**B**'.

In fact, the underlying theory posits four types of *rigid* and *extreme* beliefs that underpin unhealthy negative emotions:

1 *Rigid beliefs* or *'demands'* - e.g. 'I *mustn't* get a bad mark'.
2 *'Awfulising' beliefs* - e.g. 'It would be *awful* if I got a bad mark!'
3 *Discomfort intolerance beliefs* - e.g. 'I *can't bear* getting a bad mark!'
4 *Depreciation beliefs* - e.g. 'I'm *hopeless* (if I get a bad mark)'.

If you have worked with students for any amount of time, you will have come across these types of belief. All too often students make demands ('I *have* to get an A!'), 'awfulise' about outcomes ('My oral was *dreadful!*'), express discomfort intolerance ('I *can't bear* writing essays!') and depreciate themselves, others or the world around them ('I'm *useless*', 'My teacher's *rubbish*,' 'School is a *nightmare*!'). According to the ABC model it is these rigid and extreme beliefs that ultimately lead to anger, anxiety, dejection and so on.

Fortunately, there is another way of thinking. For each of the four rigid and extreme beliefs, there is a more *flexible* or *non-extreme* alternative. Table 14.3 compares and contrasts the two types of thinking:

Table 14.3 Rational and Irrational beliefs

Irrational beliefs	*Rational beliefs*
Rigid belief or **Demand:** I *mustn't* get a bad mark!	**Flexible belief** or **Preference:** I *don't want* to get a bad mark but that doesn't mean I *mustn't*.
'Awfulising' belief: It would be *awful* if I got a bad mark.	**'Non-awfulising' belief:** It would be *a shame* if I got a bad mark, but *not the end of the world*.
Discomfort intolerance belief: I *can't bear* getting a bad mark.	**Discomfort *tolerance* belief:** Getting a bad mark *isn't easy* to bear, but I obviously *can* bear it and will.
Depreciation belief: I'm *totally hopeless* (for getting a bad mark).	**Acceptance belief:** Getting a bad mark means I'm a *fallible human being*, not 'totally hopeless.'

As you can see from Table 14.3, the first type of irrational[5] belief is the *rigid belief* or *demand*. This type of belief normally involves expressions such as *'must'*, *'should'*, *'have to'* and the like. The three other types of irrational belief ('Awfulising', 'Discomfort intolerance' and 'Depreciation') are all examples of *extreme* beliefs. In terms of the ABC model, these *rigid* and *extreme* ('irrational') beliefs at B - lead to unhealthy negative emotions and behaviour at C.

Now consider the *rational* beliefs in the right-hand column. The first type of belief is a *flexible* belief or *preference*. This type of belief is normally expressed in terms such as 'I'd *like to* X, but I don't *have to*.' The other three types of belief are *non-extreme* versions of their irrational counterparts. For example, compare 'It would be *awful*. . .' (an extreme belief) with 'It would be *a shame*. . .but *not the end of the world*' (a non-extreme belief). If students held *flexible* and *non-extreme* beliefs, what sorts of emotions would they experience? And how would they behave? You may want to think about this before reading on.

As you may have deduced, *flexible* and *non-extreme* beliefs are likely to lead to healthier emotions and more constructive behaviour. Let's go back to Abby and her ABCs. However, let's now assume that instead of holding the rigid belief - 'I *mustn't* get a bad mark' - and the extreme belief - 'It would be *awful* if I got a bad mark' - she holds the following *flexible* and *non-extreme* beliefs:

- I *don't want* to get a bad mark but that doesn't mean I *mustn't*. **(flexible).**
- It would be *a shame* if I got a bad mark, but *not the end of the world*. **(non-extreme).**

Table 14.4 features these 'rational' beliefs:

Table 14.4 Abby's ABCs with flexible and non-extreme beliefs.

A *Aspect of the situation*	*B* *Beliefs about 'A'*	*C* *Consequences*
'I might get a bad mark.'	'I *don't want* to get a bad mark but that doesn't mean I *mustn't*.' 'It would be *a shame* if I got a bad mark, but *not the end of the world*.'	• Feeling of concern, but not anxiety (*emotional consequence*) • Abby revises diligently until 8pm, then enjoys the rest of her evening and goes to bed at 10pm. (*behavioural consequence*)

Situation: Abby is revising for a test.

Note first of all that the *A* in the table is exactly the same as before. Abby still thinks that she 'might get a bad mark'. However, this time she has different *beliefs* about that prospect. Rather than reasoning that she '*mustn't* get a bad mark', she acknowledges that a bad mark is undesirable but realises that there is no rule or law that forbids it. Similarly, rather than assuming that a bad mark would be '*awful*', Abby is able to see that it would certainly be a shame but 'not the end of the world'.

Notice what happens to the emotional and behavioural consequences now that Abby has different beliefs. Firstly, Abby's anxiety has changed into 'concern'. It seems healthy for a student to be *concerned* about getting a bad mark, but not particularly healthy for her to be anxious. Next consider Abby's behaviour. Instead of revising until late at night (as she did when she was anxious), she works diligently until 8pm, then enjoys the rest of her evening and goes to bed at 10pm. She thus not only prepares well for her test but also achieves the work-life balance that she was looking for.

How has this transformation come about? The key is the *B* column. By modifying our beliefs at B we can bring about healthier consequences at *C*. This too needs to be emphasised:

Box 14.2 Changing the Bs helps to change the Cs.

A change in the Bs facilitates a change in the Cs

When we replace **rigid** and **extreme** beliefs with **flexible** and **non-extreme** alternatives, we pave the way for healthier emotions and more constructive behaviour.

Recall our two other students – Rachel and Saima. If they too could modify their beliefs, they would experience healthier emotions and engage in more constructive behaviour. Most importantly for coaching, they would be able to overcome their 'emotional obstacles' and achieve their goals.

In the next chapter, we look more closely at Rachel. We shall see how a coach uses the ABC model to help her overcome her emotional obstacle.

Chapter summary

- If students can achieve their goals by following a simple action plan, then there is no need for psychological coaching.
- Occasionally students run into emotional obstacles. These are experienced by all human beings and should not be confused with emotional *disorders* or mental health issues.
- A coach can help a student with problematic emotions if: (i) the issue is an everyday emotional obstacle (not a mental health problem); (ii) the obstacle is preventing the student from achieving her coaching goals; (iii) the student needs help in overcoming the obstacle; (iv) the student wants the coach to help her; and (v) the coach has been trained in an appropriate approach (e.g. cognitive behavioural coaching – CBC).
- CBC uses the ABC model to help coachees overcome emotional obstacles. 'A' stands for the aspect of the situation about which the coachee feels most anxious, angry, dejected etc. 'B' stands for the coachee's beliefs about the A. 'C' stands for the consequences of holding those beliefs (in terms of emotion and behaviour).
- Situations or even 'critical' aspects of situations do not *on their own* make people angry, dejected, etc. A does not cause C. Rather, a person's *beliefs* at B largely determine the consequences at C. This is known as the B-C connection.
- There are four categories of 'irrational' beliefs: (1) Rigid beliefs or 'demands', (2) 'Awfulising' beliefs, (3) Discomfort intolerance beliefs and (4) Depreciation beliefs. Categories (2), (3) and (4) are also known as 'extreme' beliefs.
- There are four categories of 'rational' beliefs: (1) Flexible beliefs or 'Preferences', (2) 'Non-awfulising' beliefs, (3) Discomfort tolerance beliefs, and (4) Acceptance beliefs. Categories (2), (3) and (4) are also known as 'non-extreme' beliefs.

- Rigid and extreme beliefs lead to unhealthy negative emotions such as anxiety.
- Flexible and non-extreme beliefs lead to healthy emotions, such as concern.
- In order to help a student overcome an emotional obstacle, the coach needs to help her replace rigid and extreme beliefs with flexible and non-extreme alternatives.

Notes

1 In this part of the book 'dejection' describes an unhealthy negative emotion. It should be contrasted with 'sadness', which is often a natural and healthy response, and 'depression', which is an emotional disorder.
2 What distinguishes 'normal' from '*pathological*' anxiety? Experts sometimes think in terms of duration, intensity and frequency (e.g. Greene and Goodrich-Dunn, 2013). If a student feels somewhat anxious before a test but relieved when it is over, this may be considered 'normal'. But if her anxiety lasts for a considerable amount of time, reaches a highly distressing level and occurs on a fairly regular basis, then it is more than an 'emotional obstacle'. In such a case counselling would be more appropriate than coaching.
3 Of course, if Saima's 'dejection' starts to look like *depression*, then a referral to the school's counselling service will be necessary.
4 For some practitioners 'C' also includes *cognitive* consequences (i.e. how the student subsequently *thought*). For the sake of simplicity, cognitive consequences are not included in this book.
5 According to Palmer and Szymanska (2008), some coachees may be offended by the expression 'irrational belief'. They propose 'performance-interfering thought' as an alternative.

References

Buckley, A. and Buckley, C. (2006). *A guide to coaching and mental health: The recognition and management of psychological issues*. London: Routledge.

Cavanagh, M. (2005). Mental-health issues and challenging clients in executive coaching. In M. Cavanagh, A.M. Grant and T. Kemp (eds), *Evidence-based coaching* (vol. 1): *Contributions from the behavioural sciences*. Bowen Hills, QLD: Australian Academic Press.

Dikel, W. (2014). *The Teacher's Guide to Student Mental Health*. New York: W.W. Norton & Company.

Dryden, W. (2011). *Dealing with Emotional Problems in Life Coaching*. Hove: Routledge.

Greene, E. and Goodrich-Dunn, B. (2013). *The Psychology of the Body* (2nd edn). Philadelphia: Lippincott Williams & Wilkins.

Neenan, M. (2008). From cognitive behavioural therapy (CBT) to cognitive behavioural coaching (CBC). *Journal of Rational-Emotive and Behavioral Psychotherapies*, 26, 3-15.

Neenan, M. (2016). Cognitive-Behavioural Coaching. In J. Passmore (ed.), *Excellence in Coaching: The Industry Guide* (3rd edn). London: Kogan Page.

Palmer, S. and Szymanska, K. (2008). Cognitive behavioural coaching: An integrative approach. In S. Palmer and A. Whybrow (eds), *Handbook of coaching psychology: A guide for practitioners*. London: Routledge.

Williams, H., Edgerton, N. and Palmer, S. (2014). Cognitive behavioural coaching. In E. Cox, T. Bachkirova and D. Clutterbuck (eds), *The Complete handbook of Coaching* (2nd edn). London: Sage.

15 Introducing students to the 'ABCs'

In this chapter

- Discovering an emotional obstacle
- Trying a solution-focused approach
- Introducing the student to the 'ABCs'.

Discovering an emotional obstacle

In the last chapter, we met three different students, including Rachel. At the beginning of coaching, Rachel set her ultimate goal, which was to have revised effectively for her English mock exam. Part of the exam is on Thomas Hardy's *Tess of the D'Urbervilles* (*Tess* from now on). Rachel's first proximal goal was therefore to have read the first three chapters and made notes on the main themes. In the dialogue below her coach finds out how she got on:

Coach: 'On a scale from 0 to 10, how much of last week's goal did you achieve?
Rachel: *(looking annoyed)* 'Zero.'
Coach: 'What got in your way?'
Rachel: 'I just couldn't get into it. The book's so *boring*.'
Coach: 'So what did you do?'
Rachel: 'I got angry and gave up.'

At this point the coach is wondering whether Rachel has run into an emotional obstacle. Is her angry response to *Tess* going to prevent her from achieving her goals? The coach needs to check this with Rachel:

Coach: 'Do you think you'll be able to get through the first three chapters *this* week?'
Rachel: 'I doubt it. It'll still be too boring.'
Coach: 'Ok, if nothing changes how likely is it that you'll revise effectively for your mock?'
Rachel: 'Unlikely. I'll probably just leave it to the last minute.'

It seems fair to say that Rachel has indeed run into an emotional obstacle that threatens her coaching goals. However, nothing Rachel has said suggests an emotional *disorder* or mental health issue. In fact, what Rachel is experiencing is fairly common. In any school, there are students who find it difficult to engage in tasks that are unpleasant or boring. This is sometimes known as 'low frustration tolerance' (e.g. Dryden, 2001).

In the last chapter, we outlined five conditions that had to be satisfied before a coach could help a student with her emotions. Two of these conditions have now been met. First, the student's issue appears to be an everyday 'emotional obstacle' (not a mental health issue). Second, that obstacle is preventing her from achieving her coaching goals. We shall also assume that the coach has been trained to deal with emotional obstacles using cognitive behavioural coaching (CBC). The two remaining conditions were as follows:

(i) The student needs a little help to overcome the obstacle
(ii) The student *wants* the coach's help.

The coach now checks whether (i) and (ii) are the case:

Coach: 'Suppose we don't address this in coaching. Do you think you'll be able to find your own solution?'
Rachel: 'Not really. I *can't bear* it when it's boring. I just end up doing it at the last minute.'
Coach: 'Ok. I may be able to help you. Would you like to tackle this in coaching?'
Rachel: 'Definitely.'

All necessary conditions have now been met. The coach is therefore entitled to intervene. Indeed, he may *have* to do so if Rachel is to achieve her goals.

Trying a solution-focused approach

In the last chapter, we introduced the ABC model. However, it is not the *only* way to deal with emotional obstacles. At times a simpler *solution-focused* approach might be effective. Recall that the solution-focused approach assumes that *no 'problem' exists all the time* and that *people are already succeeding to some extent*. If Rachel's coach tried to be solution-focused, he would ask Rachel questions such as:

- *'When do you feel* ***different*** *about reading 'Tess'?'*
- *'When* ***do*** *you manage to read it?'*
- *'What do you do when you're* ***having more success****?'*

In the dialogue below the coach takes this approach but does not make much headway:

Coach: 'Ok, so when you tried to read 'Tess' you got angry and gave up.'
Rachel: 'Yes.'
Coach: 'When do you feel *different* about reading it?'
Rachel: 'I don't. I really *can't bear* it.'

Coach: 'Alright. When *do* you manage to read it?'
Rachel: 'I don't. I just get angry and stop reading.'
Coach: 'Ok. What do you do to get through *other* boring tasks?'
Rachel: *(sounding frustrated)* 'I dunno. The point is it *shouldn't* be that boring!'

Here the coach is trying to be solution-focused, which is to be commended. However, students may struggle to think of solutions, exceptions or what's already 'working'. It is therefore important to be flexible. Some practitioners may want to be solution-focused at all times (e.g. Ratner and Yusuf, 2015). In this book, however, we are more aligned with those who see the solution-focused approach as '*one strand* of their coaching practice, to be drawn upon as appropriate to the coaching conversation and to the needs of the coachee' (O'Connell, Palmer and Williams, 2012, p. 142, italics added).

As we saw above, Rachel did not respond well to solution-focused questions. Rather than persisting with this approach, the coach should change tack. He will now try to use the ABC model. In some ways, this is a *problem*-focused approach since it initially pays attention to the *un*-helpful aspects of a student's thinking and behaviour. However, as we shall see, it then enables her to develop helpful alternatives. Moreover, some commentators believe that the two approaches can be integrated, i.e. that one can attend to a person's problematic beliefs whilst still being solution-focused (e.g. Guterman and Rudes, 2005). At times, therefore, the coach in our example will be giving his work a solution-focused flavour.

Setting a goal using the ABCs – using the student's 'Cs'

In the ABC model '*C*' stands for 'consequences'. These are *emotional* and *behavioural*. Although Rachel and her coach have not yet drawn up an ABC table, Rachel has already revealed the 'Cs'. When she was reading *Tess* she got angry (emotional consequence) and gave up (behavioural consequence). The coach now needs to help Rachel set a goal with regard to this obstacle. It is a good idea to do this in terms of the Cs:

Coach: 'So when you tried to read 'Tess' you got angry and gave up.'
Rachel: 'Yep.'
Coach: (*helping the student set an emotional goal*) 'How would you *like* to feel in that situation?'
Rachel: 'Not angry, I guess.'
Coach: 'What would you feel instead?'
Rachel: 'Well, I'm not gonna feel *happy* about it, that's for sure!'
Coach: 'Ok. So what would be a more realistic feeling?'
Rachel: *(thinks for a moment)* 'Maybe a little bit annoyed. . .but not angry.'
Coach: 'So you'd feel a little bit annoyed but not angry?'
Rachel: 'Yeah. That'd be better.'
Coach: 'In what way?'
Rachel: 'Well I can *live* with 'annoyed'. I probably wouldn't give up.'
Coach: *(focusing on the behavioural goal)*' Ok. And what would you like to *do* in that situation?'

Rachel: 'Get on with reading the book.'

Coach: *(checking the goals)* 'Ok. So our aim will be to help you (1) feel a little but annoyed rather than angry and (2) get on with reading the book. Is that right?'

Rachel: 'Yeah, that'd be good.'

Coach: 'What would that do for you?'

Rachel: 'It would help me achieve my goal - to revise well for the mock.'

Rachel and her coach are now clear about their aim. Rather than feeling angry, Rachel would prefer to be just 'a little bit annoyed'. And rather than giving up she would like to get on with reading the book. You may wonder why her emotional goal - to feel 'a little bit annoyed' - is still negative in nature. Shouldn't coach and student aim at something more positive? Perhaps. But perhaps not. The aim of CBC is to help coachees overcome problematic negative emotions. But this does not mean turning every negative emotion into a *positive* emotion - something that would be as unhealthy as it is unrealistic. If Rachel can find a way to *enjoy* reading *Tess*, then so much the better. However, in the likely event that she continues to find it boring, feeling 'a little bit annoyed' (rather than angry) should at least enable her to get through it.

Introducing the student to the ABCs

Starting with C

The coach now introduces Rachel to the ABCs:

Coach: 'One way to help you change the way you *feel* is to change the way you *think*. There's a simple model you can use, which we call the ABC model.'

Rachel: 'Ok.'

Coach: *(the coach takes out a piece of paper and draws an ABC table)* 'First we need to be clear about the situation. What were you doing when you had this issue?'

Rachel: 'I was trying to read 'Tess'.'

Coach: *(the coach writes 'Trying to read 'Tess'' above the table)* 'Now we start with the C column. "C" stands for "consequences". There are two consequences, *emotional* and *behavioural*.'

Rachel: 'Ok.'

Coach: 'The emotional consequence is just how you felt. And the behavioural consequence is what you actually did. Does that make sense?'

Rachel: 'I think so, yeah.'

Coach: 'Ok, so how did you feel in that situation?

Rachel: 'Angry.'

Coach: 'Where should we put that?'

Rachel: 'In the C column.'

Coach: 'Exactly - would you like to write it in yourself?'

Rachel: 'Sure.'

Coach: 'Great. Now the behavioural C – what did you *do* when you felt angry?'
Rachel: 'I gave up and stopped reading. Can I write that in too?'
Coach: 'Please do.'

The dialogue above may seem a little didactic. However, this is to be expected when a new model is being introduced. At the end of Part IV we shall consider just how 'didactic' this approach really is. For now, note that Rachel is filling out her own ABCs, which currently look like this:

Situation: *Trying to read* Tess.

Table 15.1 Rachel's ABC table with C filled in.

A *Aspect of the situation*	*B* *Beliefs about 'A'*	*C* *Consequences*
		• felt angry • gave up and stopped reading

Identifying A

The next step is for Rachel and her coach to identify the (critical) A – i.e. the *aspect* of the situation about which she was most angry. The most basic way to help a student identify the A is to ask the following question, filling in the blank with the relevant emotion (see Dryden, 2011):

'What were you most ____________ about in that situation?'

The coach would therefore ask Rachel: '*What were you most* ***angry*** *about when you were trying to read* Tess?' However, as a preliminary step it is often helpful to ask the coachee to *relive* the situation as if it were happening now:

Coach: 'The next step is to find out what you were most angry about. This will go under A.'
Rachel: 'Ok.'
Coach: 'Imagine for a moment that you're back in your room trying to read *Tess*.'
Rachel: *(closing her eyes)* 'Ok.'
Coach: 'How are you feeling?'
Rachel: 'Angry.'
Coach: *(trying to identify the 'A')* 'What are you most angry about?'
Rachel: *(speaking emphatically)* 'The fact that it's so *boring*!'
Coach: 'So what you're most angry about is the fact that it's so boring?'
Rachel: 'Definitely. Do I write that under A?'
Coach: 'Yes.'

Rachel identifies her A as 'it's so boring!' Note that this A is Rachel's own *subjective interpretation* of the situation. This is often the case with As. It is crucial to realise that it is *not the coach's job to challenge the A*. Instead the student should be allowed to 'have' her A so she can identify her Bs (i.e. beliefs). It is her *beliefs* at B that largely determine the consequences at C. Rachel's ABC table now looks like this:

Situation: *Trying to read* Tess.

Table 15.2 Rachel's ABC table with A and C filled in.

A *Aspect of the situation*	B *Beliefs about 'A'*	C *Consequences*
It's so boring!		• felt angry • gave up and stopped reading

Identifying the Bs (Beliefs)

So far Rachel has filled in the A and C in her ABCs. It is now time for the coach to help her identify the all-important Bs, i.e. her *beliefs*. There are, you will remember, four types of 'irrational' belief that are thought to underpin unhealthy negative emotions. The first is the *rigid* belief and the other three - 'Awfulising', 'Discomfort Intolerance' and 'Depreciation' - are the *extreme* beliefs. These are all presented in Table 15.3:

Table 15.3 Irrational beliefs.

Type of belief	*Form of belief*
Rigid belief (or 'Demand')	• 'I *must*...' • 'I've *got to*...' • 'It *shouldn't*...'[1]
'Awfulising'	• 'It's *awful* that' • 'It'd be *terrible* if...' • 'It's *dreadful* when...'
Discomfort Intolerance	• 'I *can't bear*...' • 'I *can't stand*...' • 'I *can't face*...'
Depreciation (of self, others, the world, etc.)	• 'I'm *hopeless*' • 'He's *useless*!' • 'School is a *nightmare*!'

How will the coach help Rachel identify her own irrational beliefs? First, he will ask Rachel to look through Table 15.3. There are then at least two approaches he could take:

Approach 1: *The coach could invite Rachel to imagine the situation in her mind's eye. He could then ask her theory-driven questions to elicit any irrational beliefs (see Dryden, 2009).*

First the coach would invite Rachel to put herself back in the situation, i.e. imagine getting angry whilst trying to read *Tess*. Then he could ask the following questions:

- 'What, if anything, are you *demanding* right now?' (= rigid belief)
- 'What, if anything, do you think is *awful*?' (= 'awfulising' belief)
- 'What do you think you *can't bear*?' (= discomfort intolerance belief)
- 'What or whom are you *putting down*? (= depreciation belief)

Approach 2: *The coach could reflect back any rigid or extreme beliefs that he has heard the student express.*

You may have noticed that Rachel has already verbalised a number of rigid and extreme beliefs. For example, on more than one occasion she has expressed discomfort intolerance beliefs, e.g. 'I *can't bear* it when it's boring.' She also expressed a rigid belief: 'It *shouldn't* be that boring.' A well-trained cognitive behavioural coach listens out for such statements and reflects them back when appropriate. The coach in our example made a mental note of the rigid and extreme beliefs that Rachel expressed. He now gives Rachel Table 15.3 and combines Approach 1 and Approach 2:

Coach: 'So there's only one column left to fill in - "B" for beliefs.'

Rachel: 'Ok.'

Coach: 'In the ABC model the idea is that we largely make *ourselves* angry by holding certain rigid or extreme beliefs. Have a look at this table and see if anything looks familiar' (*gives Rachel a copy of Table 15.3).*

Rachel: (*smiling)* 'Some of those definitely sound like me. . .'

Coach: 'Which ones in particular?

Rachel: (*pointing to the 'Discomfort Intolerance' beliefs)* 'Those ones for sure.'

Coach: 'The "I *can't bear* it". . .beliefs?'

Rachel: 'Yep.'

Coach: 'OK, imagine you're trying to read *Tess*. Close your eyes if it helps. *(Rachel closes her eyes)* How are you feeling?'

Rachel: 'Angry.'

Coach: 'Ok, what, if anything, do you think you *"can't bear"*?'

Rachel: (*speaking forcefully)* 'I can't bear it being so boring!'

Coach: 'So when you're reading *Tess* and finding it boring you have the belief - "I *can't bear* it being so boring!"'

Rachel: 'Definitely.'

Coach: 'Earlier you also said: "It *shouldn't* be so boring!"'

Rachel: (*speaking forcefully)* 'No, it shouldn't!'

Coach: 'Have a look at the handout again. What type of belief is "It *shouldn't* be so boring!"?'

Rachel: (*looking through Table 15.3)* 'A rigid belief?'

Coach: 'It certainly sounds like it. Are you saying it *"absolutely"* shouldn't be so boring?'

Rachel: 'Yep.'

Coach: 'Then yes, that would qualify as a rigid belief. So when you found *Tess* boring you held the beliefs: "It *shouldn't* be so boring" and "I *can't bear* it being so boring?"'

Rachel: 'True.'

Rachel can now fill in the 'Bs'. Her completed table looks like this:

Situation: *Trying to read* Tess.

Table 15.4 Rachel's completed ABC table.

A *Aspect of the situation*	*B* *Beliefs about 'A'*	*C* *Consequences*
It's so boring!	It *shouldn't* be so boring I *can't bear* it being so boring.	• felt angry • gave up and stopped reading

Highlighting the B-C connection

In order to overcome her emotional obstacle Rachel needs to understand the *B-C connection*, i.e. the fact that it is *largely her own beliefs that leave her feeling angry*. The coach can help her to appreciate this by contrasting two scenarios - one in which she holds rigid and extreme beliefs and another in which she holds flexible and non-extreme alternatives:

Coach: 'Alright, let's see what mainly causes the anger. Imagine two scenarios. In both scenarios, you find *Tess* boring.'
Rachel: 'Ok.'
Coach: 'But in each scenario, you have different beliefs.'
Rachel: 'Ok.'
Coach: 'In Scenario 1 you believe: (*speaking in a measured tone)* "I *don't like* it being this boring, but it doesn't *have* to be the way I want. I find it *hard* to bear when it's this boring, but I definitely *can* bear it." How would you feel if you thought like that?'
Rachel: 'Probably ok. . .a bit annoyed, maybe.'
Coach: 'A bit annoyed, but not angry?'
Rachel: 'No, not angry.'
Coach: 'And how would you *act*?'
Rachel: 'I'd probably carry on reading the book.'
Coach: 'Ok, here's Scenario 2. This time you believe: (*speaking forcefully*) "It *shouldn't* be so boring. . .I *can't bear* it being this boring!" How would you feel if you thought like that?'
Rachel: *(smiling sheepishly)* 'Angry.'
Coach: 'And how would you *act*?'
Rachel: 'I'd give up on the book. Ok, I get the point.'
Coach: 'What's that?'
Rachel: 'I guess I was working myself up. . .'
Coach: 'How?'
Rachel: 'By telling myself "it *shouldn't*. . ." and "I *can't bear* it. . ."'
Coach: 'Ok, so let's think about what's really driving the anger. Is it (A) the fact that the book's boring - or (B) what you *tell* yourself about that?'
Rachel: 'It's what I tell myself - those beliefs (*pointing to the B column).*'
Coach: 'Ok, so here's an even more important question. If you want to stop feeling angry, what do you need to do?'
Rachel: 'Change those beliefs, I guess.'
Coach: 'And if you want to get on with reading the book, what do you need to do?'
Rachel: 'Same thing - change the beliefs. Stop telling myself "I *can't bear* it. . ."'

Coach: 'And do what instead?'
Rachel: 'Tell myself I *can* bear it. . .like in that first scenario.'

The coach has helped Rachel to reach a crucial insight. She is beginning to see that it is largely her own thinking that leads to her emotional reactions. She also realises that if she wants to change the way she feels she will have to change the way she thinks, i.e. modify the Bs in her ABCs. In the next chapter, we shall see how the coach helps her do this.

Chapter summary

- When a student runs into an emotional obstacle the coach can try a simple solution-focused approach. However, if this is ineffective, he can try the ABC model instead.
- When using the ABC model, coach and student begin by describing the situation and identifying the Cs - how the student felt and how she behaved.
- The next step is to identify the A - the aspect of the situation about which the student was most angry, dejected, anxious etc.
- The coach then helps the student identify her beliefs - B. He can provide the student with a handout of 'irrational beliefs', reflect back any beliefs she has articulated, and/or ask her to work out for herself what rigid and extreme beliefs she held in the situation.
- Once the ABC table has been completed, the coach helps the student see the 'B-C connection', i.e. the fact that she largely makes *herself* angry (or anxious or dejected, etc.) by holding rigid and extreme beliefs.
- The coach also introduces the idea of 'rational' beliefs, which are flexible and non-extreme. He helps the student to see that holding such beliefs would lead to a healthier emotional (and behavioural) response.
- Finally, the coach helps the student to see that if she wants to overcome her emotional obstacle, then she will need to modify her beliefs.

Note

1 Some commentators point out that 'should' beliefs are rigid only if the word 'absolutely' can be inserted, i.e. 'it *absolutely* shouldn't. . .' (e.g. Dryden, 2001).

References

Dryden, W. (2001). *Reason to change: A Rational Emotive Behaviour Therapy (REBT) workbook*. Hove: Brunner-Routledge.
Dryden, W. (2009). *Self-Discipline: How to Get It and How to Keep It*. London: Sheldon.
Dryden, W. (2011). *Dealing with Clients' Emotional Problems in Life Coaching*. Hove: Routledge.
Guterman, J.T. and Rudes, J. (2005). A solution-focused approach to rational-emotive behaviour therapy: Toward a theoretical integration. *Journal of Rational - Emotive & Cognitive - Behavior Therapy*, 23, 3, 223-244.
O'Connell, B., Palmer, S. and Williams, H. (2012). *Solution Focused Coaching in Practice*. Hove: Routledge.
Ratner, H. and Yusuf, D. (2015). *Brief Coaching with Children and Young People: A Solution focused approach*. London: Routledge.

16 Challenging and replacing unhelpful beliefs

In this chapter

- Disputing rigid and extreme beliefs
- Strengthening flexible and non-extreme beliefs
- Adding 'D' and 'E' to the 'ABCs'
- Putting new beliefs into action
- Research and evidence.

Disputing rigid and extreme beliefs

In the last chapter Rachel began to see that she largely *made herself* angry by holding certain beliefs. When reading *Tess of the D'Urbervilles* - a book she found boring - Rachel held two irrational beliefs:

1. **'It *shouldn't* be so boring!'** (a rigid belief)
2. **'I *can't bear* it being so boring!'** (a discomfort intolerance belief)

As Rachel realised in the last chapter, the key to overcoming her obstacle lies in modifying those 'irrational' beliefs. In cognitive behavioural coaching (CBC), there are at least four ways to challenge or dispute beliefs. These are presented in Table 16.1:

Table 16.1 Four ways to challenge beliefs.

Type of challenge	*Typical questions*
Rigidity/extremism	• 'How flexible is that belief?' • 'How extreme is that belief?'
Empiricism	• 'Where is the evidence that...?' • 'Is there a law or rule that...?'
Logic	• 'How logical is that?' • 'How does it follow that...?'
Pragmatism	• 'What effect does that belief have on you?' • 'How does it help you achieve your goal?'

The coach would invite Rachel to look through Table 16.1. The process of 'disputing' beliefs can then begin. Rachel and her coach begin with her *rigid* belief: 'It *shouldn't* be this boring.'

Approach 1: Rigidity/extremism

If the student's belief is extreme (e.g. 'It would be *awful* if I got a bad mark') then the appropriate challenge is extremism. If the student's belief is rigid (e.g. 'I've *got to* get a good mark') then the appropriate challenge is rigidity. When we hold rigid beliefs, we *insist* that things should be a certain way. A rigid belief allows for no other outcome than the one we demand (Neenan, 2012). When we hold *flexible* beliefs, on the other hand, we accept that we may not always get what we want. In a world where frustration is inevitable, flexible beliefs are more useful than rigid ones.

Coach: 'So when you were trying to read *Tess* you had the belief: "It *shouldn't* be so boring"?'
Rachel: 'Yep.'
Coach: 'How *flexible* is that belief?'
Rachel: 'What do you mean?'
Coach: 'Well remember those two scenarios. Scenario 1 is: "I *don't like it* being this boring, but it doesn't *have* to be the way I want." Scenario 2 is: "It absolutely *shouldn't* be this boring!"'
Rachel: 'Ok, it's not that flexible.'
Coach: 'In what sense?'
Rachel: 'Well I guess I'm saying it *has* to be the way I want.'
Coach: 'How do you want it to be?'
Rachel: 'Exciting.'
Coach: 'So the book *has* to be exciting?'
Rachel: 'Yeah.'
Coach: 'At all times?'
Rachel: *(starting to sound uncertain)* 'Yeah.'
Coach: 'So you're saying that the book *shouldn't* be boring, that it *has* to be the way you want and that it *has* to be exciting at all times?'
Rachel: *(laughing)* 'Ok, I get it. That's not flexible at all. Makes me sound like a baby.'

Here Rachel comes to see that her belief is 'not flexible at all', i.e. that it is supremely rigid. This is a good starting point. The coach can now move on to the second approach.

Approach 2: Empiricism

Challenging a belief empirically involves asking for the *evidence*. This helps the student to determine whether her belief is a fact or an idea of her own making:

Coach: 'Let's try the second approach - empiricism.'
Rachel: 'Is that where you ask for evidence?'
Coach: 'Exactly. What evidence is there that *Tess* "*shouldn't* be so boring"?'
Rachel: 'Well literature's supposed to be *fun*, isn't it?'

Coach: 'Where's the evidence for that?'
Rachel: *(looking puzzled)* 'I don't know. But *shouldn't* it be fun?'
Coach: 'Well I think we'd all *like* it to be fun. And if we're lucky, it is. But is there a rule that says that it *should* be?'
Rachel: *(thinks for a second)* 'No, I guess not.'
Coach: 'And is there a law that says *Tess shouldn't* be boring!'?'
Rachel: *(laughing)* 'No, but it would be nice if there was.'
Coach: 'True, but *is* there such a law?'
Rachel: 'No.'
Coach: 'So where's the evidence that the book *shouldn't* be so boring?'
Rachel: 'I guess there isn't any. I just don't *want* it to be boring!'

When taking the empirical approach, coach and student act like scientists. That is, they look around for any evidence that supports her belief. If it is a rigid belief, the coach can ask whether there is a rule or law that says things must be the way the student wants. Rachel comes to see that there is nothing to say that *Tess 'shouldn't* be so boring' except the fact that she doesn't *want* it to be. The stage is now set for the third approach - Logic.

Approach 3: Logic

Coach: 'Do you remember what the third approach to challenging was?'
Rachel: 'Logic.'
Coach: 'That's right. Shall we try that approach?'
Rachel: 'Sure.'
Coach: 'Ok. So we've established that you don't *want Tess* to be boring.'
Rachel: 'No, I don't.'
Coach: 'Ok, how does it follow that it *shouldn't* be?'
Rachel: 'Because I really hate it when it's boring.'
Coach: 'And that means it *shouldn't* be so boring?'
Rachel: 'Yeah.'
Coach: 'How logical is that?'
Rachel: *(looking puzzled)* 'I don't know.'
Coach: 'Let's look at that argument. *(Coach gets out a piece of paper and writes:*
1. *I really* ***hate*** *it when* Tess *is boring.*
Therefore:
2. *It* ***shouldn't*** *be so boring'.)*
Is that a good, logical argument?'
Rachel: *(beginning to smile)* 'No.'
Coach: 'What about this one?' *(Coach writes)*
1. *I* ***don't want*** *'Tess' to be so boring*
Therefore
2. *It* ***shouldn't*** *be so boring.'*
Is that a good argument?'
Rachel: *(smiling more broadly)* 'No.'

Coach: 'Would your English teacher be impressed by the logic?'

Rachel: *(laughing)* 'Definitely not.'

Coach: 'Why not?'

Rachel: 'Because it's a jump.'

Coach: 'In what way?'

Rachel: 'Well the first bit is just what I want. And the second bit is like a rule.'

Coach: 'So you're jumping from what you want to a rule?' *(Rachel nods)*. How logical is that?

Rachel: 'Not very logical.'

Coach: 'Let's check. How logical is this argument: Rachel doesn't want it to be X, therefore it *shouldn't* be X?'

Rachel: *(laughing)* 'Ok, that's silly. Makes me sound like a baby again.'

The logical approach helps the student see that the fact that she *doesn't want* something to happen hardly entails that it *shouldn't*. It is often helpful for the coach to write down the student's thoughts so that she can see the leap she is making. As the dialogue above illustrates, a dose of humour can also be effective. Of course, the target of the humour is the coachee's unhelpful belief, never the coachee herself (Dryden and Neenan, 2012).

Approach 4: Pragmatism

The last approach is pragmatism. This often puts the nail in the coffin of the irrational belief:

Coach: 'The last way to test a belief is through "pragmatism." What does that mean to you?'

Rachel: 'How *useful* the belief is?'

Coach: 'Exactly. One way to do this is to look at the Cs in your ABC table. Another way is to see if it helps you achieve your goal.'

Rachel: 'Ok.'

Coach: 'When you tell yourself "it *shouldn't* be so boring!" how do you feel?'

Rachel: *(pointing to the emotional C)*. 'Angry.'

Coach: 'And what do you do?'

Rachel: *(pointing to the behavioural C)* 'I give up and stop reading.'

Coach: 'To what extent does that help you achieve your goal of revising effectively for your English mock?'

Rachel: 'Doesn't help at all. . .makes it harder.'

Coach: 'In what way?'

Rachel: 'Well I just get angry and give up reading, which means I won't have revised for the mock and will probably get a bad grade.'

Coach: 'So when you tell yourself "it *shouldn't* be so boring!" you get angry, give up and stop reading. That means you won't know the book, which means you won't have revised for the mock, which means you'll probably get a bad grade.'

Rachel: *(looking regretful)* 'Yeah. It's not great.'

Coach: 'So how *useful* to you is the belief "it *shouldn't* be so boring!"?'

Rachel: 'Not useful at all.'

The pragmatic approach to challenging a belief involves asking the student where it *gets* her. What effect does it have on her emotions and behaviour? And *to what extent does it help her to achieve her goal*? Having gone through all four challenges, Rachel is now in a position to see that 'it *shouldn't* be so boring' has the following characteristics:

- It has little or no flexibility.
- It is not supported by any evidence.
- It represents an illogical leap (from a preference to a 'rule').
- It has a negative effect on her emotions and behaviour.
- It prevents her from achieving her goal.

Establishing a new belief

It is not enough to challenge an 'irrational' belief. The coachee needs a 'rational' alternative to replace it (DiGiuseppe, 1991). It is helpful at this point to give Rachel another handout. The table below appeared in Chapter 14. It contrasts 'irrational' beliefs with 'rational' alternatives.

Rachel needs to find an alternative to her belief 'It *shouldn't* be so boring.' Looking at Table 16.2 may help her. In addition, the coach could now try to be *solution-focused* by asking her when she *already* thinks flexibly:

Coach: 'For every irrational belief, there's a rational alternative. Have a look at this handout *(gives Rachel Table 16.2)*. Check out the first row - the rigid belief versus the flexible belief.'

Rachel: 'Ok.'

Coach: 'You said that "it *shouldn't* be so boring" is rigid?'

Rachel: 'Yep.'

Coach: 'When do you think more like *that*?' *(pointing to the 'Flexible belief')*.

Table 16.2 Rational vs. irrational beliefs.

Irrational beliefs	*Rational beliefs*
Rigid belief or **'Demand':** I *mustn't* get a bad mark!	**Flexible belief** or **Preference:** I *don't want* to get a bad mark but that doesn't mean I *mustn't*.
'Awfulising' belief: It would be *awful* if I got a bad mark.	**'Non-awfulising' belief:** It would be *a shame* if I got a bad mark, but *not the end of the world.*
Discomfort intolerance belief: I *can't bear* getting a bad mark.	**Discomfort *tolerance* belief:** Getting a bad mark *isn't easy* to bear, but I obviously *can* bear it and will.
Depreciation belief: I'm *totally hopeless* (for getting a bad mark).	**Acceptance belief:** Getting a bad mark means I'm a *fallible human being*, not 'totally hopeless'.

Rachel: *(thinks for a moment)* 'Well not when I'm trying to read *Tess* but maybe when I have to babysit my brother.'

Coach: 'Interesting. How do you think when you have to babysit your brother?'

Rachel: 'Well I don't *like* having to do it. . .but it is what it is.'

Coach: 'So you tell yourself "I don't *like* having to do it, but it is what it is?"'

Rachel: 'Yeah.'

Coach: 'That sounds like a nice flexible belief. With that sort of attitude, how would you change "It *shouldn't* be so boring?"'

Rachel: 'You mean make it flexible?

Coach: 'Exactly.'

Rachel: 'I don't *like* it being this boring.'

Coach: 'But. . .'

Rachel: 'but that doesn't mean it *shouldn't* be.'

Coach: 'Ok.'

Rachel: '. . .it is what it is.'

Coach: 'Great. So if you're thinking flexibly you believe: "I *don't like* it being this boring but that doesn't mean it shouldn't be. It is what it is".'

Rachel: 'Yeah. That sounds good.'

Coach: 'Would you like to write it down?'

Rachel: 'Sure.'

In this example, the coach is using Table 16.2 to help the student develop a 'rational' belief. However, notice that he is encouraging Rachel to formulate that belief *in her own words*. This is crucial. For a belief to resonate with a student it must be expressed in her own words. The coach's role is simply to ensure that it is flexible. In essence, a flexible belief is made up of two parts: a statement of the student's preferences (e.g. 'I *don't like* it being this boring'), but also a negation of the 'irrational' demand (e.g. 'but that doesn't mean it shouldn't be').

Note too the *solution-focused* slant in the coach's approach. He assumes that there are times when Rachel already *does* think flexibly and asks her to describe these occasions. Like all human beings, a student will engage in both 'rational' and 'irrational' thinking. The coach's job is to help her accentuate the former and reduce the latter (see Guterman and Rudes, 2005).

Testing the new belief: the four challenges again

Rachel has now formulated an alternative to 'It *shouldn't* be so boring':

Box 16.1 Rachel's flexible preference.

'I *don't like* it being this boring but that doesn't mean it shouldn't be. It is what it is.'

The coach should now help Rachel to test her new belief, using the four challenges:

Rigidity (vs. flexibility)

Coach: 'Let's see whether your new belief passes the four tests.'
Rachel: 'Ok.'
Coach: 'How flexible would you say it is?'
Rachel: 'More flexible than the other one.'
Coach: 'In what way?'
Rachel: 'Well I'm saying what I like but I'm not demanding it.'

Empiricism

Coach: 'What evidence is there for your new belief?'
Rachel: 'Well it's *true* that I don't like it being boring.'
Coach: 'And what about the second half of the belief?'
Rachel: 'That's true as well – there's no law that says it shouldn't be boring.'
Coach: 'So there's evidence for both parts of your new belief?'
Rachel: 'Yep. It is what it is.'

Logic

Coach: 'How logical is the new belief?'
Rachel: 'More logical than the other one.'
Coach: 'In what way?'
Rachel: 'I'm not jumping from what I want to a rule.'

Pragmatism

Coach: 'Let's see how useful your new belief is. Imagine you're reading *Tess*.'
Rachel: *(closing her eyes)* 'Ok.'
Coach: 'How do you find the book?'
Rachel: *(frowning)* 'Still boring.'
Coach: 'Ok. Now imagine telling yourself: "I *don't like* it being this boring but that doesn't mean it shouldn't be. It is what it is".'
Rachel: *(rehearsing the belief in her mind)* 'Ok.'
Coach: 'How do you feel?'
Rachel: 'A bit annoyed. . .but not too bad.'
Coach: 'Could you keep reading right now?'
Rachel: 'Yeah, I think so.' *(Rachel opens her eyes)*
Coach: 'So when you hold this new belief in your mind, you feel a bit annoyed, but not too bad. And you could probably keep reading.'
Rachel: *(looking hopeful)* 'Yeah.'
Coach: 'To what extent will this help you achieve your goal?
Rachel: 'Well if I can get through *Tess* then I can revise for the mock.'

Having gone through the four challenges, Rachel can now see that her new belief has the following characteristics:

- It is flexible.
- It is supported by evidence.
- It contains no illogical leaps.
- It has a positive effect on (i) how she feels and (ii) how she's inclined to behave.
- It will help her to achieve her goals.

Recall that Rachel had another irrational belief, namely the discomfort intolerance belief: '*I* ***can't bear*** *it being so boring!*' The coach would now guide Rachel through exactly the same process with regard to this belief, i.e. dispute it using the four approaches, ask Rachel to formulate an alternative belief, test the alternative and so on. Let's suppose that Rachel comes up with the following discomfort *tolerance* belief:

Box 16.2 Rachel's discomfort tolerance belief.

'It's *tough* to bear when it's boring, but I *can* bear it and I *will* – I want to be prepared for the mock!'

Rachel now has *two* new beliefs, a *flexible preference* and a *discomfort tolerance* belief. It is time to put these into action.

Putting new beliefs into action

Coach: 'Alright, do you think you can get back to work on your goal?'
Rachel: 'Yeah.'
Coach: 'So your ultimate goal is to have revised effectively for your English mock. What would you like to have achieved by next week?'
Rachel: 'Same goal as last week – to have read the first three chapters of *Tess* and made notes on the key themes.'
Coach: 'Even if it's boring?'
Rachel: *(smiling)* 'Even if it's boring.'
Coach: 'What will you do if it seems boring?'
Rachel: 'Remind myself of the new beliefs.'
Coach: 'How?'
Rachel: 'I've written them in my diary. I can read them before I start.'

As we said in Chapter 1, coaching is ultimately about action. In the dialogue above the coach is trying to help Rachel *act* on her new beliefs. In addition to writing them down and reading them before she starts, she may find it useful to *say* them forcefully out loud (Dryden, 2001).

She may also want to create abbreviated versions that are easier to keep in mind, e.g. '*It is what it is*' and '*This is tough but I can bear it.*' As is so often the case, it would be a good idea to form an 'if. . .then' plan:

'If I find it boring, then I will tell myself: "This is tough but I can bear it".'

Imagine that a week has passed. At the beginning of her next session, Rachel's coach asks about progress:

Coach: 'On a scale from 0 to 10, to what extent did you achieve last week's goal?'
Rachel: 'A good 8. I got through the chapters. And made pretty good notes.'
Coach: 'How did you do that?'
Rachel: 'It wasn't easy. I still found it boring.'
Coach: 'So how did you manage?'
Rachel: 'I just told myself "*it is what it is*" instead of getting angry.'
Coach: 'Anything else?'
Rachel: 'Well there was a bit that was *really* boring. . ..'
Coach: 'What did you do then?'
Rachel: 'I read the thing in my diary *(opening her diary)*: "It's *tough* to bear when it's boring, but I *can* bear it and I *will* – I want to be prepared for my mock!"'
Coach: 'And what did you do then?'
Rachel: 'I got on with the book.'
Coach: 'Rachel, that's really impressive.'

Final thoughts on emotional obstacles and the ABC model

We have now come to the end of Part IV. The approach we have explored – including the ABC model – derives from Rational Emotive Behaviour Therapy – REBT. When used in coaching, it is better to call it Rational Emotive Behaviour *Coaching* – REBC (Neenan, 2012). The most thorough guide is provided by Dryden (2011). As we have seen, a rational emotive behaviour approach involves:

- *understanding emotional obstacles in terms of A, B and C*
- *identifying and challenging 'irrational' (i.e. rigid and extreme) beliefs*
- *developing 'rational' (i.e. flexible and non-extreme) alternatives.*

Does a rational emotive behaviour approach actually help students? Consider a sample of the evidence. Lupu and Iftene (2009) found that a rational emotive education intervention led to a reduction in students' anxiety.[1] Mahfar and colleagues (2014) found that a rational emotive education module reduced students' levels of stress. Shannon and Allen (1998) found that students who were shown how to manage their emotions using a rational emotive behaviour approach not only experienced less attachment to self-defeating beliefs but also improved their performance in maths.

REBT and REBC are often described as having an 'educational' emphasis (e.g. Dryden, 2001). The coachee is *taught* the ABC model and shown how to challenge and replace unhelpful beliefs. You may be thinking: 'Isn't that a little didactic for coaching? Isn't coaching about letting the *coachee* take charge?'

Actually, there is every reason to think that this approach *does* let the student take charge. True, there is (initially) an element of teaching involved. But let us not forget the very active role played by the student. It is the student, not the coach, who:

- Identifies the key thoughts, beliefs, emotions and behaviour ('A,' 'B' and 'C')
- Decides whether beliefs are flexible, true, logical and helpful
- Puts new functional beliefs into her own words
- Creates her own abbreviations of those beliefs
- Rehearses those beliefs in her own time and in her own manner
- Chooses whether to apply the ABC model in future

It can therefore be argued that the approach we have considered actually *empowers* the student. With time, practice and a little support she should eventually be able to fill out ABC forms on her own. To facilitate this process, she can be given 'ABC*DE*' forms, in which the '*D*' reminds her to *dispute* irrational beliefs and the '*E*' urges her to construct '*effective*' alternatives (e.g. Palmer and Szymanska, 2008).

Taking a cognitive-behavioural approach has additional benefits. For one thing, the student will have begun to understand the impact of her thinking on her emotions and behaviour. She will also have developed her ability to:

- examine beliefs
- weigh up evidence
- evaluate 'logic'
- think flexibly about adversities

These are skills that every school wants students to develop. A cognitive-behavioural approach therefore fits nicely into a school's agenda and ethos (Platts and Williamson, 2000).

Chapter summary

- Cognitive behavioural coaching suggests at least four ways to challenge unhelpful beliefs: (1) Rigidity/Extremism, (2) Empiricism, (3) Logic, and (4) Pragmatism.
- Students can be shown how to turn rigid and extreme beliefs into flexible and non-extreme alternatives. A solution-focused approach would emphasise that they *already* think in ways that are flexible and non-extreme.
- Once the student has put new beliefs into her own words, the coach will encourage her to *act* on them. This will normally involve rehearsing the beliefs as she works on her goals. She may also find it useful to create abbreviated versions.

- The ABC model derives from Rational Emotive Behaviour Therapy (REBT) but is now widely used in Cognitive Behavioural Coaching (CBC). Evidence shows that a rational emotive behaviour approach can reduce students' anxiety and stress and enhance academic performance.
- Although there is an element of teaching involved, the student is an active participant in the process.
- A cognitive-behavioural approach not only enables students to overcome emotional obstacles but also helps them to develop important 'thinking skills'.

Note

1 It is important to realise that students in this study were experiencing *normal* (not clinical) anxiety. I would like to thank Professor Lupu for confirming this.

References

DiGiuseppe, R. (1991). Comprehensive cognitive disputing in RET. In M. Bernard (ed.), *Using rational emotive therapy effectively*. New York: Plenum.

Dryden, W. (2001). *Reason to change: A Rational Emotive Behaviour Therapy (REBT) workbook*. Hove: Brunner-Routledge.

Dryden, W. (2011). *Dealing with Emotional Problems in Life Coaching*. Hove: Routledge.

Dryden, W. and Neenan, M. (2012). *Learning from Mistakes in Rational Emotive Behaviour Therapy*. New York: Routledge.

Guterman, J.T. and Rudes, J. (2005). A solution-focused approach to rational-emotive behaviour therapy: Toward a theoretical integration. *Journal of Rational - Emotive & Cognitive - Behavior Therapy*, 23, 3, 223-244.

Lupu, V. and Iftene, F. (2009). The impact of rational emotive behaviour education on anxiety in teenagers. *Journal of Cognitive and Behavioral Psychotherapies*. 9, 1, 95-105.

Mahfar, M., Aslan, A.S., Noah, S.M., Ahmad, J. and Jaafar, W.M.W. (2014). Effects of rational emotive education module on irrational beliefs and stress among fully residential school students in Malaysia. *Procedia Social & Behavioral Sciences*, 114, 239-243.

Neenan, M. (2012). Understanding and tackling procrastination. In M. Neenan and S. Palmer (eds), *Cognitive Behavioural Coaching in Practice: An Evidence Based approach*. Hove: Routledge.

Palmer, S. and Szymanska, K. (2008). Cognitive behavioural coaching: An integrative approach. In S. Palmer and A. Whybrow (eds), *Handbook of coaching psychology: A guide for practitioners*. London: Routledge.

Platts, J. and Williamson, Y. (2000). The use of cognitive-behavioural therapy for counselling in schools in Barwick, N. (ed.), *Clinical Counselling in Schools*. London: Routledge.

Shannon, H.D. and Allen, T.H. (1998). The Effectiveness of a REBT Training Program in Increasing the Performance of High School Students in Mathematics. *Journal of Rational-Emotive & Cognitive-Behavior Therapy*, 16, 197-209.

Part V

The practicalities of coaching

17 Practicalities and logistics

In this chapter

- The practicalities of launching a coaching programme
- Consistency vs. flexibility.

Launching a coaching programme: practical issues

We noted in Part I that a teacher can 'coach' a student without conducting a formal session. Coaching – as a non-directive style of communication – can take place during report readings, parents' evenings, tutorials and indeed almost any conversation a teacher has with a student. We might call this 'corridor coaching' (Greene and Grant, 2003). If this is the only coaching that takes place, then there are very few practical matters to consider.

On the other hand, if a school is launching a coaching *programme* (involving formal coaching *sessions*), then a number of issues need to be addressed. Andreanoff (2016) deals thoroughly with these issues as they apply to a university. Although there is considerable overlap between school and university, secondary school coaching deserves its own treatment. Any school wishing to launch a coaching programme needs to consider the following:

1. *How will students enrol?*
2. *When and where will sessions take place?*
3. *How long will sessions last?*
4. *How many sessions will each student have?*
5. *What kind of paperwork will be kept?*
6. *How will coaches be trained?*
7. *How will success be measured?*

The aim of this chapter is to suggest answers to the above. Of course, every school has its own culture, values, systems and procedures. A universal approach is therefore out of the question. The following should be taken not as a set of rules to be followed, but simply as a starting point.

1. How will students enrol?

If a school is launching a formal coaching programme, then there must be a clear way for students to enrol. First, students will have to know *what coaching is* and *what it can do for them*. There are many ways in which a school can raise awareness of coaching. Assemblies, year meetings, registrations and form periods are all good opportunities to introduce the idea of coaching. The school might then simply wait for students to apply.

On the other hand, teachers and staff may prefer to take a more active approach. For example, if it is felt that particular students would benefit from coaching, then teachers or form tutors could suggest that they enrol. However, it is important not to exert too much pressure. Students should never be forced into coaching. Referring to Flaherty's (1999) model, Cox (2006, p. 195) notes that 'for coaching to succeed, there must be true enrolment into the coaching process; that is, there must be voluntary, intrinsic motivation - it must not be coerced or extrinsic.' Of course, this does not prevent teachers from making *recommendations*. When a teacher *recommends* coaching to a student he should:

- explain what coaching is
- explain how it might help the student
- ask the student if she has any questions or reservations about coaching
- allow the student to make her own decision about enrolment.

In addition, I have found that students become much more enthusiastic about coaching when they realise that they are the ones in control - *they* decide what to work on; *they* set the goals; *they* choose the action-steps. The coach is there to address the student's agenda, not the other way around.

Suppose that a number of students want to be coached. What happens next? Normally there will be some sort of *central coordinator*. Interested students contact the coordinator and explain - in general terms - what they want to be coached on. The coordinator then pairs each student with a suitable coach. Some commentators argue that students should be able to choose their own coaches (e.g. Dawson and Guare, 2012). In this case, the coordinator would give students a list of available coaches and ask them for their first (and perhaps second) choice.

Should *all* students be able to enrol at once? To make things manageable, it is a good idea to begin with a particular year group or section, e.g. Years 10–11 (GCSE), or 12–13 (A-level). Once coaching has been established for a particular group (and any teething problems have been solved), a wider roll-out may be considered. Schools may, however, need to obtain parental consent. An email or letter could be sent to parents, explaining the nature and benefits of coaching and asking permission for their children to enrol.

2. When and where will sessions take place?

Clearly, sessions will have to take place at a time when student and coach are both available. If prospective coachees indicate their free periods, then the central coordinator may be able to match them with available coaches. However, this can be a time-consuming task for the coordinator. It may be helpful to stipulate that all sessions should take place during 'universal' free time, e.g. before school, at break, at lunch, or after school. Of course, even this is no guarantee that student and coach will be available at the same time. In practice, therefore, the coordinator may simply assign students to coaches and then leave it to them to find a time for sessions.

The next question to consider is *how often* coach and student should meet. In my experience, *weekly* or at least fortnightly sessions are best. If any more time is allowed to elapse between sessions, the coaching may lose momentum. In addition, it is a very good idea for sessions to take place at the same time each week (or fortnight), e.g. at 3pm on Wednesdays. If the school or coordinator has not arranged a time for sessions, then coach and student should agree on one in the 'Contracting' phase (see Chapter 18). They should then stick to it throughout the programme.

Where should sessions take place? Once again, consistency is important. Ideally coaching sessions should take place in the same room each week (or fortnight). The location should be quiet and there should be enough space for both coach and student to feel comfortable. In addition, coaches will need to adhere to any child protection or safeguarding procedures. For example, they may need to ensure that passers-by can see into the room or that the door is kept open at all times. The school should ensure that coaches are aware of safeguarding procedures before they conduct their sessions.

3. How long will sessions last?

Coaching sessions could last anywhere between 25 minutes and 1 hour. On the one hand, sessions need to be long enough to allow students to work through their challenges and achieve their goals. On the other hand, there is a limited amount of time in the school day. Very short sessions (e.g. 15 minutes) may not be effective. I would suggest, as a rule of thumb, that sessions should last at least 25 minutes. This is normally enough time to go through the GROW model.

Should all sessions be of the same length? Or should the duration be allowed to vary? There are pros and cons to each approach. On the one hand, some parents, teachers and schools may want every student to be given the same amount of attention. On the other hand, coaching is at its best when it is tailored to a student's needs. In my own experience, I have found that some students have thrived on 25 minutes sessions whilst others have needed 40 minutes or more. Schools will therefore have to decide which is more important - having a consistent framework that applies across the board, or adapting to the needs of each student.

4. How many sessions will each student have?

In some cases, the school may stipulate the number of sessions that a coach can offer. If not, there are two options:

a Coach and coachee agree in advance on a *fixed number of sessions.*
b Coaching continues *until the student no longer needs it.*

Each of these approaches finds endorsement in the literature. Those who favour the 'fixed' approach may argue that coaching is best when it has a clear beginning and end (e.g. Wilson, 2014). Once coach and student have agreed on the number of sessions, they stick to this number (or negotiate a new contract). This, it is said, prevents the coachee from becoming dependent on the coach.

On the other hand, solution-focused practitioners often prefer not to fix the number of sessions in advance (e.g. O'Connell, Palmer and Williams, 2012). In support of this 'fluid' approach it may be argued that the number of sessions a coachee requires depends on how quickly (or slowly) she makes progress. If she is satisfied with her achievement at the end of the third session, then coaching can come to an end. On the other hand, if she believes that she needs additional support, then another session could be scheduled.

So which of these two approaches - 'fluid' or 'fixed' - should a school take? The decision will depend on a number of factors including how much time teachers and students can (or want to) commit to coaching, and how much uniformity a school wants in its coaching programme. One advantage of the fluid approach is that it takes account of the coachee's actual progress. As a result, she is likely to receive as many sessions as she actually needs. On the other hand, one advantage of the 'fixed' approach is that the teacher and student both know what they're in for. That is, both teacher and student know at the outset that they have, say, six sessions together and that coaching will finish on a specific date. This makes it easier for the student to set her ultimate goal. She simply has to decide what she wants to have achieved *by the end of the sixth session.* Moreover, being aware of a clear end point may help the student to stay focused and encourage her to work hard for her goal (Cox, 2009).

5. What kind of paperwork will be kept?

Most schools will want to have a record of the sessions that take place. However, even if this is not the case every coach should keep his own notes. In fact, coaches who are members of professional bodies are normally advised to keep some sort of log. Paperwork will include at least the following:

(i) **The contract between coach and student** - This is discussed in more detail in the next chapter. The 'Coaching Contract' states the terms and conditions of the coaching programme.

(ii) **Session notes** - Some coaches like to make notes during the session. Others prefer to write things up *after* the session. In either case, coaches need to be aware of data protection principles (St John-Brooks, 2014). If the coach is taking notes during the session, it is good practice to make these visible to the coachee. If the coach writes with his right hand, the student should be sitting on his right; if he writes with his left hand then she should be sitting on his left. This enables her to see what he is writing and promotes transparency.

(iii) **The student's coaching forms** - Certain details are crucial in coaching, e.g. the student's ultimate goal, proximal goals, and action-plans. The student records all of these things on her *coaching form* (see Appendix C). Coaches must have copies of these forms. If the student is filling them out on a laptop or tablet, she should email them to her coach once they are completed. If she is filling them out on paper, the coach will need to make copies for himself.

(iv) **Post-coaching Questionnaires** - It is essential to find out what coachees think of coaching. As we saw in Chapter 13, the coach will ask for the student's overall thoughts in the last session. However, students should also fill out post-coaching questionnaires and hand them in to the central coordinator.

6. How will coaches be trained?

It goes without saying that coaches need to be competent. Schools should ensure that coaches receive:

(i) **Initial coach training** - A book such as this can be a useful guide. But it is no substitute for professional training. Guidance and feedback from an experienced trainer are essential for any would-be coach.

(ii) **Supervision** - All coaches should periodically discuss their coaching with experienced practitioners. When undertaken formally this is known as 'supervision'. Supervisors may be external coaches or trainers (i.e. professionals not working in the school). But they may also be other internal coaches so long as these other coaches have been well-trained and are more experienced (Greene and Grant, 2003). Some coaches choose to engage in *peer supervision*. In this case, individuals with *equal* levels of coaching experience will discuss how they can improve their coaching. Admittedly, peer supervision lacks the element of expertise that a more experienced professional provides. However, it can be a helpful and cost-effective way for teacher-coaches to support one another and develop their practice.

7. How will success be measured?

In the executive coaching world, there is often a focus on ROI - 'return on investment' (e.g. Phillips *et al.*, 2012). At the end of a coaching programme sponsors normally ask: 'Was the money well spent?' A coachee's subjective sense of fulfilment is not considered enough. Business objectives must be met and key stakeholders (e.g. line managers, HR directors) must be satisfied. Of course, *executive* coaching is not the same as student coaching. However, evaluation is still extremely important. Every school will want to know that students are actually benefitting from coaching. We consider various approaches to evaluation in Part VI, focusing on quantitative methods.

We have now briefly surveyed some of the main practical issues a school will face in setting up a coaching programme. In the next chapter, we consider the process every coach and student must go through before coaching begins: 'Contracting'.

Chapter summary

- The enrolment process should educate students about the nature and benefits of coaching. Whilst students should never be *forced* into coaching, teachers should feel free to make recommendations.
- A central coordinator will be responsible for the administration of the programme. Interested students contact the coordinator so that (s)he can pair them with available coaches.
- If the school does not stipulate when sessions should take place, then coach and student should decide on this in the 'Contracting' phase. They should stick to the agreed time throughout the programme. Ideally sessions will take place once a week or once a fortnight.
- Sessions need to take place in a location that is quiet and comfortable. Coaches must abide by the school's child protection and safeguarding regulations.
- Sessions of at least 25 minutes should allow coach and student sufficient time to go through the GROW model. Some schools may want to allow coaches the freedom to vary the length of sessions according to students' needs. Others may prefer uniformity.
- A coaching programme may either (i) include a fixed number of sessions or (ii) continue until the student no longer needs (or wants) coaching. The former approach may enhance commitment and prevent the student from becoming dependent on the coach. On the other hand, the latter approach allows coaching to be tailored to the student's needs.
- A coaching programme will involve certain paperwork. This includes the Coaching Contract, students' coaching forms, session notes and post-coaching questionnaires.
- Coaches need to be properly trained and engage in supervision. Supervision normally involves a more experienced practitioner. However, peer supervision is also possible.
- Schools need to think carefully about how they will *evaluate* their coaching programmes.

References

Andreanoff, J. (2016). *Coaching and mentoring in higher education: A step-by-step guide to exemplary practice*. London: Palgrave.

Cox, E. (2006). An adult learning approach to coaching. In D.R. Stober, and A.M. Grant (eds), *Evidence based coaching handbook: Putting best practices to work for your clients*. Hoboken, NJ: John Wiley & Sons.

Cox, E. (2009). Last things first. In S. Palmer and A. McDowall (eds), *The coaching relationship: Putting people first*. Hove: Routledge.

Dawson, P. and Guare, R. (2012). *Coaching students with executive skill deficits*. New York: Guilford Press.

Flaherty, J. (1999). *Coaching: Evoking excellence in others*. Oxford: Butterworth Heinemann.

Greene, J. and Grant, A.M. (2003). *Solution-focused Coaching: Managing people in a complex world.* Harlow: Pearson Education Limited.

O'Connell, B., Palmer, S. and Williams, H. (2012). *Solution Focused Coaching in Practice.* Hove: Routledge.

Phillips, P.P., Phillips, J.J. and Edwards, L.A. (2012). *Measuring the success of coaching: A step-by-step guide for measuring impact and calculating ROI.* Alexandria, VA: ASTD Press.

St John-Brooks, K. (2014). *Internal coaching: The inside story.* London: Karnac.

Wilson, C. (2014). *Performance Coaching: A Complete Guide to Best Practice Coaching and Training.* London: Kogan Page.

18 Contracting

In this chapter

- The importance of contracting
- The Coaching Contract
- The responsibilities of the coach
- The responsibilities of the student.

The importance of contracting

Effective coaching depends on a collaborative relationship between the coach and the coachee. Each has responsibilities to the other. And each will have preferred ways of working. Stober and Grant (2006, p. 361) therefore argue that coach and coachee should 'spend some discussing the nature of their relationship, and that they [should] jointly design the dynamics of their working alliance'. This process is sometimes known as **contracting** (e.g. Passmore, 2016; Leimon, Moscovici and McMahon, 2005). The word 'contracting' may sound overly stiff or formal in a secondary school context. And yet the process is essential. Contracting helps to ensure that:

- Coach and student are clear about how they will work together.
- Coach and student are aware of the limits of their alliance.
- The student knows what she can expect from her coach.
- The student knows what her coach can expect from her.
- Safe-guarding procedures are observed.
- Problems and misunderstandings are prevented.

Appendix D provides an example of a Coaching Contract. If you do not like the word 'Contract' then 'Agreement' can be used instead. Any contract or agreement should cover the following:

- what coaching involves and what it does *not* involve
- when, where and how often sessions will take place
- the responsibilities of the coach
- the responsibilities of the coachee
- confidentiality and its limits.

What to discuss when contracting

The following points should be discussed in the contracting phase.

1. The non-directive nature of coaching should be emphasised

Students who are new to coaching may want guidance or advice. However, as you know, coaches do not (on the whole) provide this. If a student turns up to sessions expecting to be told what to do, she is likely to leave disappointed. Any contract should therefore make it clear that coaching is *non-directive*, i.e. based on the *student's* input, not the coach's.

2. Coaching should be distinguished from counselling or therapy

Before any coaching begins, students need to be disabused of the idea that coaching is "like counselling". As argued in Chapter 1, if a student's primary concern is to *alleviate emotional distress*, then counselling is more appropriate than coaching. The coach needs to make it clear to the student that the purpose of coaching is to help her *improve her performance* or *achieve practical goals*. As we have said elsewhere, this is true not only of behavioural coaching but also of *cognitive*-behavioural coaching (CBC). If coaching is likely to address emotional obstacles (e.g. through CBC), then the contract should distinguish these obstacles from mental health issues:

> *As you work towards your goals, it is normal to experience negative emotions, e.g. dejection. If you believe these are obstacles to achieving your goal, your coach may help you to overcome them. However, if you find that you are experiencing significant emotional distress (for example you feel overly anxious or depressed), then it is a good idea to contact the school counsellor.*

Of course, if the coach is not trained to deal with "emotional obstacles" then the second sentence in the above ('. . .your coach may help you to overcome them') should be omitted, as it is in Appendix D.

3. Contracting should address confidentiality and its limits

For coaching to work, students need to be honest. For example, if a student is not enjoying French, then it is important for her to say so. She may, however, be reluctant to reveal this if she believes her coach is going to communicate with her French teacher. During the contracting phase, the coach should therefore point out that *in normal circumstances* what she says in coaching will not be shared with others. Of course, the phase "in normal circumstances" is crucial. The coach needs to explain that in some cases he may be obliged to pass on information (for example, if there is a safeguarding concern). He can never promise complete confidentiality.

4. Practical and logistical details should be negotiated with the student

As far as possible, the contracting process should reflect the collaborative nature of coaching (Wisker *et al.*, 2008). Practical arrangements - such as when sessions will take place - should therefore be negotiated with the student. Some things may already have been decided by the school, e.g. the length of sessions. Even then, however, there will normally be room for negotiation: *'We could do our sessions before lunch or after lunch - what would suit you best?'* Another important issue to negotiate is how the student will complete her coaching form (Appendix C). Does she want to fill this out on paper? Or would she prefer to do it on her laptop? As long as the coach has a copy, she should be free to do as she wishes.

5. The contract should spell out the responsibilities of both coach and coachee

Without a formal contract, some students may treat coaching lightly. For example, they may turn up late for sessions or cancel at the last minute. A good contract should spell out the coachee's *responsibilities*. These will include attendance and punctuality. They will also include completing coaching forms and making some sort of effort between sessions. Of course, the contract will make it clear that the coach has responsibilities as well. These will include being non-judgemental and supportive and accommodating the student's preferences whenever possible.

6. The contract should spell out the consequences of ignoring responsibilities

What should a coach do if a student is repeatedly late for sessions? And what if she fails to show up at all? I have known coaches who accept this behaviour and carry on with coaching. This is a mistake. For coaching to work, students must show respect. This means respect for the coach, respect for themselves and respect for the process. If a student regularly arrives 10 minutes late or agrees to sessions but does not turn up, then there is (normally) no reason why coaching should continue. The contract should make this explicit, e.g. *'If you are late on more than two occasions (without good reason), then the programme may have to be terminated.'* There may be *some* circumstances in which this rule can be relaxed. For example, a student may have sought coaching precisely to address punctuality. If so, then rather than terminating the programme the coach should try to *help* the student: 'What could you do to ensure you're on time for our next session?'

7. The coach should stress the importance of taking action outside sessions

If the student has one hour of coaching a week, then it is actually the remaining 167 hours that are the most important. Her success will depend on what she does *outside sessions*. It is essential for the student to grasp this. Does she merely want to *talk* about her challenges? Is she aware that she will have steps to carry out? How does she feel about consistently taking action? These are things to discuss in the contracting phase.

8. The coach should invite the student to ask questions about coaching and do his best to answer them

The contracting phase is the student's opportunity to ask questions about coaching. Since the contract will have been sent to the student in advance, she should already have questions in mind. But it is the coach's responsibility to say something like: *'What would you like to know about coaching?'* Or *'what concerns do you have?'* He should then do his best to answer her questions and/or address her concerns.

9. The contract should be signed by both coach and student

The final step in the contracting phase is to sign the contract. By signing the contract, student and coach are indicating that they are aware of the terms of the programme and that they agree to abide by them. If substantial changes need to be made later on (e.g. if sessions need to be shortened), then a new contract should be drawn up and signed.

We have now explained the contracting process. Appendix D is an example of a Coaching Contract. You should feel free to adapt this to suit your needs. However, if you are a school leader or coaching coordinator then it is a good idea to ensure that all coaches in the school use the same template.

Chapter summary

- Contracting helps to ensure that coach and student are clear about how they will collaborate.
- The non-directive nature of coaching must be highlighted in the contracting phase.
- The coach (and contract) should distinguish coaching from counselling or therapy.
- The coach should explain the nature and limits of confidentiality in coaching. The student should know that in certain circumstances the coach is obliged to pass on information.
- Some practical details should be negotiated with the student, e.g. how she would like to complete her forms.

(continued)

(continued)

- The contract should spell out the student's responsibilities, e.g. punctuality. However, it should also specify the responsibilities of the coach, e.g. having a non-judgemental attitude.
- The contract should state the consequences of ignoring responsibilities (e.g. that coaching will be terminated if the student is persistently late).
- The contract should make it clear that the most important part of coaching is what the student does *outside sessions*.
- The coach should ask the student what questions she has about coaching. He should then answer these as thoroughly as possible.
- The contract should be signed by both coach and student before coaching begins. If significant changes need to be made later on, then a new contract should be drawn up and signed.
- Schools should give all coaches the same contract (template) to use. This ensures consistency throughout the programme.

References

Leimon, A., Moscovici, F. and McMahon, G. (2005). *Essential business coaching*. London: Routledge.

Passmore, J. (ed.) (2016). *Excellence in coaching: The Industry Guide* (3rd edn). London: Kogan Page.

Stober, D. and Grant, A.M. (2006). Toward a contextual approach to coaching. In D.R. Stober and A.M. Grant (eds), *Evidence based coaching handbook: Putting best practices to work for your clients*. Hoboken, NJ: John Wiley & Sons.

Wisker, G., Exley, K., Antoniou, M. and Ridley, P. (2008). *Working one-to-one with students*. Abingdon: Routledge.

Part VI

Evaluating impact

19 Randomised controlled trials

In this chapter

- Evaluating impact
- Goal attainment and beyond
- The importance of a control group
- The pre-test post-test control group design
- Waiting list control groups
- Statistical significance and effect size.

Evaluating the success of your coaching programme

In this final part of the book - Part VI - we consider how a school can evaluate the impact of coaching. Perhaps you are a senior leader and have just launched a coaching programme in your school. If so, you are presumably responsible for (a) assessing the value of the programme, and (b) demonstrating that value to stakeholders. Launching a coaching programme requires time, effort and (sometimes) money. Heads, governors, teachers and parents will generally want to know that the investment is worthwhile. Sadly, however, coaching evaluation is 'often neglected in the perpetual rush to get things done' (Carter, 2006, p. ix). Moreover, much of what passes for 'evaluation' is not particularly thorough or rigorous. In this chapter, we therefore focus on arguably the most rigorous approach of all - the 'Randomised Controlled Trial' (RCT).

RCTs are thought to provide the most reliable evidence for the effectiveness of an intervention. Importantly, they do so in terms of *quantitative* data. Speaking of coaching and mentoring, Andreanoff (2016, p. 118) notes that '[t]here is continuing pressure to demonstrate efficacy of these types of intervention in *quantitative* rather than qualitative terms, particularly if using government funding' (italics added). Schools may not require funding to launch their coaching programmes. But they will almost certainly want solid evidence that coaching is effective. RCTs can provide this. Before we examine RCTs, however, we need to consider *why* a school is introducing coaching. What does it want students to gain?

Goal attainment and beyond

Coaching, as we know, is a goal-focused process. At the beginning of her programme, the student sets her *ultimate goal*, i.e. what she wants to achieve by the end of the programme. In every session thereafter (except the last) she sets herself a *proximal goal*, i.e. what she wants to have achieved by the next session. Given the centrality of goals, it is natural to make *goal attainment* a key outcome measure of any coaching intervention (Spence, 2007). After all, what else is coaching for if not to help students achieve their goals? Goal attainment is clearly not the *only* measure that should be considered. But it is an excellent place to start.

How can a school tell whether coaching has helped students to achieve their goals? Consider one simple approach. Despite some shortcomings, versions of this approach have been adopted in many coaching studies (e.g. Grant, 2001; Spence and Grant, 2007; Grant, 2014).

Step 1: Ask the student to record her ultimate goal

In Part III, Zara's ultimate goal was:

> *'To have completed my English coursework by 21 October, having worked on it bit-by-bit each week.'*

Step 2: Obtain a goal attainment score before the coaching programme begins

The student rates how successful she has been in achieving her goal *before the coaching programme begins*. She might do this on a scale from 0 per cent (no success) to 100 per cent (complete attainment of the goal). Before coaching Zara had done very little of her coursework. She might therefore have given herself a goal attainment score of 20 per cent (= not much attainment). This is known as the **pre-test** score.

Step 3: Obtain a goal attainment score after the coaching programme ends

At the end of the programme, the student once again rates the amount of success she has had with regard to her goal. In Part III, we saw that Zara managed to achieve her ultimate goal - she finished her coursework. Let us assume that, by and large, she also succeeded in working on it 'bit-by-bit each week'. She might therefore give herself a **post-test** goal attainment score of 90 per cent (= highly successful).

In a randomised controlled trial, however, we do not consider one student in isolation. Instead we randomly select a number of students and randomly assign them to one of two groups - a *coaching group* and a *control group*. Both groups set ultimate goals and measure attainment before and after the coaching programme. However, *only the coaching group receives coaching*. We calculate mean goal attainment scores for each group *before* and *after* the programme. What would we expect to see if coaching has worked? You may want to think about this before reading on.

Table 19.1 Mean goal attainment scores for the control group and coaching group.

	Goal Attainment Score (PRE-TEST)	*Goal Attainment Score (POST-TEST)*
Control group	25	45
Coaching group	20	75

Table 19.1 presents hypothetical results. The numbers are mean goal attainment scores for the two groups *before* the coaching programme begins (i.e. at *pre-test*) and *after* the programme ends (i.e. at *post-test*).

Notice, first of all, that the coaching group has a higher mean goal attainment score at post-test than the control group (75 compared to 45). Notice too that the coaching group made greater *progress* from pre-test to post-test. Whereas the control group's mean improved by 20 (i.e. from 25 to 45), the coaching group's mean improved by 55 (i.e. from 20 to 75). Students in the coaching group were therefore - on average - more successful in attaining their goals.

Figure 19.1 presents these results graphically. Notice how the height of the bars change for each group. For the control group, there is a moderate increase in height from pre-test to post-test. For the coaching group, however, the height of the bars increases dramatically. This illustrates, once again, that students in the coaching group made (on average) greater progress towards their goals than students in the control group.

If we assume that the experiment has been properly conducted and that the results are *statistically significant*, then we can conclude that coaching helped students to achieve their goals. As we shall see later, we could also calculate an *effect size* to estimate *how large* the effect of coaching actually was. This is probably what stakeholders want to know.

It is important to consider how goal attainment is actually measured in the above approach. Students are asked to estimate for themselves how much success they have had.

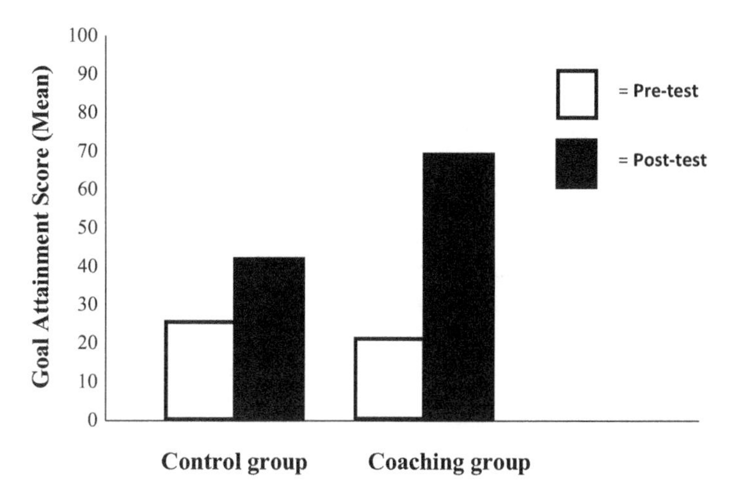

Figure 19.1 Mean scores for the coaching group and control group at pre-test and post-test.

It could therefore be argued that we are really measuring students' *perceptions* of goal attainment rather than 'objective' success (Grant, 2001). One way to overcome this issue is to use a more objective measure of goal attainment (see Spence, 2007).

However, goal attainment should not be a school's sole focus. Of course, we want students to achieve their goals. But presumably we also want them to improve their skills, become more resilient, feel a greater sense of self-efficacy and so on. Schools will therefore be interested in other outcome measures in addition to goal attainment. These might include:

- commitment
- resilience
- perceived self-efficacy
- time management
- satisfaction with school life.

Obviously, there are many other possibilities. Since we have already discussed goal attainment we can now focus on the other variables. Clearly one crucial question is how these things should be measured. 'Commitment', 'resilience', 'perceived self-efficacy' - these are abstract constructs. Fortunately, researchers have constructed psychometric scales to measure them, e.g. the 'Academic Resilience Scale' (Cassidy, 2016) or 'Self-efficacy for Academic achievement' scale (e.g. Zimmerman, Bandura and Martinez-Pons, 1992). Students typically have to fill out self-report questionnaires, many of which can be obtained and used for free. From now on, when we are discussing an abstract construct such as perceived self-efficacy, we shall assume that it is being measured by means of a suitable psychometric instrument, e.g. a tried-and-tested self-efficacy scale (see Bandura, 2006).

Do we really need a control group?

As we have seen, a randomised controlled trial involves a *control group*. You may be wondering, however, whether a control group is necessary. Surely a simpler approach would suffice. For example, suppose a number of students want coaching. Couldn't we just measure their perceived self-efficacy *before* coaching, give them coaching, and then measure their perceived self-efficacy again *after* coaching? And if their scores have improved, surely we can declare success. Unfortunately, things are not so simple, as the following dialogue makes clear:

Head Teacher: 'How did the coaching programme go?'
Senior Leader: 'Great - the students had higher self-efficacy scores at the end than at the beginning.'
Head Teacher: 'Ok, but how do we know that had anything to do with coaching?'
Senior Leader: 'What do you mean?'
Head Teacher: 'Well, perhaps they all just matured. Students develop over time. Maybe their scores would have improved even *without* the coaching.'
Senior Leader: 'Ah, I see what you mean. I guess that's possible.'

Ideally, when we assess the results of an intervention we know what would have happened *without* the intervention. In the dialogue above, the senior leader reports that students had higher self-efficacy scores at the end of coaching than they did at the beginning. However, as the head teacher points out, perhaps they simply matured. Perhaps the improvement in their scores was due not to the coaching but merely to time and experience.

A *control group* allows us to rule out this explanation. If we can compare the results of students who are coached with the results of students who are *not* coached (but who are otherwise treated identically) then we can answer the Head Teacher's objection:

Head Teacher: 'Well, perhaps they all just matured. Students develop over time. Maybe their scores would have improved even *without* the coaching.'
Senior Leader: 'Actually, we're pretty certain they wouldn't have.'
Head Teacher: 'How can you be so sure?'
Senior Leader: 'We used a control group. Half of the students were in the coaching group and half were in the control group. If it was just down to time, then the students in the control group should have improved just as much.'
Head Teacher: 'And they didn't?'
Senior Leader: 'No. Their self-efficacy scores hardly changed.'
Head Teacher: 'So the scores improved considerably for the coaching group but hardly at all for the control group?'
Senior Leader: 'Exactly.'
Head Teacher: 'And the only difference between the groups was the coaching?'
Senior Leader: 'Yes.'
Head Teacher: 'Well I suppose the improvement must have been due to the coaching then.'
Senior Leader: 'That's the conclusion we're drawing.'

You should now be able to see the value of a control group. In theory, the control group tells us what *would* have happened to the intervention group *if it had not received the intervention* (e.g. Hammond and Wellington, 2013). Without this information, it is difficult to know what to make of the results. Many of those writing about coaching evaluation therefore strongly recommend the use of a control group (Carter, 2006; Peterson and Kraiger, 2004; Carter and Peterson, 2016).

A randomised controlled trial: the impact of coaching on students' perceived self-efficacy

We are now in a position to discuss how a randomised controlled trial (RCT) actually unfolds. Several recent commentators have argued that RCTs have a crucial role to play in evidence-based education (e.g. Goldacre, 2013). They are thought to be the most powerful way of establishing that an intervention actually *caused* an improvement (Cohen, Manion and Morrison, 2017). Of course, they are not perfect. But even critics who point out their limitations agree that RCTs have an important place in education (e.g. Morrison, 2001).

Suppose that a school wants coaching to improve students' perceived self-efficacy. The school therefore needs a suitable *self-efficacy scale*, such as Bandura's 'Self-efficacy for Academic Achievement' or 'Self-efficacy for Self-regulated learning' (see Bandura, 2006). Let us assume that the school decides to focus on the latter – self-efficacy for self-regulated learning.[1] Students are then given the appropriate scale in the form of a questionnaire. Box 19.1 provides an example.

Box 19.1 A 'self-efficacy for self-regulated learning' scale – adapted from Bandura (2006).

Read through the tasks below. How *confident* are you that you can do each one? Rate your confidence from 0 to 100, using the following scale:

0 10 20 30 40 50 60 70 80 90 100

0 = I can't do this at all.
10-30 = I'm not (very) confident I can do this.
40-60 = I'm fairly confident I can do this.
70-90 = I'm (very) confident I can do this.
100 = I am certain I can do this.

1 Prepare effectively for tests ____
2 Meet deadlines ____
3 Plan my work for the week ____
4 Find a suitable time and place to study ____
5 Motivate myself to work when I'd rather be doing something else ____

As you can see from Box 19.1 the questionnaire presents a number of learning-related tasks and asks students to indicate how confident they are that they can do each one on a scale from 0 per cent ('I can't do this at all') to 100 per cent ('I have total confidence in my ability to do this'). We shall assume that the students are sixth formers, since the school's coaching programme is currently confined to the sixth form. The school wants to find out (i) whether coaching improves sixth formers[2] perceived self-efficacy, and (ii) if so, by how much?

We can now consider each of the steps in the school's randomised controlled trial. The school has chosen to use a *pre-test-post-test control group design* – see Figure 19.2. It is a good idea to study this diagram before reading on.

Step 1: Take a random sample from the 'population of interest'

In a true randomised controlled trial, the first step is to draw a random sample from the population of interest. This allows the researcher to generalise from the sample to the population. For the sake of argument, let's assume that most of the school's sixth formers are willing to try coaching. However, not all students can enter the programme at once. For

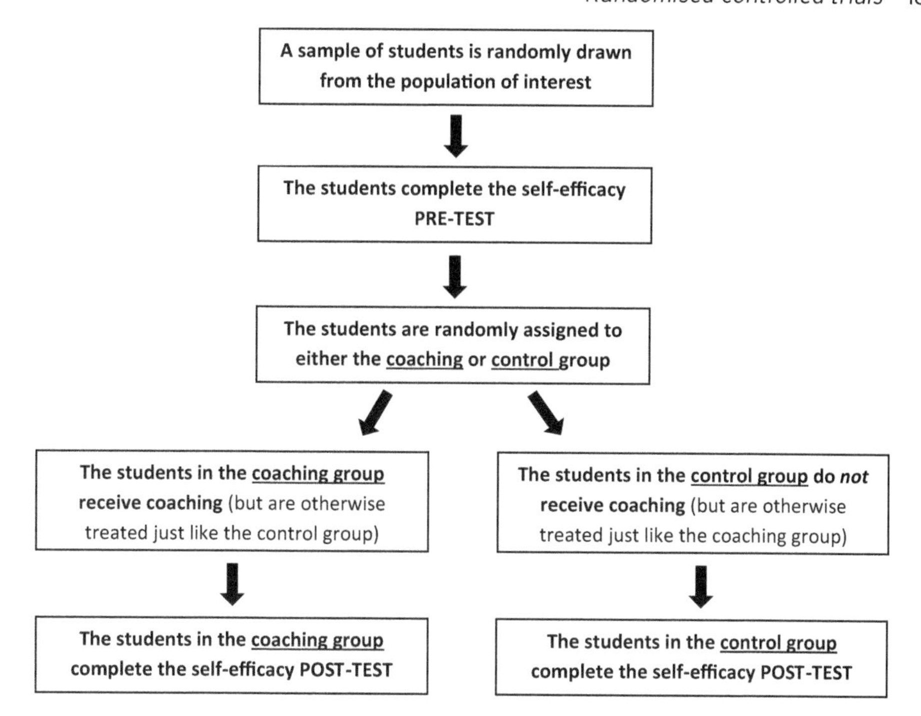

Figure 19.2 A randomised controlled trial using a pre-test post-test control group design.

now, therefore, the school randomly selects 60 sixth formers to participate. As we shall see, however, not all of these students receive coaching immediately.

Step 2: Get all students to complete the self-efficacy pre-test

The next step is to get all 60 students to complete the self-efficacy *pre-test* (see Box 19.1). It is known as a *pre*-test because it takes place before the intervention (i.e. coaching).

Step 3: Randomly assign half the students to the coaching group and half to the control group

The school now[3] randomly assigns half of the students to the *coaching group* and half to the *control group*, thus creating two groups of equal size (30 students in each). This random assignment should help to ensure that the two groups are equivalent at the outset, i.e. that neither group contains a preponderance of, say, highly able or highly confident students. A simple statistical test (known as an 'independent samples t-test') can be used to ensure that there is no statistically significant difference between the groups in terms of self-efficacy pre-test scores.

Step 4: Give coaching to the coaching group but not to the control group

This is the step that sometimes causes concern. Isn't it unfair to deprive half of the students of the coaching? Why should the control group have to miss out? Actually, these concerns are easily allayed. The control group does *not* have to miss out. The school can use a *waiting-list* control group, which means that the students in this group *will* be given coaching but at a later date. In fact, this may be unavoidable. The school may simply not have enough coaches to cater for 60 students at once. Some students will therefore *have* to wait for coaching. In the meantime, why shouldn't they serve as a control group?

Step 5: Get all students to complete the self-efficacy post-test

At the end of the coaching programme, the sixth formers once again complete the same self-efficacy questionnaire. This is called the '*post*-test' since it takes place *after* the intervention. Cohen et al. (2017) point out that the timing of the post-test should be carefully considered. The effects of coaching may not reveal themselves immediately. It may therefore be a good idea for the students to complete more than one post-test. The first could be completed as soon as coaching has finished. The second could be administered a few weeks later to uncover any effects that may have taken longer to emerge and to see whether immediate effects were enduring.

Step 6: Analyse the results

This is the most exciting step. The mean self-efficacy scores of the two groups are now compared. To simplify matters we shall assume that only one post-test has been administered so far. Table 19.2 displays hypothetical results.

As we can see from Table 19.2, the coaching group had a higher post-test self-efficacy mean than the control group (85 compared to 60). In addition, whereas the control group showed only a +5 improvement from pre-test to post-test (from 55 to 60), the *coaching* group's mean improved by +35 (from 50 to 85). These differences may be easier to appreciate when they are presented graphically. See Figure 19.3.

Visual inspection of Figure 19.3 suggests that coaching had an effect. However, statistical analysis is required to confirm this. Researchers generally look for *statistical significance*, i.e. an indication that differences are (probably) *too great to have arisen through chance alone*. But which figures should be compared? For pre-test post-test control group designs more than one analytical approach is possible (e.g. Pituch, Whittaker and Stevens, 2013).

Table 19.2 Means and standard deviations for the control group and coaching group.

	Self-efficacy (Pre-test)	*Self-efficacy (Post-test)*
Control group	**55** (SD = 15.64)	**60** (SD = 13.51)
Coaching group	**50** (SD = 14.50)	**85** (SD = 14.62)

(SD = Standard Deviation)

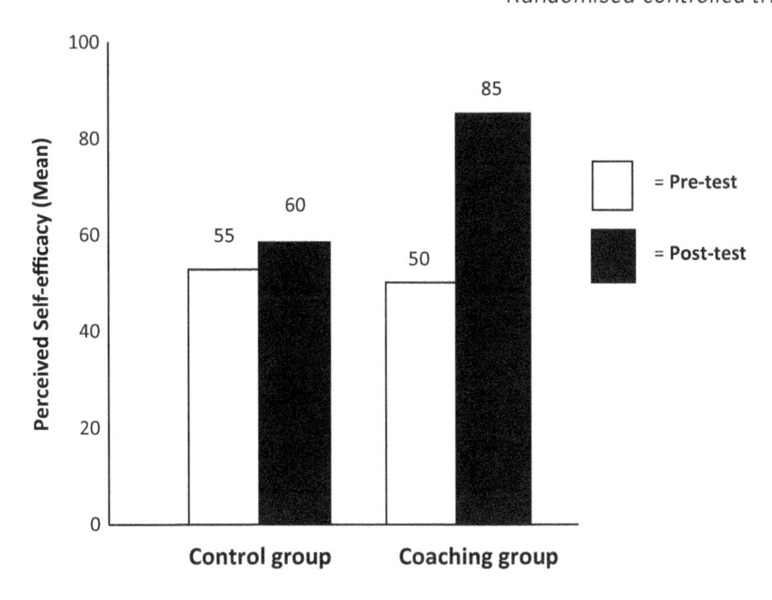

Figure 19.3 Pre-test and post-test means for the control group and coaching group.

The simplest approach would be to compare just the two *post-test means* - *60* for the control group as against *85* for the coaching group - using the 'independent samples t-test' (Cohen *et al.*, 2017). A second approach would be to compare the mean *change* of the two groups from pre-test to post-test: + *5* for the control group as against + *35* for the coaching group (e.g. Pituch *et al.*, 2013). This difference in improvement may seem considerable but we need to know whether it is statistically significant. Finally, some researchers advocate a third approach known as the 'analysis of covariance' (e.g. Dugard and Todman, 1995; Martella *et al.*, 2013). Like the first approach, this compares the two post-test means but it does so whilst taking into account students' scores on the *pre-test*.

So far, we have been talking about statistical significance. If a difference is statistically significant, then the probability of obtaining it *by chance alone* is very small indeed. We therefore conclude that it was (probably) the coaching - rather than chance - that brought it about. Let us assume that the results of the RCT were statistically significant. Further, the only difference between the two groups was that the coaching group received coaching. Given these facts, the school can be confident that coaching did indeed have a positive effect on student's perceived self-efficacy.

Statistical significance is not everything, however. The school will presumably want to know not merely that coaching had an effect but also how *large* that effect was. Fortunately, it is very easy to calculate an *effect size*.[4]

A standard way to calculate an effect size[5] would be as follows:

$$\textbf{Effect size} = \frac{\textbf{Post-test Mean of Coaching Group - Post-test Mean of Control group}}{\textbf{Pooled Pre-test Standard Deviation.}}$$

Table 19.2 provided all of the data required to make this calculation:

- The post-test means were 85 for the coaching group and 60 for the control group.
- The pre-test standard deviations were 14.50 and 15.64 for the coaching and control group respectively. The 'pooled' pre-test standard deviation is simply the average of these, which is 15.07.
- The effect size is therefore simply:

$$\frac{85-60}{15.07} = 1.66$$

As noted in Chapter 3, many researchers use Cohen's (1988) thresholds to give meaning to an effect size. Those thresholds are as follows: 0.2 = small effect, 0.5 = medium effect, and 0.8 = large effect. Cohen says that a 'large' effect (0.8) is equivalent to the mean difference in height between 13- and 18- year-old girls, a difference that is 'grossly perceptible' (Cohen, 1988, p. 27), as secondary school teachers will know. In our example, the school found an effect size of 1.66, which can therefore be considered a large (or even *very* large) effect. The data therefore suggest that coaching had a substantial impact on students' perceived self-efficacy.

Suppose now that the school administers a *second* post-test two months later and finds that the difference between the two groups is more or less the same. That is, students who were in the coaching group *still* have (on average) higher self-efficacy scores than students who were in the control group. This would suggest that the coaching has had a *lasting* effect on students' perceived self-efficacy.

Final thoughts on randomised controlled trials

By now you should be able to appreciate the power of a properly conducted randomised controlled trial. If a school wants or needs hard evidence for the effectiveness of its coaching programme, then an RCT should be considered. Randomised controlled trials are often seen as the 'gold standard' for educational researchers (Cohen *et al.*, 2017). However, they are not without drawbacks (Morrison, 2001). For one thing, they do not tell the whole story. We will often need some sort of *qualitative* data to explain the quantitative findings. For example, if coaching did indeed enhance students' perceived self-efficacy, *how* did it do so? Post-coaching interviews might shed light on this question.

Another issue may be finding enough students to participate. Cohen *et al.* (2017) point out that a sample size of 30 is normally considered to be the *minimum* if researchers want to perform statistical analysis on the data. For some schools, a sample size of 30 may not be realistic.

What should you do if there are not enough students to conduct a randomised controlled trial? And what if you are more interested in the effect of coaching on *individual* students than in its (average) effect on groups? The next chapter suggests an answer - *single-case design*.

Chapter summary

- Randomised controlled trials (RCTs) arguably provide the most reliable evidence for the effectiveness of coaching.
- 'Goal attainment' is a natural outcome measure for any coaching intervention.
- Schools will also be interested in other variables such as commitment, resilience and perceived self-efficacy. In order to measure these things schools will need a suitable psychometric instrument, e.g. a tried-and-tested 'Academic self-efficacy scale.'
- Without a control group, it can be difficult to attribute improvements to coaching. To ensure that all students eventually receive coaching, a school can use a waiting list control group.
- In the pre-test post-test control group design the school randomly selects a sample of students and then randomly assigns those students to either the coaching or control group. All students complete a pre-test before the programme begins and a post-test when the programme ends. Only the students in the coaching group are given coaching. In all other respects, the two groups are treated identically.
- Analysis of results normally involves looking for statistical significance, i.e. an indication that any observed differences are (probably) too large to have arisen through chance alone.
- In addition to testing for statistical significance, schools will want to calculate an effect size. This indicates how much of an effect coaching had.
- Randomised controlled trials are often described as the 'gold standard' for educational researchers. However, they tend to require fairly large samples. An RCT may therefore not always be feasible. A useful alternative is single-case design.

Notes

1 It is important to note that perceived self-efficacy (PSE) is domain-specific. Students may have high PSE in one domain (e.g. their extra-curricular activities) but low PSE in another (e.g. self-regulated learning). From now on in this chapter 'self-efficacy' should be taken to mean 'self-efficacy *for self-regulated learning*'.

2 Actually, this needs to be qualified. Since the population from which the school is sampling is 'sixth formers *who are willing to engage in coaching*', any generalisations can be made *only to that population*. The question the school can answer, therefore, is: 'Does coaching improve perceived self-efficacy in sixth formers *who are willing to engage in coaching*?'

3 Steps 2 and 3 can be reversed (Cohen *et al.*, 2017). In many expositions of the pre-test post-test control group design, the pre-test comes *after* random assignment to groups.

4 There are even free websites that will calculate the effect size for you, e.g. http://www.uccs.edu/~lbecker/

5 Morris (2008) recommends a slightly different effect size formula, in which the numerator would be: [Post-test mean of coaching group - Pre-test mean of coaching group] - [Post-test mean of control group - Pre-test mean of control group]. This approach has some advantages and is equally easy to calculate.

References

Andreanoff, J. (2016). *Coaching and mentoring in higher education: A step-by-step guide to exemplary practice*. London: Palgrave.

Bandura, A. (2006). Guide for constructing self-efficacy scales. In F. Pajares and T. Urdan (eds) *Self-efficacy beliefs of adolescents*. Greenwich, CT: Information Age Publishing.

Carter, A. (2006). Practical Methods for Evaluating Coaching. *IES Research Report No. 430*. Brighton, UK: Institute for Employment Studies.

Carter, A. and Peterson, D.B. (2016). Evaluating Coaching Programs. In J. Passmore (ed.) *Excellence in Coaching* (3rd edn). London: Kogan Page.

Cassidy, S. (2016). The Academic Resilience Scale (ARS-30): A New Multidimensional Construct Measure. *Frontiers in Psychology*, 7, 1787.

Cohen, J. (1988). *Statistical power analysis for the behavioral sciences*. Hillsdale, NJ: Lawrence Erlbaum Associates.

Cohen, L., Manion, L. and Morrison, K. (2017). *Research Methods in Education* (8th edn). New York: Routledge.

Dugard, P. and Todman, J. (1995). Analysis of pre-test post-test control group designs in educational research. *Educational Psychology*, 15, 181–198.

Goldacre, B. (2013). Building Evidence into Education, available at: www.gov.uk/goverment/news/building-evidence-into-education (accessed 13 February 2016).

Grant, A. (2001). Towards a Psychology of coaching. Unpublished PhD thesis, University of Sydney.

Grant, A.M. (2014). The Efficacy of Executive Coaching in Times of Organisational Change. *Journal of Change Management*, 14, 2, 258-280.

Hammond, M. and Wellington, J.J. (2013). *Research methods: The key concepts*. London: Routledge.

Martella, R.C., Nelson, J.R., Morgan, R.L. and Marchand-Martella, N.E. (2013). *Understanding and interpreting educational research*. New York: Guilford.

Morris, S.B. (2008). Estimating effect sizes from pretest-posttest-control group designs. *Organizational Research Methods*, 11, 364-386.

Morrison, K. (2001). Randomised controlled trials for evidence-based education: Some problems in judging what works. *Evaluation and Research in Education*, 15, 2, 69-83.

Peterson, D.B. and Kraiger, K. (2004). A practical guide to evaluating coaching: Translating state-of-the-art techniques to the real world. In J.E. Edwards, J.C. Scott and N.S. Raju (eds), *The human resources program evaluation handbook*. Thousand Oaks, CA: Sage.

Pituch, K.A., Whittaker, T.A. and Stevens, J.P. (2013). *Intermediate statistics: A modern approach* (3rd edn). New York/London: Lawrence Erlbaum Associates.

Spence, G.B. (2007). Gas powered coaching: Goal attainment scaling and its use in coaching research and practice. *International Coaching Psychology Review*, 2, 2, 155–167.

Spence, G.B. and Grant, A.M. (2007). Professional and peer life coaching and the enhancement of goal striving and well-being: An exploratory study. *Journal of Positive Psychology*, *2*, 3, 185–194.

Zimmerman, B.J., Bandura, A. and Martinez-Pons, M. (1992). Self-motivation for academic attainment: The role of self-efficacy beliefs and personal goal setting. *American Educational Research Journal*, 29, 663-676.

20 Other approaches to evaluation

In this chapter

- Single-case design
- The A-B design, multiple baseline design, and changing criterion design
- Using control items instead of a control group
- Qualitative data.

Single-case design - an alternative to RCTs

At the end of the last chapter we said that, for all their power, randomised controlled trials do have some drawbacks. For example, it may difficult for your school to recruit the required number of students. In the hypothetical experiment we described, 30 students were assigned to each of the two groups (i.e. a total of 60 students). But what if you are dealing with a much smaller number of participants?

One option you have is to use *single-case design*. Single-case design - also known as 'single *subject* design' - allows you to evaluate the effect of coaching on a single student or small group of students. Whereas randomised controlled trials can sometimes be difficult to carry out, single-case design 'is a highly feasible method of conducting applied research, as it does not require the use of a control group or randomization of subjects' (Riley-Tillman and Burns, 2009, p. viii).

In this chapter, we cover two fairly well-known single-case designs: the *A-B design* and the *multiple baseline design*. We also briefly consider the *changing criterion design*. After that we explore an approach that involves control *items* rather than a control group. This too can be considered a type of single-case design.

First, let us see how single-case design can be used with a single student. Imagine that a school is providing coaching for one of its sixth formers - Iona. Although Iona understands a fair amount of the subject matter in her courses, she says that she is 'hopeless' at planning her work, arranging a time to study, taking notes, revising for tests and so on. Iona and her coach will therefore be measuring her perceived *self-efficacy for self-regulated learning* - a variable that appeared in the last chapter.

The school will be asking Iona to fill out the 'self-efficacy for self-regulated learning' questionnaire (see Box 19.1 in Chapter 19). However, unlike in an RCT, Iona's perceived self-efficacy will be measured on *multiple* occasions both before and after she begins coaching. Recall that in an RCT, Iona would be part of a coaching (or control) group. The mean scores of the coaching group would be compared with those of the control group. In single-case design there is no control group. Instead students serve *as their own controls.* That is, we compare Iona's perceived self-efficacy during coaching with *her own* perceived self-efficacy *before* coaching. The simplest way to do this is the so-called *A-B design.* From now on the abbreviation 'PSE' stands for 'Perceived Self-efficacy'. 'Perceived self-efficacy', in turn, is an abbreviation for 'perceived self-efficacy *for self-regulated learning*'.

The A-B design

The A-B design involves a *baseline* phase - A - in which Iona is not coached and then an *intervention* phase - B - in which she *is* coached. To evaluate the effectiveness of the coaching, we simply look at what happens to Iona's PSE from A to B. In this design, there are therefore only two major steps:

Step 1: Measure Iona's PSE before coaching begins (A - baseline phase)

Step 2: Measure Iona's PSE once coaching has begun (B - intervention phase)

As already noted, in single-case design we measure the variable on *multiple* occasions in each phase. Imagine that Iona's coaching is due to begin in week 4 of a given term. In weeks 1 to 3 she will complete the PSE questionnaire, once a week. This is the 'A' phase. The data collected in this phase give us a *baseline*, i.e. an estimate of Iona's current sense of self-efficacy against which future data can be compared. The baseline data help us to answer the question: 'What would Iona's PSE be like *if we didn't intervene*?' Let us assume that Iona's PSE is very stable in these first three weeks, i.e. that she has virtually the same low mean score in weeks 1-3. Coaching then begins in week 4. Iona's PSE now continues to be measured once a week until coaching comes to an end. What would we expect to see if coaching 'works'? Well, firstly, does Iona's PSE go up once the coaching phase (B) begins? If so, by how much? And how stable is the improvement? Figure 20.1 presents hypothetical results.

First look at the baseline phase, i.e. weeks 1-3. In this phase Iona's perceived self-efficacy scores were at a low, stable level between 20 and 25. However, when coaching began, her PSE immediately rose to 60 and then remained between 60 and 70 for the next three weeks. What conclusions can we draw from this? There are two questions we can ask:

1 *Was there an improvement after coaching was introduced?*
2 *Was that improvement* ***due*** *to coaching?*

The A-B design allows us to answer the first question. It is clear from Figure 20.1 that Iona's PSE is much higher on average during the coaching phase (B) than it was during the baseline phase (A). Moreover, it is *consistently* higher throughout the coaching phase (i.e. it at no

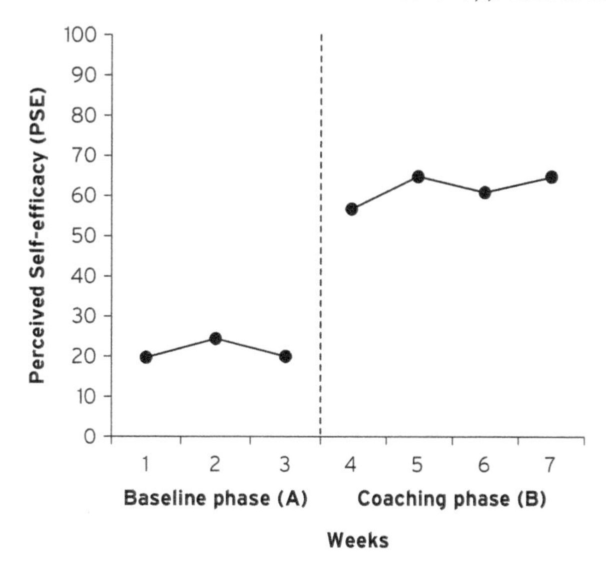

Figure 20.1 The A-B design.

point drops down to baseline levels). The school can therefore confidently assert that there was an improvement in Iona's PSE after coaching was introduced.

What about the second question? Can we be certain that the improvement in Iona's PSE was due to the coaching? Unfortunately, we cannot. The improvement *may* have been due to the coaching but equally it may have been caused by something else. Iona's coaching began in week 4. Imagine that at precisely that point in the term sixth form tutors began to teach 'study skills' in form periods. Perhaps it was these study skills tutorials that led to the improvement in Iona's PSE. The A-B design does not allow us to rule out this explanation.

You may not see this as a problem. So as long as things improve when coaching is introduced, you may not care whether that improvement can confidently be attributed to the coaching. As Riley-Tillman and Burns (2009, p. 24) point out: 'Causal statements are critical for the researcher, but may or may not be essential for the practitioner.' On the other hand, your school (or stakeholders) may be more demanding. Perhaps you are required to show that it was coaching that made the difference. Fortunately, there are more advanced single-case designs that can help you to do this.

The multiple baseline design

Iona is not the only sixth former receiving coaching. Consider two other students - Mary and Charis. Like Iona, Mary and Charis have low perceived self-efficacy. They have very little confidence in their ability to manage their time, plan their work etc. They too are therefore given coaching. To evaluate effectiveness the school will be using not the simple A-B design but a *multiple baseline design*. The multiple-baseline design is essentially a series of staggered A-B designs. Iona, Mary and Charis will all (eventually) receive coaching but they will not all start at the same time. Instead there will be a *time lag* between introductions of the intervention. The importance of this will become clear when we consider results. Have a look at Figure 20.2.

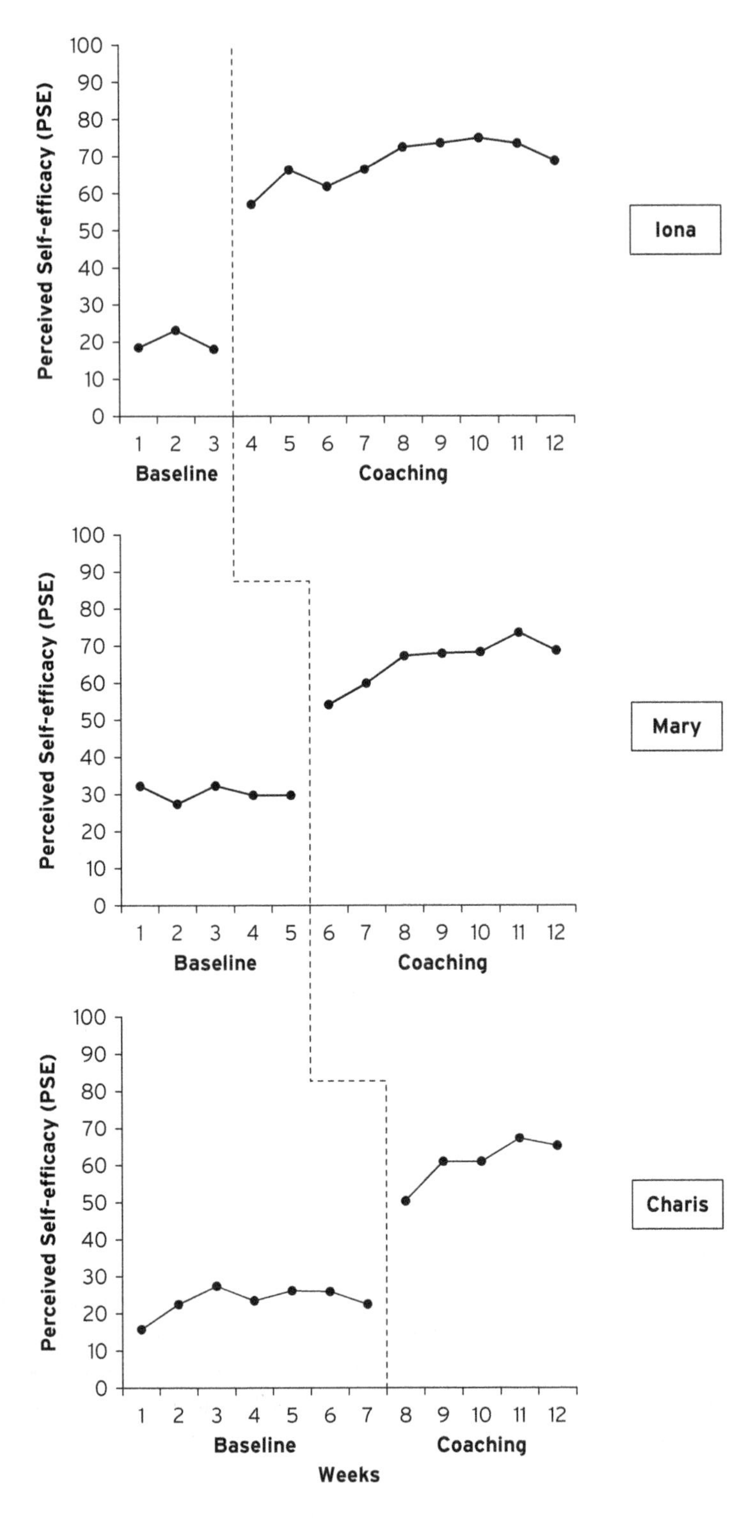

Figure 20.2 Multiple baseline design (across participants)

Figure 20.2 displays the results for Iona, Mary and Charis. Notice, first of all, that for each of the three students PSE improves as soon as coaching is introduced. But now consider the crucial point in the multiple baseline design. When coaching is introduced for Iona *her* PSE improves but *there is no improvement for Mary or Charis*, both of whom are still in their baseline phases. And when coaching is introduced for Mary, *her* PSE improves but there is *no improvement for Charis*, who is still in her baseline phase. This is exactly what we would expect to see if coaching is causing the improvements. We can explain this a little further.

As we have said, multiple baseline designs involve a *time lag*. When student 1 - Iona - starts coaching, students 2 and 3 - Mary and Charis - are still in their baseline phase. And when student 2 - Mary - starts coaching, student 3 - Charis - is still in her baseline phase. This time lag allows us to 'catch' external variables that might be responsible for a student's improvement (Riley-Tillman and Burns, 2009). Recall the alternative explanation for Iona's improvement, i.e. that her PSE improved *not* because of coaching but because of the 'study skills' tutorials that were provided in form periods. Let's see how the multiple baseline design allows us to rule this out:

Senior Leader: 'It looks like coaching has improved Iona's perceived self-efficacy.'

Head Teacher: 'What makes you say that?'

Senior Leader: 'Well as you can see from the graph *(pointing to the top of Figure 20.2)* Iona's PSE goes up as soon as she starts coaching.'

Head Teacher: 'Yes, but that was in week 4. That's when we started giving the girls study skills in form periods. Maybe it was the form periods that caused the improvement.'

Senior Leader: 'Actually, that's unlikely. If it was the form periods that caused the improvement, then Mary's and Charis' PSE should have gone up as well.'

Head Teacher: 'What makes you say that?'

Senior Leader: 'Well Mary and Charis were in form periods too. They also got the study skills training from week 4.'

Head Teacher: 'And their PSE didn't go up?'

Senior Leader: 'No, not until they started coaching. If you look at their graphs *(pointing to the middle and bottom of Figure 20.2)* you can see that nothing happens to Mary's PSE when Iona's goes up in week 4. And at that point nothing happens to Charis' PSE either.'

Head Teacher: 'I see.'

Senior Leader: 'In fact, Iona's PSE only starts to improve in week 6, which is when she started coaching. It's the same for Charis. Her PSE doesn't start to improve until week 8, which is when *she* started coaching.'

Head Teacher: 'So their PSE improves *only when they start coaching*?'

Senior Leader: 'Exactly.'

Head Teacher: 'I suppose it must be the coaching that's causing the improvement.'

Senior Leader: 'That's the conclusion we're drawing.'

You should now be able to appreciate the underlying logic of the multiple baseline design. To consolidate your understanding, you may wish to have another look at Figure 20.2. Note that each student's PSE improves when and only when coaching is introduced *for that student*. This very much suggests that it is the coaching that is causing the improvement.

Remember the two questions we asked before:

1 *Was there an improvement after coaching was introduced?*
2 *Was that improvement* ***due*** *to the coaching?*

With the simple A-B design only the first question could be answered. The multiple baseline design also allows us to answer this question. It is clear from Figure 20.2 that, as soon as coaching is introduced for a student, PSE improves. However, the multiple baseline design allows us to address the second question as well. Although we cannot be *certain* that the improvements were due to coaching, the results in Figure 20.2 are strong evidence for that conclusion. PSE improves when coaching is introduced. Otherwise it does not improve.

The changing criterion design

The A-B design and the multiple baseline design are not the only examples of single-case design. Another useful approach is the *changing criterion design*. Imagine a coachee whose weekly proximal goals become more and more challenging. Her proximal goal for weeks 1-2 is to submit at least 50 per cent of her work on time. For weeks 3-4 it is to submit at least 75 per cent on time. Finally, for weeks 5-6 it is to submit 100 per cent of her work on time. This is what we mean by 'changing criterion.'

Now imagine that in weeks 1-2 she does indeed submit 50 per cent of her work on time (but no more). In weeks 3-4 she manages to submit approximately 75 per cent (but no more). And in weeks 5-6, she succeeds in submitting 100 per cent on time. In other words, every time she sets a new goal in coaching she manages to increase her percentage. However, the percentage does not increase *until* she sets a coaching goal. This would very much suggest that coaching has been effective. As Behar and Borkovec (2003 p. 235) point out: 'If the behaviour changes as the criterion changes, then it is likely that the intervention and not some extraneous variable caused the change.' For more on the changing criterion design, see Richards, Taylor and Ramasamy (2014).

Using control items instead of control groups

The last quantitative approach we cover in this chapter has been given various names, including the 'Internal Referencing Strategy' (Haccoun and Hamtiaux, 1994) and the 'Nonequivalent dependent variable design' (Shadish, Cook and Campbell, 2002). Peterson (1993b)[1] used this approach to evaluate coaching in an organisational setting. The key feature is the use of control **items** rather than a control **group**. The reason for including this approach in the present chapter is that it is actually a variant of the multiple baseline design, which we have already discussed (Haccoun and Hamtiaux, 1994).

Have a look at Table 20.1. This is a form filled out by a student - Nancy - before coaching begins (i.e. a 'pre-test'). Nancy's *coaching objectives* are in bold. The so-called 'control

Table 20.1 Nancy's ratings before coaching (pre-test)

		Current Confidence Level
1	**Completing assignments by deadlines**	**10%**
2	Structuring and formatting essays	30%
3	**Preparing effectively for tests**	**20%**
4	Using the internet for research	10%
5	**Finding a suitable time and place for work**	**30%**
6	Making presentations in class	20%

items' are in normal font. 'Current confidence level' effectively means 'perceived self-efficacy'. As before, the student will be rating her confidence on a scale from 0 to 100.

The ratings below reflect Nancy's confidence in each area *before she has received coaching.* First consider the *coaching objectives* in bold - completing assignments by deadlines, preparing effectively for tests, and finding a suitable time and place for work. These are things that Nancy is going to cover in coaching. If coaching is effective we should expect Nancy's 'current confidence level' on these items to improve from pre-test to post-test.

Now consider the control items in normal font - structuring and formatting essays, using the internet for research, and making presentations in class. We shall assume that these are all important tasks for Nancy. However, they are *not part of her coaching programme.* That is, they feature neither in her ultimate goal nor in any of her proximal goals. To be clear, Nancy *could* have chosen to work on these areas (they are, after all, perfectly reasonable coaching objectives). However, they were, as a matter of fact, not covered in the programme. Nancy's 'current confidence level' for these items should therefore *not show much improvement over the course of coaching.* Put differently, since the *coaching objectives* are targeted in coaching whereas the control items are not, Nancy's ratings should improve more for the former than they do for the latter.

Table 20.2 displays Nancy's effectiveness ratings *after* coaching has ended, i.e. at post-test. Once again, coaching objectives are in bold:

Table 20.2 Nancy's ratings after coaching (post-test)

		Current Confidence Level
1	**Completing assignments by deadlines**	**60%**
2	Structuring and formatting essays	30%
3	**Preparing effectively for tests**	**50%**
4	Using the internet for research	20%
5	**Finding a suitable time and place for work**	**70%**
6	Making presentations in class	10%

If you compare Table 20.2 with Table 20.1, you will see that there has not been much change in Nancy's scores for the control items. On the other hand, the scores for her coaching objectives have improved markedly. Table 20.3 - illustrating all of Nancy's scores - should help to make this clear:

Table 20.3 Nancy's pre-test and post-test ratings on coaching objectives and control items.

	Pre-test Rating	Post-test Rating	Pre-to-post Change
Coaching objectives	10%	60%	+50
	20%	50%	+30
	30%	70%	+40
	Mean = **20**	Mean = **60**	Mean = +**40**
Control items	30%	30%	0
	10%	20%	+10
	20%	10%	–10
	Mean: **20**	Mean: **20**	Mean = **0**

As you can see from Table 20.3, the pre-test mean for Nancy's *coaching objectives* was 20 per cent whilst the post-test mean was 60 per cent - a mean improvement of + 40. On the other hand, there was *no overall mean change* for the control items. This pattern of results suggests that coaching was effective.

So far, we have been considering just one student - Nancy. But perhaps Nancy's results were a one-off. Researchers using this approach therefore apply it not just to one person but to *groups* of people. Imagine several other students, also involved in coaching. To keep things simple for now, suppose that their coaching objectives and control items are the same as Nancy's. These other students will therefore complete exactly the same pre-test and post-test forms, rating their confidence both before and after coaching. The evaluator can then use the data from all of these students. Figure 20.3 displays hypothetical results.

If you look at the height of the bars in Figure 20.3, you will see that the mean for *coaching objectives* improves dramatically from pre-test to post-test. On the other hand, the

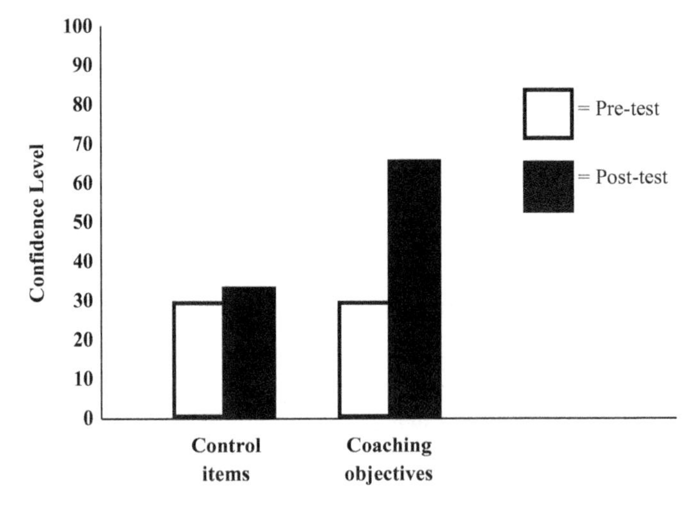

Figure 20.3 Mean scores for control items and coaching objectives at pre-test and post-test

improvement on control items appears negligible. This is exactly what we would expect if coaching was effective. Once again, a hypothetical dialogue may be helpful:

Senior Leader: 'I think the coaching was a success.'
Head Teacher: 'What makes you say that?'
Senior Leader: 'Look at the effectiveness ratings. For coaching objectives, there was a big improvement from pre-test to post-test. . .'
Head Teacher: *(interrupting)* 'What makes you think that had anything to do with coaching? Maybe it was just natural improvement. Students mature.'
Senior Leader: 'That's actually quite unlikely.'
Head Teacher: 'What do you mean?'
Senior Leader: 'Well if it was just a case of maturing, then students' control item scores should have improved just as much.'
Head Teacher: 'And they didn't?'
Senior Leader: 'No, they didn't. On the whole, there was hardly any improvement from pre-test to post-test.'
Head Teacher: 'So the coaching objectives improved more than the control items?'
Senior Leader: 'Yes, much more.'
Head Teacher: 'Well, I suppose coaching must have had an effect then.'

The logic of the senior leader's argument should be clear. Consider the alternative explanation offered by the head teacher, namely that students simply 'matured'. If that were truly the case, then we should expect to see an improvement on students' *control items* as well as their coaching objectives - or did the 'maturation' miraculously affect only the areas in which students were coached? That seems more than a little fortuitous. It is much more reasonable to suppose that coaching caused the improvement.

Figure 20.3 may have reminded you of the graphs in the previous chapter. This is no coincidence. In the last chapter, we were contrasting the performance of a *coaching group* with the performance of a *control group*. Here we are contrasting performance on *coaching objectives* with performance on *control items*. The logic is much the same in the two cases. If coaching is making a difference, then the group (or items) exposed to coaching should improve but the group (or items) *not* exposed to coaching should not show the same improvement (Peterson, 1993a, 1993b).

What about *statistical significance*? Couldn't the pattern of results in Figure 20.3 have arisen through chance alone? In the last chapter, we said that a school could use a statistical test to compare the improvement of the coaching group with that of the control group. The same sort of approach can be used here. That is, a statistical test can be used to compare improvement on coaching objectives with improvement on coaching items (Haccoun and Hamtiaux, 1994; Peterson, 1993b). If there is a greater improvement on the coaching objectives than on the control items and if the difference is *statistically significant*, then we can infer that coaching was effective. An effect size can also be calculated to quantify the size of the difference.

In one sense, this strategy has a major advantage over randomised controlled trials - there is no need to create a control group. All students can start coaching at the same time. The basis for comparison will be control *items* rather than a control *group*. For many schools, this may be more practical or appealing.

That brings us to the end of our survey of quantitative approaches to evaluation. We now conclude this chapter by considering *qualitative* data.

Qualitative data

So far in Part VI, we have concerned ourselves with quantitative approaches to evaluation, i.e. randomised controlled trials and single-case design. As powerful as these are, you may feel that something is missing. Percentages, mean scores and effect sizes may be extremely informative. But what about students' *opinions*?

Qualitative approaches to evaluation usually involve words rather than numbers. For example, a school might arrange short *interviews* with students at the end of coaching. Or it could organise *focus groups* comprising recent coachees. Perhaps most simply, students could be asked to complete *qualitative surveys* or *questionnaires* at the end of coaching. Simple qualitative surveys 'consist of a series of open-ended questions about a topic, and participants type or hand-write their responses to each question' (Braun and Clarke, 2013, p. 135). A very basic survey might include these questions:

1 *What did you get out of coaching?*
2 *What was most helpful about coaching?*
3 *What, if anything, would you change about coaching?*

The coachee could be given a hard copy of the survey at the end of coaching and asked to complete and return it by a certain date. Alternatively, it could be emailed to students or set up online using a service such as *SurveyMonkey*. For the pros and cons of each of these approaches see Braun and Clarke (2013). In my own practice, I normally email coachees a copy of the questionnaire I would like them to complete.

I would like to end this book with an extract from a post-coaching questionnaire. The student in question was a sixth former who sought coaching because she had been struggling to manage her time. Although proper evaluation[2] would involve *analysing* her comments, in this case I would prefer to let them speak for themselves. After all, coaching is ultimately about the coachee not the coach. In my view, therefore, it is only right that the last words in this book should belong to a student:

> *I have managed to achieve some things due to these coaching sessions which I would not have thought I could do before (however small they were). It has given me a new confidence and outlook on approaching organisation and time-management when faced with a mountain of work - skills which I had struggled with throughout my school career. I feel much more in control of my work and workload and have discovered I am able to do far more than I had given myself credit for!*
>
> *Much of coaching was self-directed allowing the advice to be tailored to you as an individual rather than the generic tips we hear so often. Also the weekly meetings*

created a sense of accountability and consistency, which motivated me personally to stick to my objectives and tasks. As well as this, it made me approach time-management and procrastination with a new mindset that has greatly helped me.

Coaching has been tremendously useful and I have developed many skills and techniques which I am sure I shall continue to use well into the rest of sixth form, university and beyond.

Chapter summary

- Single-case design (SCD) allows you to evaluate the impact of coaching on a single student or small group of students.
- In SCD, there is no control group. Students act as their own controls. The variable of interest (e.g. perceived self-efficacy) is measured repeatedly in a baseline phase and an intervention phase. Results are displayed in a line graph.
- The A-B design can show whether a student improves once she starts coaching. However, it cannot prove that the coaching caused the improvement. The multiple baseline design *can* provide evidence of a causal relationship.
- The changing criterion design involves steadily increasing the amount expected of the student. If she makes an improvement when (and only when) the criterion changes in coaching, this suggests that the intervention (i.e. coaching) was effective.
- Another approach involves using control items rather than a control group. If students improve more on coaching objectives than on control items (and if the difference is statistically significant), we infer that coaching was effective.
- Qualitative data can be collected by means of an interview, focus group or qualitative questionnaire. Such data can shed considerable light on students' experience of coaching.

Notes

1 Peterson's approach is a little more sophisticated than the one outlined here. For one thing, coachees not only rate themselves but also receive ratings from other individuals, e.g. their line managers. In a school setting, ratings could be supplied not just by the student but also by her teachers and coach. This might provide a more rounded and accurate view of her progress. For more details see Peterson (1993a, 1993b).

2 For an overview of qualitative methods of evaluation see Cohen, Manion and Morrison (2017).

References

Behar, E.S. and Borkovec, T.D. (2003). Psychotherapy outcome research. In J.A. Schinka and W.F. Velicer (eds), *Handbook of psychology: Research methods in psychology*, vol. 2. Hoboken, NJ: John Wiley & Sons.

Braun, V. and Clarke, V. (2013). *Successful Qualitative Research: A Practical Guide for Beginners*. London: Sage.

Cohen, L., Manion, L. and Morrison, K. (2017). *Research Methods in Education* (8th edn). New York: Routledge.

Haccoun, R.R. and Hamtiaux, T. (1994). Optimizing knowledge tests for inferring learning acquisition levels in single group training effectiveness designs: The internal referencing strategy. *Personnel Psychology*, 47, 3, 593–604.

Peterson, D.B. (1993a). Measuring change: A psychometric approach to evaluating individual coaching outcomes. Paper Presented at the annual conference of the Society for Industrial and Organizational Psychology, San Francisco.

Peterson, D.B. (1993b). Skill learning and behavior change in an individually tailored management coaching program. Unpublished doctoral dissertation, University of Minnesota, Minneapolis.

Richards, S.B., Taylor, R.L. and Ramasamy, R. (2014). *Single subject research: Applications in educational and clinical settings* (2nd ed.). Belmont, CA: Wadsworth.

Riley-Tillman, T.C. and Burns, M.K. (2009). *Evaluating educational interventions: Single-case design for measuring response to intervention*. New York: Guilford Press.

Shadish, W.R., Cook, T.D. and Campbell, D.T. (2002). *Experimental and quasi-experimental designs for generalized causal inference*. Boston: Houghton Mifflin.

Appendix A

Generating options

In the 'Options' phase of GROW, the student is encouraged to think of different ways to achieve her goal. As we saw in Chapter 11, the most basic questions the coach can ask are: *'How could you achieve your goal?'* and *'What else?'* However, the student will sometimes say 'I don't know'. The following is a list of additional approaches the coach can take to help the student generate options:

Approach 1 – past successes

Step 1: 'When was the last time you achieved a similar goal?'

Step 2: 'What did you do *then*?'

The great merit of this approach is that it encourages the student to draw on her own experience. Reflecting on past successes may not only illuminate the present but also enhance the student's sense of self-efficacy.

Approach 2 – the student's 'best self'

Step 1: 'What are you like *at your best?'*

Step 2: 'What would you do when you're *like that*?'

The first question here helps the student to imagine her 'best self'. She might say that at her best she is 'energetic' or that she 'doesn't give up'. The coach then asks her how she would go about achieving her goal *in that state*.

Approach 3 – advising her best friend

Step 1: 'Suppose that your best friend were in your position.'

Step 2: 'What would you advise *him/her* to do?'

When we are considering our own predicament we often can't see the wood for the trees. This approach enables the student to step out of her own shoes and view her challenge from an external perspective. The 'solution' then often becomes apparent.

Approach 4 – learning from others

Step 1: 'Who do you know who's *achieved this goal*?'

Step 2: 'What did you see *him/her* do?'

In coaching the student is normally encouraged to draw on her *own* experience. However, there will be times when she can learn from others. She may find that she can accelerate her progress by taking a leaf out of their book.

Approach 5 - acting out of necessity

Step 1: 'Imagine you *had* to achieve this goal (or else you'd. . .)'

Step 2: 'What would you do then?'

When people have no choice but to do something, they generally find a way to do it. The coach can complete Step 1 by spelling out a scenario the student wants to avoid, e.g. '*or else you'd lose all your school privileges*'. This often triggers ideas when a 'gentler' approach has failed.

Appendix B

Performance goals and learning goals

Performance and outcome goals

In most coaching programmes coachees set *performance* or *outcome* goals (Grant, 2006). In Part III Zara's ultimate goal was: *'To have completed my English coursework by 21 October, having worked on it bit-by-bit each week.'* This is a performance goal. An outcome goal might be: *'To have achieved an A on my English coursework.'* A vast body of research confirms the effectiveness of performance and outcome goals (Locke and Latham, 1990, 2013). However, there are times when a *learning* goal is more appropriate (Seijts, Latham and Woodwark, 2013). Being overly focused on the outcome can sometimes negatively affect performance.

When should learning goals be set?

Far fewer studies have been conducted on learning goals than performance goals (Seijts *et al.*, 2013). However research is beginning to give us a fairly clear picture of the circumstances in which learning goals should be set. The most important points are as follows:

1 **Students should set learning goals rather than performance goals if they currently *lack the ability, knowledge or skills* to achieve the performance goals.**
When students are faced with new or complex tasks for which they are inadequately equipped they perform better with learning goals than with performance goals (Winters and Latham, 1996; Seijts and Latham, 2001). If a student struggles to write *any* sort of essay, then a goal such as *'To get an A on my English coursework'* will probably not do her much good. She would be better off with a learning goal that helps her to develop her essay-writing skills. A good example in this case might be: *'To have discovered 3 practical ways to make it easier to write essays.'*

2 **Students should think about setting learning goals rather than performance goals if they *see the latter as a threat.***
Challenging performance goals may lead to increased stress. A little extra stress may be a good thing. However, if students begin to see their goals as a *threat*, if they are worried about exposing their 'inadequacies', then they may become overly anxious and perform poorly as a result (Latham, Seijts and Slocum, 2016). In cases such as this a learning goal can be beneficial (Seijts *et al.*, 2013). For example, if a student feels intimidated or threatened by the performance goal - *'To have completed at least 70 per cent of my trigonometry booklet'* then she could replace it with a learning goal, e.g. *'To have learnt how to use the three trigonometric ratios.'*

3 **Students should think about setting learning goals rather than performance goals if they are likely to *respond badly to negative performance feedback.***
Imagine that a highly conscientious student is considering the following performance goal: 'To score at least 80 per cent on Maths tests this term.' Suppose further that finding out that she has scored *less* than 80 per cent would leave her feeling tense, anxious or frustrated ('Oh no, I'm underperforming! What will people think?'). In this case, it would probably be better for her to set a learning goal than a performance goal. Learning goals can act as a 'buffer' against negative performance feedback (Cianci, Klein and Seijts, 2010). People who set learning goals are more likely to see setbacks as part of the learning process. (Latham *et al.*, 2016).

When should performance goals be set?

For all their merits, learning goals are not always the right choice. Sometimes performance goals can be more effective. The key point is this:

Students should think about setting *performance* goals if they *already have the knowledge, skills and ability to achieve them.*

Recall that one of the main reasons for setting a learning goal is to help the student acquire the knowledge and skills she needs to achieve a desired outcome. However, if she already *has* the required knowledge and skills then the learning goal is in a way redundant. In fact, research shows that performance actually *suffers* when people who have the ability to achieve a performance goal set a learning goal instead (Locke and Latham, 2009; Winters and Latham, 1996). This is not difficult to explain. For people who already have the necessary knowledge and skills a learning goal 'needlessly focuses attention on rediscovering the task-relevant strategies' (Seijts *et al.*, 2013). Learning goals do a wonderful job of helping students acquire knowledge, but 'knowledge is not always applied unless *performance* goals are set' (Locke and Latham, 2009, p. 20, italics added).

Of course, students who have what it takes to achieve a performance goal will still need to make sure that they do not feel *threatened* by that goal. They must also be able to handle negative performance feedback. This is where a coach can be influential: *'Ok, so you scored lower than you would have liked. What did you* ***learn*** *that could help you in future?'*

Additional points about learning goals and performance goals

A few other points about learning and performance goals may be of interest:

i **Students of lower cognitive ability benefit more from learning goals than students of higher cognitive ability** (Latham, Seijts and Crim, 2008). Whereas students of higher cognitive ability may *automatically* focus their attention on discovering appropriate strategies, students of lower cognitive ability may need a learning goal that explicitly tells them to do so (*'To discover 3 effective strategies to. . .'*).

ii **Students will have their own preferences or 'goal orientations'** (Dweck and Leggett, 1988; Morisano, 2013). As all teachers know, students differ in motivation and personality. Research also shows that whilst some students may be naturally inclined to pursue a performance goal, others may display more of a learning orientation and yet others may adopt goals that combine both learning and performance dimensions (Harackiewicz *et al.*, 1997).

iii **Learning goals are especially effective with students who have a learning goal orientation**. As noted above, students differ in their goal orientations. Experiments suggest that the positive effect of a learning goal is actually enhanced if the student has a learning goal *orientation* (Seijts *et al.*, 2004). However, coaches should remember that even students with a performance orientation can and do benefit from learning goals. As Latham and his colleagues note, 'setting a learning goal for tasks requiring knowledge acquisition is effective for everyone' (Latham *et al.*, 2016).

iv **Learning goals and performance goals can be combined in the same coaching programme**. As already noted, most coaching programmes have traditionally focused on performance (or outcome) goals. But there is no reason why a programme focused on performance cannot feature learning goals as well.

Research has not yet made it clear whether performance goals should always come *after* learning goals or whether they should be set at the same time (Seijts *et al.*, 2013). Some evidence suggests it can be effective to have a learning and performance goal *at the same time on the same task* (Masuda, Locke and Williams, 2015). More experienced coaches may want to experiment with this approach. However, those who are new to coaching should help students set one type of goal at a time. For example, a student's first proximal goal might be to discover the most effective way of structuring her coursework (a learning goal). Her second proximal goal might then be to write the introduction and body (a performance goal).

References

Cianci, A.M., Klein, H.J. and Seijts, G. (2010). The Effect of Negative Feedback on Tension and Subsequent Performance: The Main and Interactive Effects of Goal Content and Conscientiousness. *Journal of Applied Psychology*, 95, 618-630.

Dweck, C. and Leggett, E. (1988). A social-cognitive approach to motivation and personality. *Psychological Review*, 95, 256-273.

Grant, A. (2006). An integrative goal-focused approach to executive coaching. In D.R. Stober and A.M. Grant (eds), *Evidence based coaching handbook: Putting best practices to work for your clients*. Hoboken, NJ: John Wiley & Sons.

Harackiewicz, J.M., Barron, K.E., Carter, S.M., Lehto, A.T. and Elliot, A.J. (1997). Predictors and consequences of achievement goals in the college classroom: Maintaining interest and making the grade. *Journal of Personality and Social Psychology*, 73, 1284-1295.

Latham, G.P. and Seijts, G. (2016). Similarities and Differences among Performance, Behavioral and Learning Goals. *Journal of Leadership and Organizational Studies*, 23(3), 225-233.

Latham, G.P., Seijts, G.H. and Crim, D. (2008). The effects of learning goal difficulty level and cognitive ability on strategy development and performance. *Canadian Journal of Behavioural Sciences*, 40, 220-229.

Latham, G., Seijts, G. and Slocum, J. (2016). The goal setting and goal orientation labyrinth: Effective ways for increasing employee performance. *Organizational Dynamics*, 45, 271-277.

Locke, E.A. and Latham, G.P. (1990). *A theory of goal setting and task performance*. Englewood Cliffs, NJ: Prentice Hall.

Locke, E. and Latham, G. (2013). *New Developments in Goal Setting and Task Performance*. New York: Routledge.

Locke, E.A. and Latham, G.P. (2009). Has Goal Setting Gone Wild, or Have Its Attackers Abandoned Good Scholarship? *Academy of Management Perspectives*, 23, 1, 17–23.

Masuda, A., Locke, E.A. and Williams, K.J. (2015). The effects of simultaneous learning and performance goals on performance: An inductive exploration. *Journal of Cognitive Psychology*, 27, 32–52.

Morisano, D. (2013). Goal setting in the academic arena. In E.A. Locke and G.P. Latham (eds), *New developments in goal and task performance*. New York: Routledge.

Seijts, G.H. and Latham, G.P. (2001). The effect of learning, outcome, and proximal goals on a moderately complex task. *Journal of Organizational Behavior*, 22, 291–307.

Seijts, G.H., Latham, G.P., Tasa, K. and Latham, B.W. (2004). Goal setting and goal orientation: An integration of two different yet related literatures. *Academy of Management Journal*, 47, 227–239.

Seijts, G.H., Latham, G.P. and M. Woodwark (2013). Learning goals: A qualitative and quantitative review. In E.A. Locke and G.P. Latham (eds), *New developments in goal setting and task performance*. New York: Routledge.

Winters, D. and Latham, G. (1996). The effect of learning versus outcome goals on a simple versus a complex task. *Group and Organization Management*, 21, 236–250.

Appendix C

Student's coaching form

If I *don't* work for my goal (costs)	**When I *do* work for my goal. . .** (benefits)

ULTIMATE GOAL

↑

THIS WEEK'S GOAL

↑

ACTION PLAN

	Time and date	**Action**	**Place**
1	When it is	Then I will	In ....
2	When it is	Then I will	In ....
3	When it is	Then I will	In ....
4	When it is	Then I will	In ....

I confirm that I will carry out these action-steps before our next session:

Signature: ________________________________

Appendix D

Coaching Contract

What coaching is

1 Coaching is a *non-directive, collaborative* process designed to *help you achieve your goals.*

2 Coaching is *non-directive* in the sense that your coach will never *tell* you what to do. Instead he will listen, ask questions and help you to *make your own decisions.*

3 Coaching is *collaborative* in the sense that your coach will work *with* you as you try to achieve your goals. He will help you to generate ideas, identify resources and overcome obstacles. Ultimately, however, you and you alone are responsible for your performance.

4 At the beginning of coaching, your coach will help you to set your *ultimate goal*, which is what you want to achieve *by the end of coaching.* At the beginning of each session you will then set *a smaller weekly goal*, which is what you want to achieve *by the next session.* Your coach will help you to develop plans to achieve your goals.

5 Coaching is *not counselling or therapy.* The purpose of counselling/therapy is to reduce emotional distress. The purpose of coaching is to help you improve your performance or achieve practical goals. As you work towards your goals it is normal to experience negative emotions, e.g. dejection. However, if you find that you are experiencing significant emotional distress (e.g. you feel overly anxious or depressed), then it is a good idea to contact the school counsellor.

6 The success of coaching depends on what you do *between sessions.* The sessions themselves will not lead to progress. You will need to *take action* each week.

Coaching sessions: practical details

1 Coaching sessions will take place on ______________________ at _____________ in __________________.

2 Coaching sessions will last approximately _______ mins.

3 The first session will take place on ______________. The last session will take place on ___________________.

4 There will be _____ sessions in total.

What your coach can expect from you

1 You will arrive for sessions *on time* (except in cases of emergency). If you cannot make a session, you will notify your coach *at least 48 hours in advance* (except in cases of emergency).

2 During the session, you will fill out your own *Coaching Form.* This includes *(a) your weekly goal* and *(b) the steps you will take* to achieve it (i.e. your action-plan).

3 Once you have created your action-plan, you will do your best to carry it out. Your coach will not and cannot *force* you carry it out. But it is up to you to make a genuine effort.
4 You will let your coach know what you find most (and least) helpful. This will enable him/her to tailor the coaching to suit your needs.

What you can expect from your coach

1 Your coach will arrive for coaching sessions *on time* (except in cases of emergency). If (s)he cannot make a session, (s)he will notify you *at least 48 hours in advance* (except in cases of emergency).
2 Your coach will not judge or criticise you at any point in coaching.
3 Your coach will be focused entirely on you and your goal. His/her only agenda will be to help you make progress.
4 At times - with your permission - your coach may offer suggestions. You are entirely free to ignore these if you do not consider them helpful.
5 Your coach may - with your permission - take notes during the session. You are free to see these notes whenever you wish. Indeed, you and your coach may often create them together.
6 If you are having difficulties between sessions, you may email your coach. (S)he will reply as soon as (s)he can. However an immediate response may not be possible.
7 In normal circumstances, what you discuss in coaching will not be shared with others. However, there are certain situations in which your coach is morally and legally obliged to pass on information (for example, if there is a safeguarding concern).

Coach and coachee must abide by the above terms throughout the programme. If either party fails to do so, coaching may have to come to an end.

Coach signature: ______________________________

Coachee signature: ______________________________

Appendix E

From PITS to PETs

At times our own *thinking* can make it harder to achieve our goals. If you are feeling frustrated, stuck, or pessimistic about your goal you are probably having *performance-interfering thoughts (PITs)*, e.g. *'This is too hard'*, *'I don't feel like studying.'* Use the table below to respond to your PITs with *PETs* – *performance-enhancing thoughts*, e.g. *'If I study now, I can enjoy the rest of my evening.'*

Performance Interfering Thoughts (PITs)	*Performance Enhancing Thoughts (PETs)*

Adapted from Centre for Coaching (2014)*

Step 1: If you are feeling negative about your goal, write down any thoughts that occur to you (e.g. *'I'll never be able to do this'*) in the left-hand column – *PITs*.

Step 2: Take a few slow, deep breaths and relax your muscles. Put yourself in a more positive, solution-focused state. You may want to read a motivational quote or think of something that inspires you. You may also find it helpful to *remember your goal(s)*.

Step 3: Look at each *PIT* you've written down and think about how to *respond* to it. Write your response in the *PETs* column. The questions below may help you come up with *PETs*:

- **If my *best friend* had that thought, how would I encourage *him/her*?**
- **What would my *best friend/teacher/parents/coach* say to encourage *me*?**
- **How might *other* people think about this situation?**
- **What is a more *helpful* way of looking at the situation?**
- **How do I need to think to *achieve my goal*?**

Step 4: Read through your PETs and take action! What small step could you take right now to get closer to your goal?

*Centre for Coaching (2014). Primary Certificate in Performance Coaching Training Manual. Course held by Centre for Coaching, London, on the 15-16 July, 2014.

INDEX